The HeART of Feng Shui...Simply Put

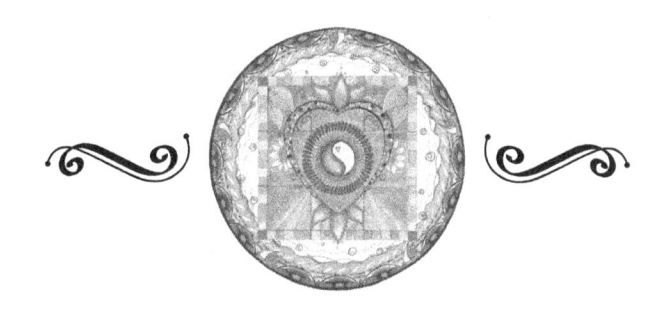

Anita Adrain

BALBOA PRESS
A DIVISION OF HAY HOUSE

Copyright © 2019 Anita Adrain.

All rights reserved. No part of this book may be used or reproduced by any means, graphic, electronic, or mechanical, including photocopying, recording, taping or by any information storage retrieval system without the written permission of the author except in the case of brief quotations embodied in critical articles and reviews.

This book is a work of non-fiction. Unless otherwise noted, the author and the publisher make no explicit guarantees as to the accuracy of the information contained in this book and in some cases, names of people and places have been altered to protect their privacy.

Scripture taken from the King James Version of the Bible.

Balboa Press books may be ordered through booksellers or by contacting:

Balboa Press
A Division of Hay House
1663 Liberty Drive
Bloomington, IN 47403
www.balboapress.com
1 (877) 407-4847

Because of the dynamic nature of the Internet, any web addresses or links contained in this book may have changed since publication and may no longer be valid. The views expressed in this work are solely those of the author and do not necessarily reflect the views of the publisher, and the publisher hereby disclaims any responsibility for them.

The author of this book does not dispense medical advice or prescribe the use of any technique as a form of treatment for physical, emotional, or medical problems without the advice of a physician, either directly or indirectly. The intent of the author is only to offer information of a general nature to help you in your quest for emotional and spiritual well-being. In the event you use any of the information in this book for yourself, which is your constitutional right, the author and the publisher assume no responsibility for your actions.

Any people depicted in stock imagery provided by Getty Images are models, and such images are being used for illustrative purposes only.
Certain stock imagery © Getty Images.

Print information available on the last page.

ISBN: 978-1-9822-3116-3 (sc)
ISBN: 978-1-9822-3115-6 (hc)
ISBN: 978-1-9822-3128-6 (e)

Library of Congress Control Number: 2019909553

Balboa Press rev. date: 09/18/2019

Contents

Dedication vii

Acknowledgements.. ix

Foreword xiii

Introduction xv

Vital Points xvii

The Journey Begins xix

One – Ancient Principles, Relevant Wisdom 1

Two – Feng Shui Defined... 15

Three – Life Force Energy 'Chi' 32

Four – Universal Symbol 43

Five – Home Is Where The Heart Lives..................................... 54

Six – Mind Over Matter 66

Seven – The Writing Is On The Wall.. 85

Eight – Live With What You Love: Out Of Chaos Comes Clarity 102

Nine – Change Your Frequency—Change Your Life 123

Ten – Nature's Building Blocks 134

Eleven – Your Home, Your Sanctuary 145

Twelve – Sacred Circle 162

Thirteen – Mirror, Mirror 172

Fourteen – Science And Spirituality 191

Fifteen – Awakening To A New View 202

Sixteen – Intentional Living.. 208

Seventeen – Using Your Inner Compass 235

Eighteen – Success Leaves Clues 243

The Journey Continues From Here In Your Home And Heart 254

H.E.A.R.T. CLUES 256

Testimonials 265

Resources 269

Dedication

The seed of life begins in the nourishing environment of the Mother's womb.

I dedicate this book to all the Mothers of the world—from our sentient Mother Gaia to all of our ancestral Mothers who honored the cycle within to give birth to our nations.

To my own dear, sweet Mother, Alida, who has taught me so much and, without her love of family, she may have stopped at child number eight.

To my mother-in-law, Edna, who gave me her only son, Calvin as my life partner. Without his unwavering belief in me, this book would have remained only a thought—unrealized potential.

Acknowledgements

The Universe always supports us; when we trust the journey and allow the process to flow. Not having a specific expectation of the outcome is trusting that everything will unfold as it is supposed to. So many times, I had to remind myself that this book was being created with a higher power at work and that I was being divinely guided. Trust … trust … trust …

Saying "Yes" and following my own Inner Compass, my intuition, has led me to so many beautiful souls who have contributed to my life and this book.

My dearest Marie, there is no question that I would still be fumbling my way through the book writing process, had I not met you.

It started when I said yes to being a presenter for the Women's Wellness Retreat in my hometown. The evening before the Saturday event, there was an opportunity to participate in a mini tradeshow, which I did. It was there, that I met a vivacious, confident, blonde, curly haired woman. She was bubbling over with enthusiasm and smiles as she greeted the attendees across the room from where I had my table. I was prompted to introduce myself and we quickly engaged in conversation. I found out that she was a published author and would also be one of the presenters for the following day's retreat. It just worked out (wink) that I was able to attend her session and she mine. We were both impressed with the other's presentation, prompting a follow up meeting several weeks later.

Wanda St. Hilaire, I am so grateful that you shared with me the contact of your incredibly talented editor and writing coach, Marie Beswick-Arthur.

I had been in contact with a few other book editors and writing coaches and hadn't yet committed to working with anyone.

Marie agreed to have an online meeting with me to see if we were a 'fit'. An hour later, it was an easy decision for me, and I was overjoyed when she agreed to take me on as a client. We immediately began to sort through the book files and fragmented chapters that had accumulated over several years. Marie's patience with me as a first-time author, was like the patience one gives a small child learning a new task; without judgement. She has expertly guided me over many months, through hundreds of emails and countless versions of the manuscript. What has emerged is a manuscript that I am super proud of, and I am awed by its completion.

I have become a better writer under Marie's excellent guidance and expert eye. We may even do another book together, something I never thought possible, before working with her.

The Universe divinely conspired to connect us in a synchronistic encounter and I now have another soul sister in my tribe. My 'heartfelt' love and appreciation to Marie for agreeing to go on this journey with me.

Editor of The HeART of Feng Shui…Simply Put: Marie Beswick-Arthur www.mariebeswickarthur.com

There are no coincidences in this life. Opportunities and potentials of something better than anything you can conjure up in your mind are always there, waiting in the wings, so to speak. Moving out of your comfort zone and taking action will always lead you exactly where you are destined to go. You just get there a lot quicker when you are consciously aware of the 'road signs' along the way.

I had an image in my mind of what I wanted for a book cover. I looked through countless 'stock' images that might convey what I was looking for. The search came up empty and a friend suggested that I paint or draw my own image. Although considered highly creative in many areas, painting and drawing, are not in my wheelhouse! That's when I decided to ask for help from the unseen forces - my guides and the creative force that permeates all things. I asked that the perfect person for the job of creating an art piece for my book cover would come to mind. I know several exceptionally talented artists, one of which is my cousin and a couple of other long-time friends. When I 'asked' if any one of them would be the one to create the art for my book cover, the answer I got back was no. I had no expectation or judgement around the answer and trusted that I would be presented with another source. Within days, someone whom I had briefly met before at our weekly 'Power of 8' meditation group, was sharing photos with one of the other attendees. *Wow* … we had no idea that she was such a talented artist. A seemingly out of the blue coincidence, that lead to asking the question, "Would you consider creating an art piece for my book?" Cynthia's answer was "Yes!"

We met later that week and I gave her a rough sketch of what was in my head and conveyed my ideas to her. It wasn't long before she was able to magically create the image that was in my mind. I wanted a mandala type image, because we naturally recognize repeating patterns on a soul level, and I also wanted it to encompass all the Feng Shui teachings represented in the book. Cynthia had no prior knowledge of Feng Shui and had not even read the manuscript and yet she was able to capture the exact essence of all that I had imagined - from the colors, to the intricate details - bringing them all to life. It is a great visual representation of the contents of The HeART of Feng Shui ... Simply Put.

Cynthia, you nailed it! I am blessed to have met you through a friend of a friend. May your creative talent ripple out into the world, adding beauty in the hearts of many.

Book cover artwork credit: Raevyn Berg Fine Art, www.raevynberg.weebly.com

You just never know who it is that the Universe has enlisted to help you; be open to receiving clues that are outside of your perception of 'how' something is supposed to show up for you.

Acknowledgements would not be complete without thanking Greg Dickson, who started the book writing process with me many moons ago. The experience taught me many things and the book you are holding in your hands is a result. Everything does happen for a reason.

Writing a book takes hundreds of hours to complete, and in doing so there are many other daily tasks that are put on the back burner. Thank you to my husband Calvin and my son Mason for allowing me the time to write this book and for your willingness to take on the extra load. My family has been immensely supportive and encouraged me every step of the way. I love you all and I am blessed beyond measure. A heart-filled thank you to: Calvin, Dillon, Vanessa, Marc, Mason, Emerson and GG for honoring my journey.

To all my brothers and sisters who have always loved me: Lloyd, Tony, Maurice, David, John, Paulette, Jeannette, Sandra, Warren and Theresa. My sister in-laws, brother in-laws, nieces, nephews, and great nieces and nephews you are included here as well. I love you and I am profoundly grateful that you are all my family.

To my spiritual family, close friends and community of clients and students: your positive encouragement for this project will always be remembered. Thank you for agreeing to share your stories.

With love and gratitude,
Anita

Foreword

I have been a fan of Anita Adrain since we were children. She always had a unique flair and innate knowledge of how everything was connected. Long before these subjects were discussed or became mainstream, Anita attracted industry thought-leaders and spoke openly of her beliefs, constantly sharing new, thought-provoking subjects.

When Anita was introduced to Feng Shui it immediately resonated with her inner-being. This was in the day when the Western world was just being introduced to this ancient, Asian practice. Many could not wrap their head around it; however, Anita shared the concept in a manner that took the "woo" out of it.

Proof is the best truth. After Anita completed her Feng Shui training, she came to my clinic and did a consultation for me. I made the changes she recommended and, shortly after, my phone began to ring... and ring. People were making appointments, and dropping in to see if I could fit them in. Eventually, we had to readjust the office so I could handle the increase in business. Wow!

Fast forward a couple of decades; not only has Anita developed a substantial client base, she is also a teacher/trainer, developing and conducting training seminars that are transforming the lives of many.

Anita is a successful businesswoman. She is in constant motion, living life to its fullest as a devoted wife, dedicated mother, active grandmother, and trusted friend. Her timing for this beautiful book is perfect: we're all hungry for peace, harmony, and the 'lessons' to move forward in joy. Anita's creative sharing of the sum of her knowledge and experience, based on progressive, proven ancient wisdom, is timely and well-expressed.

It is my belief that this book will contribute to the massive shift underway as we enter the Golden Age of Enlightenment.

My life has been enriched by Anita on so many levels. I am massively grateful for her shiny light.

Marianne Noad
Co-author of Refusing to Quit
Global Master Distributor
www.mariannenoad.gpsandyou.com or www.marianne.gpsandyou.com

Introduction

Let's start with the pronunciation: it's pronounced 'fung' 'shway.'
Now we know how to say it, what does Feng Shui mean?
Feng is wind. Shui is water.
Feng Shui represents the two forces that govern all things: unseen and seen energies.
Feng/wind/the unseen: the spirit, the soul, the breath, the feeling, the thought.
Shui/water/the seen: the physical aspects of self, the physical aspects of Earth, the seen forces representing fluid movement.

The unseen world and the seen world.
The inner world and the outer world.
The spiritual plane and the physical plane.

No matter the cultural background, tradition, symbol, or ceremony, Feng Shui references the unseen and seen energy forces present in all things animate and inanimate.

The natural world holds hope for us to live with the things we love, reduce stress, and experience a greater sense of well-being.

This book offers scientific validation, and covers ancient principles with spiritual practices for the NOW age of conscious awakening.

By the time you have moved through this guide/workbook you are likely to notice a shift in your thinking. In educating yourself about the natural world, you will have shifted a part of your 'beingness.' Making notes throughout this book will allow you to gift yourself time to think, to consider, and to go within.

The further through the book you go—and the more notes and sketches you make—the more you will be able to key into the ability to recognize the energy aspects in your physical world and create a shift in your unseen world.

We are one in spirit, we are one with the land.
We are one in the universe, come take my hand.
They will know we are warriors,
Brothers and sisters of the light,
By our love... by our love.
- Anita Adrain

Vital Points

- Feng Shui is not a religion, nor is it a fad or superstition. Feng Shui is a study and application of energy. It may well be considered physics or, more importantly, metaphysics. Indigenous cultures may have practiced Feng Shui; the Chinese just gave it the recognizable label.
- With love as the glue of the universe, the heart must be the compass—the connection—to the innate system within; the part of God or the source that is within every cell of our body. Intuitively, instinctively, you practice Feng Shui and have a built-in compass that gives you direction on a daily basis—you just haven't been taught how to use it, until now.
- Over the last two decades, self-help—now called personal growth—and personal development forums, along with spiritual teachers, have provided little information on the energy of the home environment. We spend at least 30% of our lifetime in our home. Perhaps you have witnessed participants in personal growth weekend events that are repeat attendees—you may be one yourself—continually looking to enhance their lives and yet still feeling energetically stuck or not connected to source.
- It is my observation that the seekers of spiritual wisdom, or self-development in any area, will not advance to the level desired until they recognize that the physical environment in which they live has to match or mirror the energy vibration they are seeking.
- There is no-thing that we are not connected to energetically in the universe. The word 'universe' can be broken down into 'uni' as in one, and 'verse' as in statement or voice—one whole body, and one whole world.

- ❖ It is possible to be more conscious of our thoughts—currently it is believed we are only aware of 10% of them. Greater awareness is what will bring us to co-exist in peace on Earth. This age is called the NOW age. Note: There is a parallel with the percentage (approximately 10%) of what is understood about our DNA. Perhaps, as science unravels the mystery of our DNA, we will match our cognition (knowledge of our thoughts) to this. There are many other parallels and clues throughout the pages of this book that will be a guide—a catalyst, perhaps—in reaching a new understanding of all things animate and inanimate.
- ❖ Our bodies were designed to live longer—the phrase heaven on Earth may be a reference to tuning our frequency to higher dimensions. Raising our vibration starts in the home, creating a healthy environment that supports mind, body, and spirit.

The Journey Begins

It makes sense that I felt the power and importance of the elements found in the natural environment from early childhood. Growing up in rural central Alberta, Canada—the ninth child of eleven—life was busy.

We lived in a small house in the country—a mixed farm of animals and agriculture—mostly for the purpose of sustaining our large family. We required a lot of food to feed us all: my parents, grandparents, and eleven children. Many times, there were extra guests at the table, too. My intimate relationship with Mother Nature started early. We had a garden. I am sure it was over an acre—at least it felt that way as a young child going between the rows pulling weeds; everyone was expected to contribute.

My father was a hard-working man and often put in long hours at the lumber mill, leaving my brothers to do most of the outside chores.

We had an outside well with a hand pump; we used to fill many buckets of water, daily—my older brothers would haul them to the house for drinking, cooking, and cleaning. We had an outside structure, known as an outhouse. Yes, this was the family toilet. The exception was that, in the cold winter months, a five-gallon pail sat at the top of the stairs for emergency use. Eventually, in the early 1970s, we were blessed with indoor plumbing—a real bathroom with a bathtub as well.

I think back to these times and wonder how the heck we managed with one bathroom. Even though we lacked the modern conveniences of our 'town friends,' our parents managed to instill family values, a strong work ethic, and the most important ingredient: a love for each other that would serve us all into adulthood.

Unseen and seen energy forces: It's not a surprise that I have continued to understand their relevance as 'life-changing' and 'life-giving' forces. I was immersed in all of outdoors, an infinite source of Mother Nature right outside my door—the fields, streams, mountains, and forests.

In addition to pumping the water, my older brothers were tasked with the daily chores that included milking the cows and chopping wood to fuel the large wood stove used for heating and cooking.

It was behind this huge, cast-iron fixture where I escaped the hectic, and sometimes chaotic, place called home. There was just enough space between the wall and the back of the stove that I could safely fit, finding comfort in the residual warmth from the morning fire. It became a regular place to explore an imaginary world that I created. This is my first memory of instinctively seeking a place of comfort and safety; intuitively practicing Feng Shui somewhere between three and four years old.

There were many other times during my youth that I found solace in re-arranging and beautifying the space around me. I believe I was an expert at wallpapering at the age of nine.

While I was instinctively practicing Feng Shui, it wasn't until my early 30s that I was introduced to the term.

The 'Aha!' moment came while attending a spiritual conference in Banff, Alberta, Canada, with my mom and my close friend, Trudy. This is where I first met my spiritual mentor, Lee Carroll, and where I was introduced to the work of Dr. Todd Ovakaitys, a brilliant scientist.

One of the speakers, Jan Tober, was talking about bubble bowls and how to improve a home's energy, circulating the qi (also known as Ch'i or chi, pronounced Chee) to attract abundance and good fortune in every area of life.

I immediately knew that I had to find out more about this fascinating subject and sought her out at the intermission. Jan told me that a couple of her close acquaintances, Louise Hay and Terah Kathryn Collins, whom she'd lunched with the day before, were the forerunners in introducing the Western world to the ancient practice of Feng Shui. Terah had just written her book, *The Western Guide to Feng Shui*, the first on this topic to be produced by Hay House Publishing.

I could barely contain my excitement as I confirmed and validated what I had been intuitively practicing my whole life. The profound impact of attending that weekend spiritual event would prove to be the catalyst for finding my life's purpose—including how I could show readers, through my own book (this book), that they, too, have this same instinct.

My Feng Shui journey officially began in 1996. My life has been enriched, and continues to grow, as a result of saying yes.

*****

The purpose of practicing Feng Shui is to create an environment that is safe and comfortable. Learning to become aware of the natural flow of energies in your personal environment, and their influence, can effect change in every aspect of your life.

It is my desire to share my personal experiences and observations through *The HeART of Feng Shui… Simply Put* so that all readers can come away with an understanding of this powerful practice, and experience their own 'Aha!' moments with a new view of energy.

The words and material in this book are purposefully arranged for you to experience a greater sense of well-being. I ask you to learn alongside me, come up with answers to the questions posed, use the blank spaces to make your own notes, record your own coincidences, list your own knowing, and write your own stories. Making an energetic shift in your outer world will have a profound impact on your inner world.

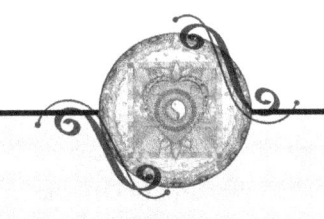

One – Ancient Principles, Relevant Wisdom

*"Increasing our personal energetic vibration
has an impact on the increased vibration of the whole, all of humanity,
so that we may return to the teachings of the ancients,
co-existing in harmony with each other and our Mother Gaia."*
Anita Adrain

Understanding the workings of a living Earth begins with this fact: there is unseen and seen energy around us. This energy is referred to in a number of ways, including Feng Shui.

Quantum physics is described by Wikipedia as 'a fundamental theory in physics which describes nature at the smallest scale of energy levels of atoms and subatomic particles.'

Softened, quantum physics is a bird's flight as it rides wind's current, and yesterday's flower bud that today, after being watered, is opened and the face of an angel.

Note: wind's current is unseen energy. The flower is seen energy.

Gaia is the name given to the personification of the Earth. Personification means giving something non-human (in this case, the Earth) human qualities. Another way of understanding the word Gaia is to simply say 'living Earth.' This is not difficult to do since every part of our Earth is 'living.' In the case of the word Gaia, we give the Earth the qualities of being a Mother or a Goddess. She is the unseen and seen energy all around us.

One – Ancient Principles, Relevant Wisdom

Ancient cultures recognized their own relationship with Gaia. They somehow knew about the connection between interdependent systems governed by the universe and the invisible field of energy that infuses all things.

All of these words: Feng Shui, quantum physics, Mother Nature, Gaia, reference energy. Additionally: qì or ch'i or chi, the latter used throughout this book, means breath, air, or gas. Symbolically in language it means life force or energy flow.

I wasn't aware of the depth of these energetic influences until I began my Feng Shui journey. Once I began learning, I 'woke up' and began to look at everything differently. It was as if invisible strings held everything in place, and that, with subtle adjustments, the effects produced dramatic results—just like puppeteers seemingly bring marionettes to life.

It was this dance between the seen objects, tangible in my home and intangible—the unseen—that produced results which intrigued and ignited my desire to search for more clues to how life exists, becomes, is.

I am not a scientist—but I respect science, and look to the organized aspects that help me understand my relationship within and without the whole space we call Earth; in this whole we call the universe.

My curiosity, and the underlying feeling of having to defend my new awareness, caused me to search for scientific parameters or rules that might help me to define and validate the teachings of Feng Shui. I read many books and scoured the internet looking for links to connect with the ancient wisdom of Feng Shui, and a specific reference defined by the scientific community that could explain the 'unseen energy.'

As I gained a deeper understanding of the 'law of cause and effect,' 'the law of vibration,' 'the law of polarity,' the 'law of gender,' and other universal truths and insights, I began to see the parallels and similarities in my Feng Shui teachings that were conveyed in science, and some that applied to the 'rules in religion' which I was taught as a young child.

Many insights have surfaced and helped me to become a better teacher of the principles of Feng Shui.

I have had many teachers, some who have been particularly spiritual, and who represent the unseen energy, and others—scientists—who represent the seen energy.

As humanity moves into uncharted territory, there are many new thoughts surfacing, that are validated by the laws of physics and science. We are indeed in the time of new discovery and self-awareness. With the click of a mouse we can glean insight, and discover much about our relationship with ancient cultures, their intimate relationship with Gaia—the living Earth as a goddess—and what that means for us.

Energetic Beings

It is my goal to help you embark on the journey of mastering your own life. Starting in your own home, you will discover that some of the same energetic qualities that reside in your physical body are also embodied in your home. It is all connected: the mind, body, and spirit.

We are energetic beings living in an energetic universe. There is NO-thing that is not vibrating, oscillating at a specific frequency, thereby connecting us to each other, to the environment around us, and to our Mother Gaia.

In the 'Now Age,' quantum physicists—those who study the science of the smallest scales of energy levels of atoms and subatomic particles—are validating the energy of consciousness and our connectedness to all things.

> *"Our continued survival on this beautiful planet*
> *is contingent on our awakening to living a conscious life."*
> *Anita Adrain*

At the end of the chapters, and within specific sections of this book, you will find interactive areas called 'Life is an interactive experience. This is Your Space.'

Participating in 'Your Space' ensures a higher probability of retaining the information in this book. When each of us speak or write about a subject—in particular with new knowledge—the stage is set for accelerated learning and clearer recall. These practices fire and re-wire new patterns in the brain. Neurons that fire together, wire together, and that strengthens brain pathways.

One – Ancient Principles, Relevant Wisdom

"When you change your beliefs, learn something new, or become mindful of your habitual reactions to unpleasant emotions, you actually alter the neurochemistry and the structure of your brain." https://medium.com/@alltopstartups/want-to-rewire-your-brain-for-meaningful-life-changes-do-these-things-immediately-119ea0904e38

Life is an interactive experience.
This is Your Space.

What is your earliest recollection of the environment you grew up in?

What was your favorite room, area or space in the family home that you remember?

One – Ancient Principles, Relevant Wisdom

Describe the space in as much detail as you can.

Before you continue, jot some ideas and thoughts, from your current understanding and/or experience, of what you think that practicing Feng Shui is.

Feng Shui is…

Lessons From Our Ancestors

Every Indigenous culture that has ever inhabited this living planet followed the natural rhythms—the ebb and flow—of Mother Nature. With no internet or satellite GPS to guide them, each group carved out a place for itself. We are proof of their survival, whether descended from them, or having benefitted from their creations and inventions. For thousands of years, ancient cultures recorded their observations and developed their beliefs around the energy flow of their natural environment. No matter where on the planet they lived, they had two things in common: The Earth below and the heavens above.

It is in this place of contemplation that we can learn a great deal more from our benevolent Mother, and from our ancestors who intimately knew and respected the connection with her.

Somewhere along the way, humanity lost the importance of the connection that all ancients knew, respected, and followed.

> In his book, *The God Code*, Gregg Braden notes: "Scholars acknowledge that through intentional edits as well as natural processes, the chain of knowledge linking our oldest traditions with the modern world has been interrupted on more than one occasion."

We now live in a period of great dis-connect. We're constantly striving to comprehend who we are, and understand our relationship to all things. When we reflect upon how we live today, and compare it to ancient cultural ways, it seems we have somehow lost our way.

I have always said that Mother Nature has been my greatest teacher. From a young age, I recall finding comfort and safety in the embrace of the outdoors. Whether I was building willow forts or snow caves with my sisters or digging in the dirt and making mud pies for Dad or Grandpa, the outdoor experience was always invigorating and inspiring. In many ways, I have been creating sacred spaces where I felt safe and nurtured—practicing Feng Shui—my entire life.

In the book, *Working with The Law*, author Raymond Holliwell points out: "All of the processes of nature are successful. Nature knows no failures. She never plans anything but success. She aims at results in every form and manner. To succeed, in the best and fullest sense of the term, we must, with nature as our model, copy her methods. In her principles and laws, we shall discover all the secrets of success."

Whatever your cultural background, religious doctrine, or faith in a higher power that you recognize to be true for you, I am sure that you will discover some universal truths when you consider your relationship with Mother Nature.

It is the home environment of the natural world that we must first learn from because 'she' never plans anything but success.

Sleeping Giants

Even though Feng Shui has been defined as an Eastern philosophy, with deep roots in Chinese culture, I am certain that all the Indigenous cultures studied the energy within their environment—that being the practice of Feng Shui.

They may have called it something else, but they, too, looked for clues to their existence, and sought continued survival from the natural surroundings of Earth, the heavens, and stars above. They recognized the natural rhythms and cycles of the planet, and the flow of energy in and around everything.

Thousands of years later, there is still an opportunity for mankind to learn a great deal more and to re-connect with, through observation and experience, the abundant resources of the natural world that sustain life itself—the flora and fauna.

From the tallest mountain to the vast prairie, the formation of the landscape has inspired many explorers, outdoor enthusiasts, artists, and writers looking to get into the flow—become one with the rhythm—of this place we call home.

Stretching from Alaska all the way to the state of New Mexico, the rugged 'Rockies,' as they are known, are the mountains that form the backbone of our continent. From a distance they appear to be sleeping giants standing guard, protecting the foothills, rivers, streams, and forests—all of which are home to many other life forms, some of whose mysteries are yet to be discovered.

On many occasions in my youth, my family would travel a couple hours from home, by car, to take special visitors and relatives to see the Rocky Mountains. The trip was never boring and always offered a new perspective. Looking out the back-seat window, I could only imagine how the early travelers of this land would have felt traversing by foot or by horse. The incredible feeling of reverence that one feels in this special energy cannot be described.

It's no wonder that one of my brothers, Hawkeye (Maurice), became an expert guide and outfitter in the Rocky Mountains. Lured, perhaps, by the whispers of the ancients, it seems only natural he decided to make a career out of taking visitors to this beautiful landscape.

In the summer of 1989, Hawkeye was getting ready to take a large group out trail riding to a remote area west of Rocky Mountain House.

I can still see the excitement in his eyes and the smile on his face when he asked me to join the excursion. "Sis, you would love it out there, plants everywhere and you won't believe the views—you never gunna see that in the city."

Well, I did ride a horse when I was a kid—but of the five girls in the family, you might say I was more of a city-girl-with-country-roots. The thought of going out into the wilderness—grizzlies and wolves live there—sleeping on goodness knows what, and being away from the safety and comfort of my home, was slightly intimidating.

The third oldest of my six brothers, Hawkeye has a way of making everyone feel like a kid; such a happy-go-lucky nature. Once he'd invited me, he remained persistent, and assured me that I would love it. He was over-the-moon-excited when I accepted his invitation.

As I discovered, my brother was right about the abundance of flora that grew in this remote landscape. Wild onions and orchids were a few surprises that I found, which led me to enquire how to identify the edible plants that seemed to have been strategically placed by Mother Nature.

One – Ancient Principles, Relevant Wisdom

My three-day trail ride turned into seven—with the promise to return someday. The bounty of the mountains—food for those who lived and traveled through there—was a discovery I was not expecting. When I returned, *Wildflowers of the Canadian Rockies,* and the *Guide to Indian Herbs,* became my summer reading material. It was in the latter that I read about ancient principles and relevant wisdom that I had previously been unaware of, not knowing the true relevance of what was revealed in the pages, for me personally, until many years later.

Relevant Wisdom

> Following excerpt from *The Guide to Indian Herbs* by Raymond Stark, published by Hancock House Publishers ISBN: 0-88839-077-7 www.hancockhouse.com
> "Before European immigration to North America, and for some time afterwards, Indians maintained an extensive stock of herbal medicines which they gathered from the forests, plains and mountains of their locales. In many Indian tribes and nations, the medicine man or medicine woman was much like a para-psychologist. Their function was to encourage the mind of an ailing person to turn toward a positive style of thinking, with (it was hoped) a corresponding start on the path to improvement. In some Indian nations - such as the Ojibwa, Cherokee, and Cree (sic) - the work of the "medicine man" was complemented by that of the herbalist, the individual who treated a patient with roots, leaves, barks, and berries. The Ojibwa had four distinct classifications of medicine people. First, and highest ranking, were the holy men of the Midewiwin, the Medicine Society; next came the Wabenos, the Men of the Dawn, who practiced a kind of magic medicine, ensuring good fortune for warriors and hunters, providing incantations and charms... all of the esoteric matters of magic. The herbs of forest and field were used in the rituals of the Wabenos, the success or failure of whose work depended upon a combination

of natural medicines and human psychology. Third in line were the Jessakid. These were the men of truth, of divination, the prophets and clairvoyants - the men who operated under the auguries of the God of Thunder. Last were the Doctors of Medicine, the Mashki-kike-winini, who knew the powers of the berries, leaves, roots, barks, resins, and flowers. These doctors of herbal medicine understood clearly that certain herbs exerted specific effects in the human body, and earnestly believed that the herbs functioned against some species of demonry held within the body.

This is somewhat analogous to the ancient Saxon belief that illnesses were caused by the evil elves of the air, land, and sea, and to be ill was to be "elf-shot." In modern medicine, we call these devils of the Indians and the elf-venom of the Saxon by such terms as bacteria, bacilli, microbes, viruses, and so on, but the basic theory appears to be much the same. None of them are fully understood, but all are treated by the best means available at the time. Among the Ojibwa, women also served as herbal doctors, members of the Mashki-kike-winini, and some were members of the holy society of the Midewiwin.

Modern psychiatry is familiar with the idea that the psychology of the patient plays an important, if rather incomprehensible, part in healing. A present-day psychiatrist, for example, has his own special methods of affecting the psychology of the patient... the supine position, sedative medication, specific questions designed to relax, and so on. The Indian medicine man, with his rattles and bear claws and awesome paint, *expected* to impress the patient with his deliberately fearsome mien. The idea was that the Indian psychiatrist would look so fearsome and act in such a threatening way that the demons and evil spirits would be frightened away from the patient's body, *and the patient understood this.* This potent assistance from the medicine man must have bolstered the mental and emotional forces of the patient and cause the physical ailment to respond positively.

More than 200 medicinal plants indigenous to the Americas have been official in the *United States Pharmacopoeia* since the first edition was published in 1820. In addition to these, perhaps another 300 herbs of the Indian world have been used by doctors, and a considerable number of these have been investigated by early pharmaceutical firms, and brought out under various names in the forms of extracts or compounds or in synthetic forms."

Indigenous Cultures Mirror the Practice of Feng Shui?

The four classes of Medicine People clearly show that there was a belief in the higher powers—in the unseen energy—through the use of divination tools. They trusted their instincts and intuition and looked to Mother Nature for clues for plant-based healing. The mental, emotional, and physical well-beingness of a patient as a 'whole person' was taken into consideration when treatment was administered.

The important role of Mother Nature's systems to human existence can be found in the physical remains and oral history of all Indigenous cultures.

Following the harmony and rhythm of nature as their guide, the Chinese developed a LuoPan; the Hopi created a ceremonial calendar; the Indigenous peoples of the Americas made a Medicine Wheel, all of which are tools and symbols; wisdom passed down through the ages that are relevant for today's understanding of nature's laws.

Imagine what North America would look like today if the Native Americans could have led and taught their ways to the new settlers. Is that when we started to lose our way? Perhaps. If we had only followed the teachings of the Medicine Wheel.

Ancient Principles

The Sacred Circle, or Medicine Wheel teachings, of the Indigenous also recognize the natural surroundings, and the goal to achieve balance. The sacred circle teachings are shared in many Aboriginal cultures, helping their people to learn about living a harmonious, holistic life.

The Medicine Wheel shows the interconnectedness of all things. Each part of the wheel is symbolic, representing the stages of life, and the four directions. Every knot that ties the whole together represents every person, every tree, every blade of grass, every river, every animal, and every rock. The string represents the connection to the people and nature around them.

The string between the knots represents the culture, the beliefs, and the values that are shared along the path.

The wisdom of the Medicine Wheel is a map for life's journey, a walk-in tune with the mind, body, heart, and spirit. It's good medicine to follow the wheel. If the four areas are not in balance in the person, it is believed that the circle will lose its shape, and the person will feel lost on life's journey.

If one of the knots, or one of the strings, is severed from the wheel, then part of the web becomes separate and disconnected from the whole.

I invite you to start on the path to your well-beingness by being open to the wisdom of the ancients and their learning principles, so that you can acquire the tools that are relevant for today's journey of self-discovery.

One – Ancient Principles, Relevant Wisdom

Life is an interactive experience.
This is Your Space.

What have you learned from your cultural past? Can you share any insights or relevant wisdom from your ancestors?

What mind, body, spirit practices have you participated in or hold an interest in?

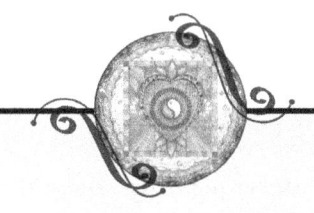

Two – Feng Shui Defined

*"Living in a state of emotional excellence, or close to it,
is the path to reaching your highest human potential."*
Anita Adrain

The Shift

There appears to be a shift occurring in which many people are demonstrating a greater caring about what happens to Planet Earth—they care about the condition of the land, the quality of water, and the air that everyone breathes.

Perhaps you have noticed, as have I, a gradual move to environmental consciousness—positive action to get back to the basics of life. There is a predominance of natural alternatives: organic foods, nature-based remedies, solar power, electric cars, windmills, responsible recycling—the list goes on.

Could it be that there is a calling from our ancestors to reconnect to our natural state of beingness, to honor that which we feel deep inside?

Mankind has never been as technologically advanced—not meaning that other civilizations were not highly intelligent in method and design—yet there is an alarming increase in dis-ease and social dis-connection within our 'tribe.'

It is disconcerting that we live in this advanced society and yet it has been reported that, in 2017, one in three deaths in the United States was related to Cardiovascular Disease (CVD).

The world Health Organization says that CVD is currently the largest single contributor to global mortality. The WHO projects it will continue to dominate mortality trends in the future.

> "95% of all dis-ease is caused by STRESS, and 100% of stress is caused by the wrong belief, and it's almost always subconscious." Bruce H. Lipton, PhD, Cellular Biologist

So, what does all this mean? What is really going on? Scientists are telling us that stress is the number one cause of disease. Could some of this stress have any relevance or relationship to our personal environment?

I admit this is one of the main reasons I wrote this book. It is my belief that when you learn to live in the flow, in an energetic, supportive environment, one that mirrors the natural environment, you can reduce stress and experience a greater sense of well-being.

The Inner World Is Connected To, And Reflected In, The Outer World

It is my desire to heighten or increase your awareness and connectedness to ALL things. People have been taught that they are: separate from the ground they walk on; separate from the circumstances that happen to other people; separate from the walls that surround them; removed from the food they use to sustain life.

The fact is, there is NO-thing that we are not connected to energetically.

Feng Shui

You know that the words Feng and Shui translate as wind and water. Well, wind and water are the natural elements of flow. Wind represents the unseen energies: intangible, subconscious, feelings, and thoughts. Water represents the physical energies: tangible, things we can experience through touch. A graceful dance exists between the unseen forces of the wind on the 'seen,' or visible, forces of water, in harmony with the elements of Mother Nature, bringing balance to the entire environment.

When you practice Feng Shui, you will become aware of, the natural flow of these two energies, the seen and unseen, in your environment, and how their influence can change every aspect of your life.

Let's get more acquainted with Feng Shui. The roots of Feng Shui are deeply embedded in the soil and culture of our Asian brothers and sisters. Whether you have read one or two books on Feng Shui, heard of it in passing, or this is your first exposure, matters not. The goal of this book and the subsequent outcomes for each reader will be unique and life affirming.

The purpose of applying Feng Shui principles is to create an environment that is safe, comfortable, and aesthetically pleasing. This puts the person(s) in a state of ease, harmony, and balance.

This simple definition is noted in the British Dictionary: *"The Chinese art of determining the most propitious design and placement of a grave, building, room, etc. so that the maximum harmony is achieved between the flow of chi of the environment and that of the user, believed to bring good fortune."*

Wikipedia adds to the definition: *"Feng Shui is one of the Five Arts of Chinese Metaphysics, classified as physiognomy (observation of appearances through formulas and calculations)."* And *"The Feng Shui practice discusses architecture in metaphoric terms of 'invisible forces' that bind the universe, Earth, and humanity together, known as qi."*

My definition and take on Feng Shui is that it is the study of energy. When we have an understanding of the fundamental aspects of energy systems as being interconnected and interdependent, only then can we make a profound impact on the human energy systems, mind, body, heart, and spirit. All are directly influenced by the environment of 'home' either positively or not so positively.

There are two main schools of thought from which many branches have formed. These two main schools of thought that have provided the foundation for all other teachings are the Form School and the Compass School Feng Shui.

The Form School of Feng Shui originated approximately 5000 BC—some 7000 years ago. In hopes of being bestowed Earthly riches from the heavens above, people in Eastern cultures would search out the most desirable natural environment in which to bury their next of kin. An area that provided all of nature's best elements was thought to be enriched with good chi (energy).

The International Feng Shui Guild recognizes that Form School is the foundational aspect of Feng Shui.

The Compass School is synonymous with Traditional or Classical Feng Shui. What differentiates this school of thought from others is the use of the directional bagua as well as the use of a directional compass. The LuoPan or LoPan (compass)—based on mathematical formulae—provides a complex, detailed reading to align the environment of the home in the most auspicious direction (traditionally) to the head of the household.

All Feng Shui practitioners begin with reading and 'seeing' energy that is apparent in physical form.

> *"When we truly approach living with what we love,*
> *and loving where we live,*
> *we have established the HeART of Feng Shui."*
> *Anita Adrain*

The GPS to navigate your life's journey doesn't require batteries, nor an electrical outlet to charge—your inner compass has always been there: your innate guide. Creating coherence, creating balance and harmony in all systems, and learning to use your heart, is one of the ways you can engage your compass.

Essential Feng Shui® teaches and honors the fluidity of Form School within Western culture. An Essential School® practitioner works with the aspects of the occupants of an individual home. Essential Feng Shui® adapts Feng Shui guidelines to a unique situation. For example, having a mirror or mirrors in the bedroom works, if it works for the occupant. Does she sleep undisturbed? Great. If not, then a practitioner might suggest covering the mirrors with a blanket or sheet to notice if that influences the quality of sleep.

I was trained at the Western School of Feng Shui, and completed my Essential Feng Shui Certification training in 2000. I am a Certified Essential Feng Shui Practitioner®. The founder of the School, and my instructor, Terah Kathryn Collins, continues to be one of my mentors. Terah is a best-selling author, the originator of Essential Feng Shui®. Her six inspirational books have sold over a million copies around the world—all honor the essence of Feng Shui's Eastern heritage and focus on the benefits Feng Shui can provide to all.

> "The most accurate definition of Essential Feng Shui isn't in a line. It's in a circle that is constantly turning, each rotation building upon the one before it to achieve perfect harmony. Life is replete with fair weather conditions such as abundant resources, good relations, and a steady stream of opportunities. In such harmonious circumstances, your health, prosperity, and happiness thrive." www.wsfs.com/what-is-feng-shui/ www.westernschooloffengshui.com

Terah continues to inspire me, and many others, to elicit the genius within, with a fluidity and grace that reflects her passion and personifies Feng Shui. I am blessed and honored to be the Canadian facilitator of her EFS program, where I gently guide students to uncover their hidden talents so that they, too, can become certified Essential Feng Shui practitioners—so that they, too, can become part of the shift in the world, one home at a time.

Even though I received my formal training at the Western School of Feng Shui, I consider myself a life-long student of Mother Nature. As a participant and an observer, I have gleaned many insights and continue to be in 'awe' of her brilliance.

My 'energetic journey of discovery' has also been hugely influenced by Lee Carroll. I was first introduced to Lee's work in 1993 by my mother, who was given his book, *Kryon Book I: The End Times*. A few years later, I met him in Banff, Alberta, during his first visit to Canada as an international speaker—he was with Jan Tober and Dr. Todd Ovakaitys. It is interesting that Jan Tober had introduced me to the term Feng Shui, and then was instrumental in my meeting Lee Carroll. This was the serendipitous event that led me to hosting Lee many times in Alberta, for similar enlightening events. The Kryon work, in written form, audio, or as received as an attendee at a live event, is always inspiring. (in-spirit-ational). I consider Lee Carroll my spiritual mentor and continue to gain

Two – Feng Shui Defined

a better understanding, and energetic awareness, of this magnificent world in which we live, through his work.

The views expressed in this book are a culmination of my personal observations, experiences, and interpretations of the world around me. My understandings are based on acquired knowledge: what I have learned through reading, attending workshops and seminars. It turns out I like aspects of science as well, and have learned and will continue to learn through that 'lens.'

I have gained many insights working with clients—while I viewed their environment energetically—who have taught me a great deal. A few of their stories will be shared to help you gain a deeper understanding of Feng Shui.

I feel we are on the precipice of a new view that will ultimately be identified as the catalyst in the evolution of mankind—a move geared to our continued existence to thrive instead of surviving.

Consider the seen, (the Shui), and unseen, (the Feng - the awareness), as the foundation of your Feng Shui house. Once you understand how all the pieces fit together, you will have a better idea of how to implement and follow the plans for lasting results.

It all starts with creating a healthy home: this means your physical body and your physical home—the place your body resides, and your physical home, Planet Earth.

Having a conscious awareness of the energetic influences of all things physical, and knowing that the subtle influences of energy can ultimately affect every area of one's life is, to me, what Feng Shui is all about.

> *"The HeART of Feng Shui... Simply Put*
> *is not about achieving a state of perfection.*
> *It is about ELEVATING your frequency*
> *and increasing your awareness of ENERGY."*
> *Anita Adrain*

As you begin to work with your space and possessions, you will begin to experience a sense of flow and harmony. You will develop an ability to observe and interpret what is going on in your home and in the lives of the people within it. With practice, you will be able to read the seen and unseen life force energy in your home.

The Seen and Unseen

Looking deeper into the meaning of Feng Shui can provide more clarity of the aspects of wind and water, and the relevance of these two forceful energies. They may have been observed in other ancient cultures providing the foundation for their doctrines.

Growing up, my family attended Catholic church regularly; it wasn't an option, it was a requirement, as my mother was two years in a convent studying to be a nun prior to meeting our father. The Catholic Church has its followers recite a Creed that includes: "I believe in the Holy Catholic Church, the communion of saints, the forgiveness of sins… I believe… in all that is seen and unseen." This mantra was ingrained deep into the mind of my youth without any cognitive awareness or explanation. Even 'the Bible' refers to the unseen and seen energies, the wind and water. Imagine that.

Wind and water are essential to life itself: it is estimated that we can live without food for three weeks, approximately three days without water, and only three minutes without air—another clue as to the importance of energies that we need to sustain our life every day that, perhaps until now, have been taken for granted. So, wind and water (Feng Shui) are essential to all living organisms.

Gaining a deeper understanding of these energies will help you to embrace the energetic study and application of Feng Shui.

Wind (Feng)

The essence of life begins with a breath—the moment we leave the warm embrace of our mother's womb. Is it any wonder that, when a child is born, it is often referred to as a miracle? We come into this world starting with a single breath, and we will leave the same way, with our last breath.

Two – Feng Shui Defined

"The wind blows where it wishes, and you hear its sound, but you do not know where it comes from or where it goes. So, it is with everyone who is born of the spirit." John 3:8

The breath of Mother Nature is the unseen energy that moves through all things tangible. It is the way the Earth has been designed to sustain life.

Breath Of Air

One morning, as I worked on this chapter, delving deep into the qualities of wind and water, and the human relationship to these unseen and seen forces, I had to pause for a breath of fresh air. That day, Mother Nature gave me a 'universal wink,' or confirmation I was on the right path, and my work was being divinely guided.

Welcoming the new day with promise and vigour, the sun graced a clear blue sky that elevated my senses and awareness to our benevolent mother. By mid-morning she beckoned and whispered with a soft, gentle breeze to invite me to escape the office; it worked—the typing stopped, and the thoughts went outdoors to dance with her.

Her summoning reminded me to reach back into the memories of childhood: the exhilarating feeling of freshness that escaped the sheets hanging on the clothesline in-between the trees. As a child, I remember putting my whole face in that heavenly scent before taking the clothes and linens into the house to be put away; an after-school chore that at the time seemed more like work than pleasure.

To really capture those memories, I put the linens in the washer, then, instead of loading the dryer, I hung them out on the banister of the deck in anticipation of recapturing the essence of 'her' scent. And so, it was that the breeze that called me outside, that also helped awaken my senses, transformed its whisper to a howl. After I'd brought in the sheets, Mother Nature began sweeping the streets, swirling remnants of Halloween treats, leaves, and dust, in the neighborhood.

I thought about a farmer friend that I'd met earlier in the morning at the grocery store. I smiled for him because Mother Nature answered his prayer and was helping him to dry and harvest the remainder of his crops.

I inhaled a deep breath and knew that the day was by perfect design. I scanned ahead, knowing my night would be blessed because of the day.

~~~~~

Breath

A perfectly orchestrated rhythm unfolds through the natural cycles of the trees, bushes, flowers, and plants through photosynthesis. They breathe in carbon dioxide and expel oxygen. A beautiful example of cyclical energy, and perfect design of nature: constantly moving, flowing, exchanging secrets.

When time is taken to 'stop and smell the roses,' nature's design draws each of us into her embrace. Have you ever really stopped to contemplate what Mother Nature had in mind? Look at a single rose or any flower. Its intricate design and vibrant color are sure to draw you in. What is your natural response? To inhale its wonderful, heavenly scent.

Have you ever watched a small child on a spring day when she sees the first dandelion in the green grass? She will immediately pluck it from the ground and put it to her nose. She will often ask the person nearest to smell it as well.

What do each of us do naturally when we bring a flower to our nose? Take a deep breath, hold it for a few seconds, and then redirect attention to the sensory experience of the fragrance of the flower. This is the power of breath, to become aware in the present moment and to experience a state of heart coherence.

Wind has the ability to shape the landscape—the physical environment over time. This is evidenced in the patterns in the sand, the hill formations, and even in the unusual shaping of trees. Repeated action determines results. Water has the same ability. Over time, it softens and polishes a stone's rough edges. Similar occurrences happen with the unseen and seen forces in your home. Over time, the subliminal messages you receive from your environment—in the way of thoughts and emotions—can 'wear' on you (and your home's occupants), creating not-so-positive results.

Water (Shui)

Imagine the world without ample water. Stop for a moment and think of all the times in a day when you use water: from the time you wake up in the morning to make your coffee, use the bathroom, make breakfast, brush your teeth, clean the dishes, and throw in a load of laundry, through to bedtime when you bathe or shower. All these tasks are performed without any consideration to the importance and the power of water—on which human existence depends.

From the time of conception, in our Mother's womb, we are each surrounded by water. The physical body is comprised of 70-80% water. Interestingly, Mother Earth is mostly comprised of water: two thirds—based on land mass versus sea. Herein lies a big clue left by the creator.

Water in Feng Shui represents all that is seen, tangible—that which can be touched and felt. In the natural environment, water is fluid and conforms to its container, be it a bed of rocks or the land mass between continents. The ocean tides ebb and flow with a continual rhythm influenced by the power of the moon. Water has a mesmerizing power that lures people to take a closer look.

When people sit by the ocean and listen to the waves, it relaxes the body and helps to release mental clutter, allowing for an 'in the present' moment.

Photo credit Vannette Keast

The stillness of water reflects the images that surround its body—trees, hills, valley, or mountains.

Again, nature provides clues to her intricate design. 'As within so without.' Each of us only has to be still in our individual body (of water) to recognize that the truths of our life are being reflected to each of us in our environment.

How water behaves and interacts with all other systems in the natural environment, be it with the seen or with the unseen (wind), these same attributes or qualities must also be present in the physical environment of the home.

Our Inner World Is Connected To, And Reflected In, Our Outer World

When you spend time in a natural environment, the outdoors (outer world), your focus, attention, and antenna tunes into your surroundings: nature's beauty, intricacy, fragrance, shape, colors, sound. That signal is received by the inner world and has the power to increase or enhance your personal energy. It evokes feelings of love, peacefulness, gratitude, stillness, wonderment, and a thousand other evocative expressions. When filled with such joy, 'this' is the energy you then reflect outward.

As you begin doing the work suggested in this book, embarking on your Feng Shui journey, you will be more in tune with your personal surroundings, even perhaps learning to mirror the qualities of the natural environment that resonate for you.

Developing an ability to observe and interpret what is going on in your home, and in the lives of the people within it, is vital and life affirming. With practice, you will be able to read the unseen (Feng) and seen (Shui) energies in your home.

Imagine yourself as a body of water (which you are)—the seen energy. Starting at the front entrance of your home, see yourself moving through your space as water flowing.

In a natural setting, water flows within the boundaries of the shoreline or banks of the river, meandering, moving, flowing either quickly or slowly depending on what other elements are present. A big boulder may cause the water to go in two different directions; a narrow passage may cause the water to move quickly until it can spread out.

The movement of water is also influenced by sharp turns and sudden drops, as seen in a waterfall. As you move through your home as water, be aware of the unseen force of wind in your thoughts, your feelings, and even in your breath. Are there areas where the obstacles of furniture cause you to make a choice to move in one direction or the other? Are there areas where you move quickly or slowly, feeling more relaxed and at ease? Notice how your body responds to your heightened awareness (muscle tension diminished, rhythmic breathing). As you become more cognitive of the energetic attributes of your home, you begin to practice Feng Shui.

Client Feng Shui Story

A long time ago, I had a client who hired me to energetically assess his home. The client really felt that he wasn't being taken seriously in his work, and sometimes in his relationship. He was hoping that a Feng Shui evaluation would help. I was able to bring to his attention several issues that I saw in his and his partner's shared space that was also mirrored in their personal lives.

My client and his girlfriend seemed very compatible. They both listened intently and joked around as we did the initial tour of the home. They were living in a house that belonged to him—he and his girlfriend in the basement suite of his home. He had a lovely, older couple renting the upstairs of the home.

I was curious why my client chose to live in the basement suite, under foot, beneath the more mature adults. When I asked why he made that choice he said, "I can get more rent for the upstairs than the suite in the basement."

I asked him if he always felt like he had to go out of his way to prove himself. His environment was reflecting that and showed that he was 'settling' in areas of his life.

The downstairs suite had a tiny kitchen—like one you would find in a university dorm. It had one bedroom that did not have a door for the closet; they were 'making do' (settling).

Without asking either one of them, I told them who had which side of the bed. They were astounded that I was correct. They thought I was psychic; I assured them I was not.

I could also see that the person who slept closest to the bedroom door was also the one who was responsible for shutting off the alarm and getting the other one up in the morning. It turned out that my client's girlfriend was taking on the 'motherly' role, being the responsible adult in the relationship. The 'outer world' was reflecting what was going on in the 'inner world.'

By observing the environment in their home, I helped them to see that their current 'basement' living arrangements were not matching their conscious desires. Instead, the energies of the environment reflected their subconscious fears of not being good enough or deserving enough.

I made some suggestions for enhancements, and recommended changes for both in their shared space. With a new awareness and a few changes, they made the conscious choice to start the necessary process to move into the upstairs space of the home and rent out the basement suite. After all, they were both consenting adults, aspiring to 'move up in the world,' and wanted to be respected by their peers. Their environment was reflecting or telling a much different story than they were experiencing.

That home evaluation was profound, not only for the client but for me as well. It validated and proved that one's home environment will always mirror an image of the conscious and subconscious energies or personality of the people who reside there.

Several months later, the client let me know that they had found a great renter for the basement suite. He and his girlfriend were looking forward to moving upstairs. They asked if I would come by and offer suggestions for arranging their possessions in the new space. I hadn't seen either of them for several months and did not know them deeply at that time. It was incredible to see the positive, empowering shift in personal energy that had occurred for both of them. It was a complete result of embarking on their Feng Shui journey, going with the flow (water), and breathing new life (wind) into their intimate environment.

A few months, moving some things around, letting go and releasing a few possessions, changed perceptions they had pertaining to their basement suite, all of which had a dynamic impact on their personal and professional lives.

Life is an interactive experience.
This is Your Space.

Imagine your favorite flower. Now take a conscious breath and smell the sweet scent. Notice your body. Did you feel your shoulders relax? Did you have a smile on your face?

What memory or emotion comes to mind?

Did this remind you of the start of a meditation exercise?

Two – Feng Shui Defined

Think back to a time when you were last near or beside water. Where were you?

Who were you with?

What were you doing?

How did you feel?

Is there something or somewhere in your home environment that elicits the same positive emotions? Please write about that.

If not, you could create a space, what would that look like?

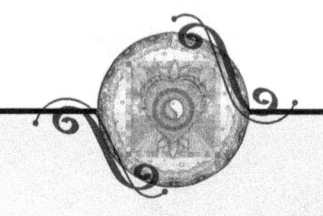

Three – Life Force Energy 'Chi'

> *"The universe is designed to support*
> *all your thoughts and ideas, and bring them to you."*
> *Anita Adrain*

You are an energetic being living in an energetic universe. If you allow yourself to become consciously aware of this truth, you have the opportunity to live an empowered life in abundant flow.

Scientists can see beyond our galaxy with powerful telescopes. They can witness the expansion, continuation, or evolution of our solar system. The macro of the universe leaves clues that it is still growing. We are the micro energy systems of the planet. Doesn't it make sense that we, too, are evolving, expanding, and growing? If you are not personally growing on some level, be it mentally or spiritually, you are doing the opposite: dying.

I do not understand the technical, scientific aspects of our cosmos, but I do recognize that the life force energy, chi, is constantly growing, changing, and connecting with everything—this is the inherent nature of all things.

> "Everything in this entire universe is connected to everything else in this entire universe through the law of vibration." *You Were Born Rich*, Bob Proctor

What Is Chi?

The universal life force energy is called chi. Other traditions refer to the Great spirit, God, Yahweh, Christ Consciousness, Buddha—the label matters not. What is true is that all traditions recognize one unifying life force.

> "In Traditional Chinese culture, qì or ch'i is an active principle forming part of any living thing. Qi literally translates as 'breath,' 'air,' or 'gas,' and figuratively as 'material energy,' 'life force,' or 'energy flow.' Qi is the central underlying principle in traditional Chinese medicine and martial arts."
>
> Excerpt from Wikipedia

> "Concepts similar to qi can be found in many cultures, for example, 'prana' in the Hindu religion, 'chi' in the Igbo religion, 'pneuma' in ancient Greece, 'mana' in Hawaiian culture, 'lüng' in Tibetan Buddhism, 'manitou' in the culture of the Indigenous of the Americas, 'ruah' in Hebrew culture, and 'vital energy' in Western philosophy. Some elements of qi can be understood in the term energy when used by writers and practitioners of various esoteric forms of spirituality and alternative medicine."
>
> Excerpt from Wikipedia

Chi is…

Sometimes we can see chi and sometimes we cannot.

> "To believe in the things you can see, and touch is no belief at all; but to believe in the unseen is a triumph and a blessing." Abraham Lincoln

It has been my experience that what we cannot see is far more powerful than what we can see. Examples of energy that we cannot see are: electricity, gas, wind, and gravity. We can witness the effects of the wind as it blows debris around in a windstorm. We use natural gas to heat our homes. We use the Earth's magnetic energy without contemplating or consciously acknowledging the source. How would we survive without electricity? At the quantum level of understanding, the human body is a conductor of electrical energy. We are so dependent on the immediate supply that operates our laptop, television, stove, fridge, and all the modern conveniences, that we don't recognize that these items use unseen energy. We can connect with anyone thousands of miles away (think: www) using technology that harnesses unseen energy. Imagine, if you were to go back in time with all these 'unseen forces of energy,' you would likely be burned at the stake for all your sorcery.

When you practice and apply Feng Shui principles to your home, you may discover the unseen forces, having a positive effect on those around you.

> "Nobody changes their life until they change their energy"
> Dr. Joe Dispenza

The intangible chi is connected to the tangible aspects of all things that we can see and touch. Examples of energy that we can see are people, animals, color, water and fire.

If chi is in everything, and everywhere, then we must be connected to and a part of this energy. Example: think about the unseen force of electricity that lights up a light bulb. What we see is the tangible result.

Speaking of light bulbs: have you ever had a light bulb moment? Suddenly, a thought enters your mind and, 'Aha!' This is another example of unseen energy.

In The Flow

Universal Life Force Energy chi is in a consistent state of movement and change; nothing sits still.

We are a part of an energy system that is moving forward in perpetual motion, in and out, expanding and contracting. Chi moves in a cycle or circle.

Every day, Mother Nature confirms the life force that permeates in and throughout all things, evident in the fresh new day complete with sunshine. She completes the day by saying goodnight with the sunset which reminds us of her beautiful cycle. This continues day in and day out, with or without us. Days accumulate into weeks and months, with four distinct seasons, until we return to start the cycle once again. We only need to look at the stars, the moon, and the sun, to witness the relationship of Mother Earth with the unseen forces connecting us to the seen forces.

Have you ever seen a golden thread connecting the moon to the Earth? I have not, yet somehow the moon has an incredible 'cause' or 'effect' upon our physiology, and on the Earth.

The moon has a powerful influence on the oceans as it controls the tides; it's remarkable how the moon affects BILLIONS of gallons of water. If the moon has such a dramatic effect on two thirds of the Earth's surface, and our bodies are comprised of 70-80% water, it makes sense that the moon would influence us as well.

On a full moon, people react to the unseen energies—simply ask a nurse or a policeman what their day is like when there is a full moon. They will tell you their shift was 'crazy,' and much busier than usual. We even have a word for it: lunacy.

The full moon represents a turning point in time, it signifies closure, and is a sign to harvest at full cycle. For centuries, humans have recognized the positive effects of the moon, taking advantage of these cycles—planting crops and sowing seeds in synchronization with the New Moon—which represents the beginning, a fresh start, and a time of initiation. This wisdom has been passed down from our ancestors. There are many examples left in history for our understanding and observation of how chi is always moving in a cycle or circle.

Indigenous people knew about the forces of the moon and seasonal cycles. They observed Mother Nature's rhythms and learned to live in harmony with her system. They honored their sacred connection with Mother Earth, using ceremonies to recognize the moon, sun, stars, and the seasons. These rituals of gratitude were to the seen and unseen energies, and the symbiotic systems which created and sustained their existence.

Members of Indigenous communities were keepers of the land, and they operated in co-operation with all Mother Earth and everything

Three – Life Force Energy 'Chi'

she offered. When they took something from the land, they always gave something back in honor and recognition of her nourishing cycle. They only took what they needed, and understood the supply and replenishment cycle. When the summer season arrived, they worked with vigor, collecting, hunting from dawn until dusk, harvesting the Earth's treasures. They honored the cycles of each season and knew when the sun would shine longest in the sky—that was their 'clue' to prepare for the seasons ahead.

> "James Knowles argued in 1834 that it was God's plan for America for New Englanders to wipe out the Native Americans, because they would not 'obey the great law of God' which 'obliged them to become civilized, and to adopt those modes of life which would enable their territory to support the greatest possible number of inhabitants.' Knowles concluded the Americans could achieve this 'by saving from ruin the helpless descendants of the savage.'" http://blog.americanindianadoptees.com/2016/11/gods-plan-mission-schools-his-story.html

Even though they had never been exposed to Christian doctrine, our Native North American tribes were in alignment with some of the teachings of the Bible long before the European settlers came to 'save them from their sins of savagery.'

> "To everything there is a season, and a time to every purpose under the heaven: A time to be born, and a time to die; a time to plant, and a time to pluck up that which is planted." Ecclesiastes 3:1-8

We often learn our greatest life lessons in retrospect. It's easy to read history books or 'google' about the trials and injustices of Indigenous peoples being forced off the land. The European settlers acted on what they knew and believed to be true for them at the time. If they had only known then what is known now, they would have understood that the land-keepers they were fighting held great insight of nature's systems, and could have taught them to live in balance and harmony.

I wonder how things would be different if the settlers had learned to honor these systems? Could we have prevented the creation of this imbalance in our environment and within our society?

Only recently does there appear to be a return to the realization that there may be a system more powerful than we know: an unseen energy system which, when we work with it in co-operation instead of in competition, allows us to achieve harmony with one another and Mother Earth.

There is NO-thing that we are not connected to energetically. As a result of our science and technological advancements, we are on the brink of re-discovering what our ancestors knew.

Energy, chi, and life-force are one and the same—metaphysical attributes of the unseen, intangible life that surrounds us, and which permeates all things.

Metaphysical describes that which is NOT physical or tangible—put simply, it cannot be seen or touched. We have been taught to put our attention on the physical aspects of life: the human body, the material things of this world, that which we can see and/or hold in our hands.

Mother Nature Leaves Clues

Over the last thirty years, as a florist and outdoor plant enthusiast, I've had the privilege of working closely with Mother Nature. Getting my hands dirty has always been an opportunity for me to feel the earth and marvel in the support it provides. I have learned a great deal by observing the intricate life force energy of nature. One instance stands out as an 'Aha!' moment.

It was during one October, as I sat on my sunny deck looking out at my beautiful Sweet Peas still blooming prolifically, that I contemplated, 'How Great Thou Art.' What began as four tiny seeds had expanded and grown into an unknown number of blooms, expressing their full potential for my enjoyment. I had planted Sweet Peas many times before but, for some reason on this day, I was in awe of the cycle of life.

The potential of those four tiny seeds would not have been realized had I not taken the action to plant them, then nurtured them in the right environment—an energy-rich space of nutrient-filled soil, exposed to the right amount of sunshine and water.

Once planted, the cycle of life had soon begun: the seeds sprouted and the shoots expanded and grew hundreds of leaves. With the support of the trellis, and with the long summer days, intensely scented, purple blooms began to emerge against the green foliage. These blooms attracted bees and other insects. I was able to bring many blooms into my home to enjoy the sweet fragrance up-close; enjoyment that spread to my neighbors. The entire process had become chi enhancing.

The plants continued well into the fall somehow averting the touch of Jack Frost—they were in a well-protected, sheltered flower bed. It was then I noticed many seed pods had accumulated on the vine, each one containing three to six seeds—some even more. Mother Nature had exponentially increased the fruits, the seeds for the cycle to start again, with the potential to be prolific. If left to the natural process, the seeds would have returned to the soil, been protected with the fallen leaves—a natural compost to replenish the soil in the spring. The cover of snow from the winter months would keep the seeds dormant—sleeping. The promise of spring, the new day, the New Year, would have supplied a new cycle for the seeds to reach their full expression once again.

Life force—chi—is constantly moving and changing, expanding and contracting, circulating throughout all living systems as was evident in my observation of my Sweet Peas.

In his book *Fractal Time,* Gregg Braden refers to the cycles of nature from other noted sources:

> "'There are cycles in everything. There are cycles in the weather, economy, sun, wars, geological formation, atomic vibrations, climate, human moods, the motions of the planets, populations of animals, the occurrence of diseases, the prices of commodities and shares and in the large-scale structure of the universe.' Ray Tomes, contemporary philosopher."

Talk about coming full circle or returning to our beginnings; as we return to our roots, so does Mother Nature literally cycle back to her own.

As a metaphor and 'guided instruction,' it appears to be a time for humanity to get back to the teachings of the ancients and celebrate its relationship with Mother Nature—Mother Earth, Gaia, the Creator.

"What you do for your brother you do for me."
(Matthew 25:40)

Like many others, I believe in a cycle of humanity. We have another chance. Just like our biological mother who gave lots of chances and forgave us for past wrong doings, so too is Mother Nature providing another opportunity to begin a new cycle and respect that she is our Life-Force.

Chi Continued

A refresher: Everything is alive with chi—the glue of the universe. Chi is constantly moving and changing, moving in a cycle or circle. Chi is tangible and intangible—seen and unseen.

We've all heard or used one or more of these expressions before, without fully being aware of the cyclical energy systems that have been in place since the beginning of time:

'Reap what you sow.'
'What goes around, comes around.'
'Ask and you shall receive.'

'What you put out there comes back to you,' is a true statement when we consider that we are energetic beings living in an energetic universe.

Your personal well-beingness (energy) reflects outward into your community, your town, your city, your country, and so on, reflecting the personal vibration that you are. Your well-beingness ripples, touching all in its path. If people were in sync with their natural environment, they would be more grounded or stable, and would radiate compassion, love, peace, and harmony. Imagine all that energy going out into the world: what joy!

The human body is a hub of electrical activity with basic biological systems dependent on electrolytes for cell-to-cell instantaneous communication. The nervous system relies on this communication to achieve optimum health. A break in the circuit can cause imbalance similar to what happens when the power circuit in your house is disrupted.

There is a field of unseen energy, an electromagnetic field, that surrounds you and expands outward, intermingling with the energy around everything, including the space of your home and all its contents. Some experts say this field radiates over twenty-five feet beyond your physical body (other scientists believe that it has no boundaries). Consider that this invisible field of energy is touching and intermingling with another person's energy field some twenty-five steps away from you.

This field of energy is called a torus—a doughnut shaped magnetic field, an invisible cloak or bubble of energy that exists around all living systems. Do you remember a school science experiment in which metal shavings came into alignment with the electrical energies of positive and negative charge? If you recall, the shavings formed a shape. This visible outline of those shavings was the torus.

> "Toroidal energy fields exist around everything: people, trees, the Earth, sun, and universe. It is the key to everything because your entire life is created by and from this place. Most torus dynamics contain two 'toruses' or 'tori'—like the male and female aspects of the whole, one is spiraling upwards and the other downwards." www.mindmovies.com

The torus field of energy has similar attributes to the Yin Yang symbol with male and female aspects of the whole. Upon closer examination, we may uncover more clues or an unspoken language that communicates this preserved knowledge of intrinsic design, a benevolent energy system left by the ancients for us to discover.

Life is an interactive experience.
This is Your Space.

The more you hear this, the more you'll understand the interconnectedness on our planet and in the universe: your outer world is connected to, and reflected in, your inner world.

Mother Nature left us 'clues' reminding us of the unlimited supply of the universe: the beautiful, perfect cycles of life that surround us each day, awakening and reaching their full potential.

What seeds have you sown in the garden of your mind (your inner world) that will return to you tenfold? Past or present.

What deep desires of yours are waiting to emerge, expand, and express themselves in your outer world?

Three – Life Force Energy 'Chi'

When you are in a state of peace-fullness, at ease, comfortable, and relaxed, what effect does that have on everything, everyone around you?

Leading to the final question—consider whether you have ever given much thought to the 'wisdom' that awakens the dormant seed in the ground. The force that makes it spring to life. The way the seed knows its potential is to become a tree, a bush, or a Sweet Pea…
Is it possible the same life force energy that shows up in nature also shows up in humankind? What evidence have you seen?

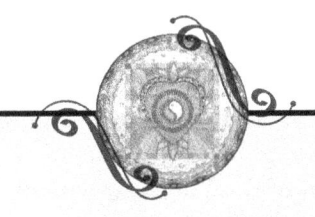

Four – Universal Symbol

"Increasing our personal energetic vibration impacts the increased vibration of the whole—all of humanity."
Anita Adrain

Everything in the universe has an opposite or opposing force: Yin and Yang, male and female, hot and cold, soft and hard.

The Yin and Yang combination—two comet-like shapes within a circle—is probably one of the most recognized, universal symbols. It's generally understood and referred to as the symbol of opposites.

Divine Design

Within the pages of a great little handbook I picked up years ago, *Awakening Your Physic Powers,* are spiritual concepts and scientific explanations for living the mind, body, spirit connection.

Based on the writings of Edgar Cayce, the book, *Awakening Your Physic Powers* by Henry Reed, is still in print, and it offers valuable insights into the inner workings of the human mind.

Edgar Cayce, noted as America's most amazing see-er, founded the Association for Research and Enlightenment (A.R.E.) over eighty-five years ago with the purpose of helping people to transform their lives in the understanding of energy systems, specifically that of the unseen: living a purposeful life with a deep connection to the divine.

Four – Universal Symbol

The divine, to me is reference to God, the Creator, the universe, the oneness that is within each of us, the part that we refer to as our essence or spirit.

Cayce may not have specifically referred to Feng Shui, but there are many similarities in the core of his teachings.

A detailed explanation of the Yin Yang symbol, and the meaning as described by Cayce—and written by Henry Reed—offers insight to the reader.

While scientists, psychiatrists, yogis, spiritual teachers, authors, and scholars offer in-depth explanations or interpretations of Yin Yang as an energy system, this simple primer, below, is the best way to begin understanding the symbol and what it represents.

Balance

The Yin Yang symbol is the black and white expression of two comet shapes which dance and intermingle in the center of a circle that represents the whole. Gazing upon, even meditating on, this universal symbol, one might come up with a deeper understanding and appreciation of what it represents.

Cayce describes the Yin Yang symbol as probably being the oldest expression of the primal creative process.

Depending on your spiritual or religious upbringing, God or the Creator would represent the circle or the energy of the oneness: the whole.

The parts of the whole—the male and female expressions—are not separate from each other, yet form another aspect from which to view or perceive the whole.

Is this universal symbol an expression of, or in reference to, the many creation stories reference the dividing of forces—the 'one' that became 'two'?

> "All creative energy results from this one source, from the central, universal vibration at the beginning of creation."
> *Awakening Your Psychic Powers* by Henry Reed.

"That flip-flop back and forth between two ways of perceiving the curve is the basic dynamic of vibration, an oscillation between two opposing perspectives. Oscillation/vibration is the basis of energy."

Awakening Your Psychic Powers by Henry Reed.

You might see this symbol as being black with a white background or white with a black background. Seemingly opposite forces, complementary in how they interrelate, they are a fusion of energy from one source.

In Eastern philosophy and the study of Feng Shui, Yin Yang represent a balance of creative energy forces within a person's intimate space: the home environment.

Yin Yang shows us that energy is always flowing, moving. It also shows us the benefit of a balanced lifestyle, creating a quality of life that can be extraordinary. The key word is balance.

A New View

I would like you to take a moment for an exercise; I'll share some wisdom as we go through it.
Please use the blank space on the next page.
First, I want you to create a Yin Yang image.
To do that, draw a circle, any size that you like.

Then, with a letter 'S' in mind, start at the top right of the circle, follow the existing curve and move your pen or pencil downward, connecting to the bottom left of the circle. It's like making a large letter S through the middle of your circle.

Now, in the larger parts that each resemble a comet shape, create a small circle—a center, if you like, to each of the curves—basically a little circle at the top and bottom of the whole.

Next, shade one 'comet' except for its little circle, and shade in the circle in the remaining unshaded 'comet.'

Four – Universal Symbol

This should resemble the Yin Yang image.

Upon closer observation of this symbol you should be able to see the inward movement of the feminine expressed as Yin energy (the black comet), and the outward movement of male expressed as Yang energy (the white comet).

The dynamics and dualities of Yin Yang are exampled by its expanding and contracting, pulling and pushing, with the sum of the two parts (created by the S curve drawn in your circle) forming a whole symbol.

Perhaps the knowledge that the ancients left in this pattern for us to recognize and realize was that of coherence?

> "The state of being coherent is formed by unifying the sum of the parts to be united, so they form a synthesized whole." (www.ascensionglossary.com)

I think that definition matches the image of the Yin Yang symbol: two unified parts united within the one circle. A symbol of balance and coherence.

> "Most people know what it feels like to be in harmonious state, the place where our hearts, minds and bodies are united in a feeling of wholeness. This state is often referred to as "the zone," "flow," "oneness." When we are in such states, we typically feel connected not only to our deepest selves but to others, even to the Earth itself. We call this state of internal and external connectedness "coherence." This overview discusses how increased personal coherence can be achieved as people learn to more consistently self-regulate their emotions from a more intuitive, intelligent, and balanced inner reference and how this state is directly associated with increased intuition and improved health and cognitive functioning." HeartMath newsletter: 10 ALTERNATIVE THERAPIES, Jul/Aug 2010, VOL. 16, NO. 4 Coherence: Bridging Personal, Social, and Global Health www.heartmath.com

Four – Universal Symbol

Practice makes permanent, so draw another Yin Yang symbol. Further to your previous drawing I would like you to take a few moments to add or enhance the image, as I would like to visually demonstrate how achieving coherence is possible for you, starting right now if you choose.

Add to your drawing by closing off the curves of the S and turning it into the number 8. You should now have a circle with the number 8 in the middle—two small circles, one in the top and one in the bottom of your original circle.

The HeART of Feng Shui... Simply Put

Take your pen or pencil and lightly mark or shade the areas of the number 8. Does it resemble an hourglass in a circle? Great if it does. Redraw if it doesn't.

This modified Yin Yang symbol is my own design, which you have now recreated. There are 3 main parts consisting of the 8, and the two spaces—one on either side of the 8.

In a later chapter you will gain insight into another energy system, that of numerology. According to numerology, there are further messages, significant in the understanding of the study of Feng Shui, within the energy of the numbers 3 and 8.

If we take the 3 parts and multiply by the number 8, it equals 24. We express our days in 24 segments. It is recommended that, to achieve a balanced healthy life, we get 8 hours a day for rest or sleep, 8 hours a day for our life's work, and the remaining 8 hours for our leisure or play. When you can recognize where you are out of balance you can move back into flow. Only then can your minutes, hours, days—cycles within cycles—form a natural expansion and contraction with night and day.

Shade the number 8. This represents your work time, the middle or active part of the day. To the left represents your 8 hours of rest, and the area to right of the 8 represent your play or leisure time.

Out of balance, the number 8 would be distorted and could be shown as being very wide, expanding outward and consuming the space that represents the 8 hours for leisure, play, creative expression, self-love and other life-delights. Or the 8 hours that represents rest.

Now, consider how your personal '24 hours' looks with the new Yin Yang symbol as your guide. Is your life in balance—in coherence? I invite you to draw an overlay on a new Yin Yang symbol to represent what your life currently looks like. Then draw a symbol of what your optimum life balance would look like. Observe this and reflect on it. Therein lies the clue for you in how you can regain or achieve balance using this new version of the Yin Yang symbol.

What works for you? Perhaps you feel balanced with a 6-hour work day, and 9 hours for rest and play.

It's important to recognize that there are times in life when we are out of balance for short periods of time. We all experience instances when we may be operating on five hours of sleep a night and working twelve-hour days, only to spend even more time—a couple of hours—working at home to finish that work project. Or, as my son the accountant does when it's tax season, leaving very little time for self-care, self-love, and spending time with loved ones. This pace can only be sustained for so long before the body's systems are stressed to the point of affecting all area of one's life.

The creative source expressed in the Yin Yang symbol, represented by the areas of play and leisure, are as important as rest and work. When you have time to play, to be creative, to live in the moment, experiencing joy doing something that makes you happy, you vibrate at a higher frequency.

Engaging in a creative process also build new neurons. Neurons are the basic functional units of the nervous system. An excellent explanation and illustration of this appears in: https://www.khanacademy.org/science/biology/human-biology/neuron-nervous-system/a/overview-of-neuron-structure-and-function

The body's nervous system responds to conditions inside and outside the body. The majority of cells that make up the nervous system's tissue are neurons. This is important because neurons are essential to body function, communicating and transmitting electrochemical signals throughout the body. If the nervous system is out of balance, it's safe to say the health of the body is in jeopardy, in a state of dis-ease, or out of ease.

If coherence implies order, structure, harmony, and being in alignment within, then incoherence would imply the opposite: chaos, dis-harmony, and out-of-balance.

Isn't it interesting to know that, if you learned to paint, dance, or build something, you would be positively affecting your nervous system? Remember practicing Feng Shui is another way in which you can support and relax the nervous system.

Living a balanced lifestyle, with the understanding and use of my version of the Yin Yang symbol, is a great place to start in achieving optimum health.

The Creative Force

These two energies—Yin and Yang—show up in all areas of our life, including our homes. When you create balance in the outside environment of your home, you increase your vital life force energy—your chi—and you thereby achieve balance in all areas of your life, including the inner environment. Doing so creates a state of coherence (balance).

Visual balance can be achieved in a particular space in the home when Yin and Yang are both represented, creating the feeling of peacefulness, calm, and inner harmony.

Four – Universal Symbol

A general guide for you to know if a room is more Yang than Yin, or more Yin than Yang, is to notice what color or item dominates or stands out more in the room.

Yang energy is very bold; it's active (male)—it's in your face. The word 'strong' is associated with Yang energy.

Yin energy is more subdued; it's passive (female). The words 'soft' and 'subtle' are associated with Yin energy.

Colors in use, in the home environment, need a complimentary expression to balance the Yin Yang energies.

Experiment with these forces of energy in any area to create balance, ultimately seeing if you can feel a shift or feel different when you, say, add a bold color in the way of throw or cushion, compared to adding a soft color.

Always consider the room's use in your determination of adding more Yin or Yang energies. Balance is essential. For example, a bedroom is one area where you will want to have more Yin energy. Soft, passive, or dark moody tones expressing the feminine.

Creating a balanced environment is having Yin and Yang energies present in a state of balance and harmony. A great way to achieve this is by becoming familiar with the five elements, and with the use of the 5-element theory that we will go over in detail in later chapters.

Further examination of the original Yin Yang image reveals what Edgar Cayce described as the magnetic energy in which the positive charge attracts, and the negative charge repels. The two smaller circles may very well represent the North and South magnetic poles. Finding your way and navigating this subject further may require the use of a compass—that instrument designed to align with the Earth's magnetic energies of North and South, enabling the user to find his or her way.

Classical Feng Shui uses a compass called the LuoPan (Lopan). It is used to provide a precise geomantic chart for the client. It has been my observation that we all have our own built in compass. In this 'New View' of understanding Feng Shui as the study of energy, we may want to refer to this Inner Compass as the LovePan.

Life is an interactive experience.
This is your space.

What area of your life is currently out of balance?

What steps could you take to restore balance in your version of the Yin Yang symbol in these 3 areas;

Work:

Rest:

Play:

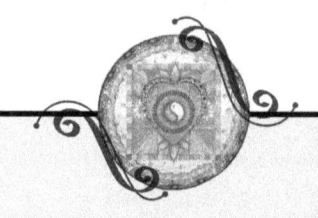

Five – Home Is Where The Heart Lives

*"Living in a state of emotional excellence, or close to it,
is the path to reaching your highest human potential"*
Anita Adrain

When we each tune into our heart, and live a consciously aware life in rhythm with the environment, it is possible to live in harmony with the Earth and its inhabitants. The Earth and the heart are indelibly connected—it's no coincidence that the same letters that appear in 'earth' also appear in 'heart.'

Have you ever considered that your heart is more than a beating organ within your body?

"Above all else, guard your heart, for it is the well spring of life."
Solomon Prov. 4.23

Have you ever heard or used the expression 'Home is where the heart is'? If home is where the heart is, then home must also be where the heart lives.

There are many references to the heart in giving advice in the matters of love; the symbol of the heart is well known and used to celebrate St. Valentine's Day.

February fourteenth, St. Valentine's Day, is the one day of the year that surpasses all others as being the biggest in floral sales. I know this first-hand; as a professional florist I have made thousands of Valentine's bouquets, all created in hopes of helping someone express the deepest emotion, that of love.

I may have exchanged money for flowers and plants, and sold my customers physical arrangements, but what I was really selling was a product that conveyed an emotion. Those emotions represented love, compassion, gratitude, appreciation, empathy, and thoughtfulness. There are many reasons people buy flowers—all represent gifts from the heart.

Home must be where your heart is, and where your heart lives. Your heartfelt thoughts, attitudes, and emotions create an energetic environment that affects perspective, relationships, and even touches those around you? Remember the torus field? That field, seemingly a natural extension of your energy, bumps, connects, interacts, and overlaps with the fields of others.

The good news is you have the power to amplify that energy with attitudes of genuine love, appreciation, care, and compassion.

> "There is biological process that involves the heart, brain, nervous and hormonal systems and sensory organs. All as a result of experiencing an emotion." www.heartmath.org

Your heart is a powerful working compass that you have not been taught how to use… until now.

What's Love Got to Do With It?

For many years, I have taught my clients and students to live with what they love, and to love where they live. I realized the importance of activating positive emotional energy in their homes, sharing with them that the word e-motion is energy in motion. When they began to activate the positive emotions in the physical environment of their home, they also began to activate more of the same in their inner world environment. This elevated state of awareness put them in a state of emotional excellence which helped them to realize a greater existence.

When I became aware of the Institute of HeartMath (thank you, Lee Carroll, for introducing me to this important and relevant work), I received scientific validation and confirmation of these practices.

Inner Compass - Lo(ve)Pan

'Listen to your heart' and 'follow your heart' are metaphors and, according to Deborah Rozman Ph.D., founding executive director of the HeartMath Institute, these statements are physiologically correct.

I was in the right place at the right time when I met Deborah at The Summer Light conference in Big Sky, Montana. Her keynote—during which I wrote frantically—and my own thoughts, combine to emphasize the importance of the heart, love, and benevolent connection.

> "Scientists at the HeartMath Institute in California have been studying the affects of the heart since 1990s. It is their belief that the next frontier of human awakening is about understanding how to better use the power of emotion to enhance the quality of our life experiences, improve health and ultimately find solutions to personal and societal problems." HeartMath Institute www.heartmath.org

We associate the word love with the heart and, until now, you may not have realized the importance of that association.

Did you know the heart generates the strongest electromagnetic field of the body?

The communication that happens between the brain and the heart—when a subject focuses his or her attention on the feeling or experience of positive thoughts such as love, gratitude, or compassion—can be measured.

An ECG (electrocardiogram) measures the heart rate variability or HRV. If you were to take a pen and draw a letter M, and repeat the M-pattern erratically, the resulting illustration might resemble the HRV chart of a stressed person.

When you have heart-focused awareness on a positive feeling or emotion, the HRV chart is similar to drawing a repeat of a letter U followed by an upside-down U. The HRV in this case is more wavy and consistent than the sharp M-pattern. The wider the gap between the peak and the valley, the more resilient we become. 'Water off a duck's back' or 'going with the flow' are clichés that example someone who is resilient and less likely to have his or her buttons pushed.

When you can learn to sustain positive emotions, a happy go lucky attitude, your nervous system is relaxed or at ease and the heart becomes coherent, in harmony with all of your other biological systems.

> "For the last 30 years Heart Math's founder, Doc Childre, has been developing the Heart Math Systems' research-based tools and techniques that are especially useful for regulating emotions. The core of Doc's system focuses on the heart, both energetically and physical, as a powerful source of innate intelligence. Neuro cardiologists have decisively established that the heart is not just a muscle. It's also a sensory organ and a sophisticated information processing center. The heart has its own nervous system which gives it the ability to sense, learn, remember and make functional decisions independent of the brain."
> HeartMath Institute www.heartmath.com

An EEG (electroencephalogram) is a test used to evaluate the electrical activity in the brain and records brain wave patterns. Different emotional states produce different outcomes.

> "Coherence is a highly efficient state in which all of the body's systems work together in harmony. Increasing personal coherence creates an alignment of mind, body, emotions and spirit through the power of the heart."
> HeartMath Newsletter: You Can Positively Change Your Personal Field Environment July 8, 2016, www.heartmath.org

Heart intelligence plays a very important role in our physical health. Five minutes of heart-focused awareness, activating positive feelings, boosts the immune system for up to six hours! Imagine the power within, with a new thought every second, if we could become aware of the thoughts, thinking only positive thoughts for three hundred seconds. Do that several times a day and chances are you could extend the length of your life, or at least the quality of your life.

Biochemically, when the heart is in coherence, the balancing hormone serotonin is released. Considered the happy hormone, serotonin is a mood regulator making us feel calm and at ease, creating emotional stability. Serotonin is also a pre-cursor for the hormone melatonin which is secreted by the pineal gland. Melatonin is mainly known for regulating sleep (synthetic versions are used to help with sleeping when your circadian rhythm has been disrupted—like through travel). Melatonin also has anti-aging properties, helping to neutralize free radicals in the body, promote DNA repair, and heighten immune response as well as other benefits.

> The HeartMath Institute teaches several powerful ways that only take a few minutes to practice in order to achieve heart/brain coherence. They are similar to the technique that I would like to share with you (on the next page) that you can practice right now. https://www.heartmath.org/resources/heartmath-tools/quick-coherence-technique-for-adults/ Note: HeartMath has two separate websites, a dot com and a dot org.

Simply put: happy thoughts create happy hormones; negative or not so positive thoughts create stress hormones. When the stress hormones go up, the level of melatonin goes down, and when stress hormones go down, melatonin levels go up. By this account it would appear that reducing stress equates to living longer in a healthier body.

The HeartMath Institute teaches several powerful techniques that only take a few minutes to practice to achieve heart brain coherence. They are similar to the technique that I would like to share with you (below) that you can practice right now.

The Energetic Heart Code Technique™ Anita Adrain

Place your hand on your heart, then bring awareness—focus your attention—in the area of your heart.

Take a deep breath in, hold to the count of 5 or 6 seconds, then exhale to the count of 5 or 6. Do this several times until you start to feel your body relax.

With each breath, FEEL the feeling of gratitude or deep appreciation and, with each exhale, FEEL the feeling of love.

Breathe in gratitude while recalling what you are grateful for. Exhale love while recalling a personal experience of giving or receiving love. Inhale gratitude, exhale love, and repeat.

Continue this pattern until you feel your body has totally relaxed and released all tension.

This exercise takes a few minutes and can be used anytime you are sensing any dis-harmonic feelings. You can practice in your car, at your office, with your eyes open or closed. The important thing is to practice being in a state of heart-brain coherence. This is a way of managing stress and transforming your state of being. In short, what this practice does is add more heart to your day.

Your heart is your built-in compass, your emotional gauge. Now that you have a better understanding of how to use it, you can attract positive results as you navigate life's journey.

The HeART of Feng Shui… Simply Put contains examples of an Energetic Heart Code™ which have been purposely created for you to practice being resilient.

When you see "H.E.A.R.T." take a few minutes, focus on the individual words or the entire phrase, whichever holds a deeper emotional connection for you personally, and FEEL the feelings that come up for you.

There are 5 letters in the word heart, a number which serves as a reminder to breathe and hold and exhale for 5 seconds or more. Focus on each of the phrases or individual words for sixty seconds or more. It is believed by doing this you can achieve a boost to your immune system for upwards of 6 hours.

H.appy **E.**motions **A.**lways **R.**adiate **T.**oward-others

You can practice this 5-minute technique anywhere, simply by inhaling gratitude and exhaling love while recalling what you are grateful for, and who or what you love.

I have also created a card deck with Energetic Heart Codes that you can place in areas of your home, or keep in your car—areas where you may experience stress and need a quick reminder to focus your attention on balancing the heart brain connection. Each card will help you to reduce stress in a short time—a few minutes.

Five – Home Is Where The Heart Lives

Heart Intelligence

The current state of the environment of your home is a contributing factor to your overall health and well-being. Considering how much time you spend in there, doesn't it make sense to start there—at home—creating a harmonious space that allows all occupants to be at ease, feel safe, nurtured and loved?

The outer world environment stimulates, supports, and/or de-presses the emotional state of the person.

All material and matter that shows up in your physical space has been created first by a thought (unseen energy) and then created from the abundant resources (seen energy) from Mother Earth. Therefore, everything is connected to everything else and contributes to the overall energy within your home.

The intimate space of your home reflects your core values, emotions, personal tastes, and experiences. The things that you value—your possessions—are an expression of the same.

If you start with a healthy home, your spiritual heart opens more easily, and kindness comes naturally, magnetizing the wisdom of our soul nature, or soul purpose, journey, and love connections. Heart-brain coherence is supported by a healthy environment.

All it takes is an open heart and mind, and a willingness to apply the principles, practices, and suggested activities in this book to embrace a healthy lifestyle. As this book's title suggests, the heart of Feng Shui is an art in which each of us can participate.

Home Is Where the Heart Is: A Love Story

Mother's Day is a day Mothers all over the world are honored and revered for their invaluable contributions to the family unit. In the floral business, it's especially busy because many expressions of love are given through bouquets and arrangements.

When my children were younger and required supervision, my Mother was my saving grace during busy holiday occasions. She would come and stay at my house for the entire week. This allowed me to render all my

Motherly duties as I worked long hours preparing bouquets for all those special people.

It was one of these times when my Mother had brought along her crocheting. She was making a little bonnet and sweater for one of her great grandchildren that was due to arrive later in the month.

One of my sons, who was nine at the time, was intrigued with the swiftness and skill his grandmother displayed as she magically transformed the ball of wool into a recognizable shape. He asked his grandmother if she could teach him and, if at all possible, could he make something for his Mom (me) for Mother's Day. So, for the remainder of the week, in-between chores and after school activities, grandma taught her grandson how to crochet.

I was not aware of the creative endeavour until the morning of Mother's Day. Everyone was up early to present their gifts as I had to open the store later in the morning to accommodate the last-minute shoppers—after all, every mother deserves a beautiful bouquet of flowers.

My middle son was beaming with pride as he handed me a small box that was obviously wrapped without the help of his grandmother. There was a hand written card—created with construction paper—that I was not allowed to read until after opening the present. He was so excited for me to see what was inside that I'm pretty sure he did most of the unwrapping.

Inside the box was a piece of tissue which, once removed, exposed the gift of 'love.' A soft-colored mauve slipper that he had crocheted. He was quick to tell me, with pride, that he had made it all by himself. "Mom, I only had time to make you one slipper." The handwritten card explained this detail along with the promise to make the other one.

It is sixteen years later, and I still have ONE crocheted slipper. Yes, I still have it, and the memory of that Mother's Day will stay with me for the rest of my life as I am sure the slipper will too.

A small pair of hands made that slipper with unconditional love and a pure heart. Once a ball of wool and, to the eyes of a stranger, just a slipper. For me, that slipper is a testament to the bond between a son and a Mother, and defines our love. Recalling this memory to share with you, my eyes are filled with tears and my heart over-filled with love, gratitude, and deep appreciation; the same feeling and response I had many years ago.

Five – Home Is Where The Heart Lives

    I have many other 'treasured' items that were handmade and given as gifts of love from my other sons. All possess-ions imbued with the deep emotion that can never be replaced. These items are personally symbolic for me; powerful reminders of energy in motion. They always put a smile on my face, and will always have a place in my home and in my heart.

Life is an interactive experience.
This is your space.

Where do we begin this heart work? We start in our home environment, creating a harmonious space that allows all occupants to be at ease, feel safe, nurtured, and loved. And we repeat that in ourselves, and ensure we are open and 'kind-hearted' to those with whom we interact. Have you ever received a gift that brought tears to your eyes? What was it? Who gave it to you? Do you still have it?

Do you feel loved? By whom?

Five – Home Is Where The Heart Lives

Make a list of 12 things seen or unseen that you are grateful for.

-
-
-
-
-
-
-
-
-
-
-
-

Make a list of the 12 things seen or unseen that you love.

-
-
-
-
-
-
-
-
-
-
-
-

ENERGETIC HEART CODES™

Focus your attention in the area of your heart.
With the intention of breathing in gratitude and exhaling love:
Take a deep breath in for 5 seconds or more.
Hold for 5 seconds. Exhale for 5 seconds or more.
Bring your awareness and attention to each word and
or phrase in the Energetic Heart Code below.
Bringing them into your heart— feel the feeling of the
word or phrase radiating to every cell of your being.
Relax and repeat, while continuing to breathe,
to create heart-brain coherence.

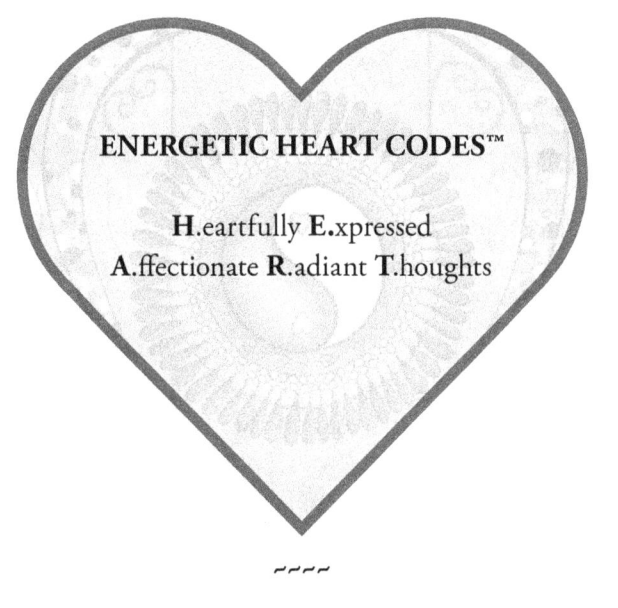

ENERGETIC HEART CODES™

H.eartfully **E.**xpressed
A.ffectionate **R.**adiant **T.**houghts

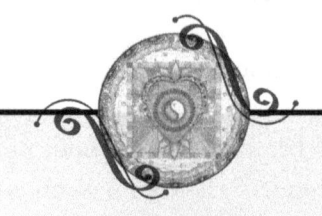

Six – Mind Over Matter

*"If you want to re-program your operating systems
you must release that which no longer serves your highest good."*
Anita Adrain

It is essential to understand that your inner world—your thoughts, beliefs, and emotions—are connected to, and reflected in, your outer world.

It is said that each person has about 60,000 thoughts a day (about a thought every second) and that each person is only consciously aware of about ten percent of those thoughts.

So that must mean that the other 54,000 thoughts, the ninety percent, are in the depths of the unconscious mind (also known as the subconscious). Could it be possible then, that the subconscious programs—those based on our past experiences and beliefs—are also being reflected in our home?

'As within, so without,' is not *just* another quote; there is profound truth in that phrase. It has always been of great interest to me to see how in fact this plays out time and time again in my clients' homes. Sometimes I am sure that they think I have some psychic gift, whereas I am just reading the energy of their home, knowing that what's going on in their minds is being expressed outwardly, and therefore reflected in their home.

It is my desire to heighten everyone's awareness and connectedness to ALL things. We have been taught that we are separate from the ground we walk on, separate from the circumstances that happen to other people, separate from the walls that surround us, and separate from the food we use to sustain our life, when in fact there is NO-thing that we are not connected to energetically.

Inner world and outer world are intricately connected, and so it is that you can 'not' work on your inner world without working on the outer world, or the other way around.

> "When there is light in the soul, there is beauty in the person, when there is beauty in the person, there is harmony in the home, when there is harmony in the home, there is honor in the nation, when there is honor in the nation, there is peace in the land."
>
> Author unknown

Creating harmony in the home starts with creating harmony in the person. Achieving this preferable state, where we can co-exist as peaceful inhabitants of planet earth, begins in the mind with the thoughts we create.

I'm not certain who really should be given the credit for the following acronym, as Bob Proctor, world-renowned speaker, motivational coach, bestselling author, and Law of Attraction teacher uses a similar version in his teachings.

T.E.A.R. Thoughts + **E**motions + **A**ction = **R**esults

Your thoughts plus your emotions plus your actions equal your results. I first learned of this equation in 2001 as a student of T.Harv Eker, founder of Peak Potentials Training Inc., and New York Times #1 bestselling author of *Secrets of the Millionaire mind, mastering the Inner Game of Wealth*. As a student of the Millionaire mind Intensive Weekend and active member at many subsequent events, I consider T.Harv one of my influential mentors.

Thoughts + Emotions + Action = Results. This mathematical and word equation has great relevance, in my opinion, in the unraveling and understanding of how powerful the practice and application of Feng Shui is, as the study of energy.

Take some simple math learned in grade school: 1+2+3=6.

From that we were probably shown—or figured it out ourselves that: if 1+2+3=6 then 6-2-1=3 or 6-3=2+1.

With the equation in mind: Thoughts + Emotions + Action = Results Your thoughts 'T' and your emotions 'E' (feelings) and your actions 'A' cause the results that are currently showing up in any area of your life, be it wealth or romance. If you are not happy with the result, then you have to determine which of the other three 'numbers' or 'factors' that make up the equation are the weak link for you.

Dis-empowering Thoughts create non-supporting Emotions which may cause you to make poor choices or take no action. If there is no action, then there is an inability to move in any direction, which has direct impact on your Results. There is a big difference between activity and inspired action.

Inspired action has the potency to amplify that which you desire or are moving toward.

I first want to take you through each one of these letters (ideas), T, E, A, R, separately, and then I will relate the relevance to Feng Shui and how you can apply this mathematical word equation to your life, producing amazing results.

T is for Thoughts

T.E.A.R. (Thoughts + Emotions + Actions = Results)

> "Therefore, as soon as you choose certain thoughts, your brain cells are affected. The cells vibrate and send off electromagnetic waves. When you concentrate on those thoughts, you increase the amplitude of vibration of those cells, and the electric waves, in turn, become much more potent." Bob Proctor, *You Were Born Rich*

I am sure you have heard thoughts are things or thoughts become things.

This is easy to believe when you consider that everything that has ever shown up in our physical world first started as a thought. Every great inventor first had an idea, a thought, about what it was he wanted to create.

That was followed with the deep desire or willingness to take action. The latter moved the thought into physical form.

If thoughts become things, then can the things be controlling or influencing the quality of our thoughts?

Many mind over matter, self-help, and personal development authors and teachers in the last century, such as: Charles F. Haanel, W. Clement Stone, Napoleon Hill, Edgar Cayce, Dale Carnegie, Louise Hay, Deepak Chopra, Ernest Holmes, Anthony Robbins, Robert Kiyosaki, Jack Canfield, Mark Victor Hansen, T.Harv Eker, and Bob Proctor have taught us about the power of our thoughts. I've read many works from these individuals. They could all be considered forerunners in the 'thought' movement in the past one hundred years, responsible, in part, for raising global consciousness and awareness.

Our thoughts originate in the mind, and it's important to understand and clarify here the different parts of the mind, and how thoughts are processed and stored.

Sigmund Freud's theory of personality divided the human mind into 3 levels: the conscious mind 10%, the subconscious 50-60% and the unconscious 30-40%.

'The conscious mind' is our 'in the moment' awareness—the think tank. It's in this place that we make decisions, use free will, reason, and imagine. The conscious mind lets us know, through our five senses, when something is hot or cold to the touch, smooth or rough to feel, or when something tastes delightful or awful. What we learned from our parents, our teachers, and mentors, through experience and reading, our intellectual faculties first processed in the conscious mind as a thought.

The conscious mind, then, accepts or discards the thought and, if it is accepted, it becomes one of our programs, similar to a program that you use on your computer.

Microsoft Word, for example, is a program that I use to write my current thoughts. Once I have my thoughts or material in a document that I am happy with, I save it to a file, and there it sits, along with a bunch of other files, until I need to retrieve the information for a useful purpose.

Another analogy might be considered: when you embark upon acquiring a new skill or specific behavior, such as riding a bike or learning to swim, it takes conscious thought, total in-the-moment awareness

Six – Mind Over Matter

concentrating on repeated action required to learn the new skill. Once the new skill becomes automatic, that is it is fully acquired, the newly learned behavior becomes integrated in the subconscious.

The next time you go to swim or take a bike ride you no longer have to have conscious thought for each actionable step as the subconscious is in the driver's seat and is the autopilot system that moves your body.

Depending on what beliefs you currently hold—based on your own personal experiences—your conscious mind is reading this book and then making a decision to accept some of these ideas or thoughts, storing them in the subconscious, to be retrieved at a later time.

As we accept a thought to be 'true' or right for us personally, that thought is impressed upon the subconscious mind, also known as the conditioned mind.

'The Subconscious mind' then becomes the storage of your programs. It acts like the hard drive of your computer, and the thought is a permanent fixture.

'The Unconscious mind' is not awake or in your present awareness. The unconscious contains memories and past experiences that are usually unpleasant: the traumas, the feelings of pain, loss, anxiety, and conflict. According to Freud, the unconscious continues to influence our behavior and experience, even though we are unaware of these underlying influences.

Note: retrieving information from the unconscious mind may require the help of a professional to heal past trauma or help to handle past or current drama.

It is said that the mind is like a super-computer and, in fact, more powerful than any artificial intelligence currently in existence. There are many mind-body scientists unraveling the psychological and neurological systems of the brain to bring to the forefront a better understanding of how the mind operates.

If this topic is of interest, I would suggest learning more from these two phenomenal individuals: Bruce H. Lipton, PhD, an internationally recognized leader in bridging science and spirituality. He is a stem cell biologist, and bestselling author of *The Biology of Belief.*

> "Yet the subconscious mind, which processes some 20 million environmental stimuli per second versus forty

environmental stimuli interpreted by the conscious mind in the same second." From page 176—*The Biology of Belief*

...and best-selling author, Dr. Joe Dispenza, *Becoming Supernatural: How Common People Are Doing the Uncommon* (Hay House, 2017), which draws on research conducted at his advanced workshops since 2012. Each of these highly aware individuals explores how common people are doing the uncommon to transform themselves and their lives.

To recap: of the approximately 60,000 thoughts a day that you think, only 10% are in your cognitive or conscious awareness. The other 90% of the approximately 60,000 thoughts a day are subconscious or subliminal messages that determine how you show up in the world today, tomorrow, and the next day.

If all the thoughts you had in a day became words, then that would be enough to write an average self-help book every day!

I'm sure you are aware that there are two parts to the brain referred to as the right brain and the left brain which are the parts of the whole brain. The left side of the brain is considered masculine, and is where our intellect, logic, analytical thoughts, science, and math concepts are stored. The right side of the brain is considered feminine, and is where the intuition, creativity, and compassionate thoughts are stored.

Most of us are more one than the other. We operate as a left-brain personality or right brain, which might help to explain why we gravitate toward one or the other as personality traits.

Of note: what's interesting to me is if we were to take a topical picture (a bird's eye view) of the brain it resembles the universal Yin Yang symbol. The concept of Yin Yang, to describe the complementary forces found in all things in the universe, has been used in Chinese Philosophy for thousands of years.

> "The Yin Yang symbol is probably the oldest expression of the primal creative process. You can look at the Yin Yang symbol and see how the original One, a circle, was divided into two comet-shaped parts, each apparently spinning about the other." Henry Reed, describing Cayce's description of Yin Yang.

Hemispheric Synchronization is the term used in neuroscience and metaphysics to describe the brain when it is balanced, an unusual condition when the electrical activity of the whole brain is in sync.

Coherence is another word used when the left and right brain hemispheres are in balance. This is a state we can strive for, as it's in this place where the magic happens, and our lives can truly reach extraordinary levels. Considering the Yin Yang symbol has been used for thousands of years, perhaps it also represents the pre-understanding of how the brain worked long before we had the scientific equipment to validate it—another clue from the ancients that we were designed to live in balance.

Once you understand the science behind your thoughts, and how your thoughts elicit emotions that affect your behaviors, you'll soon discover you are more powerful than you ever could have imagined.

E is for Emotions

T.E.A.R. (Thoughts + Emotions + Actions = Results)

Of the thousands of thoughts that we have every single day, some of those thoughts become the words that we speak. It is important to understand what impact those words could be having on the life that you are currently experiencing.

There are many variations of the following statement of wisdom—from Gandhi to Margaret Thatcher. This one was written on a wall in a small town in Mexico that my family visited. I was impressed that it was in a location as a visual reminder for passersby, visitors and locals alike.

Be careful of your thoughts, they become your words.
Be careful of your words, they become your actions.
Be careful of your actions, they become your destiny.

Dr. Andrew Newberg, a neuroscientist at Thomas Jefferson University, and Mark Robert Waldman, a communications expert, wrote a life-changing book together called *Words Can Change Your Brain*. In this book, they wrote: "A single word has the power to influence the expression of genes that regulate physical and emotional stress."

The Power Of Words

Using uplifting words like 'love,' 'amazing,' 'grateful,' and 'peace' in our everyday lives can literally change pathways in our brains by boosting our cognitive reasoning and making areas of the frontal lobes more effective. Using positive words in place of negative words can provide each of us the energy and motivation to start taking charge in life, and will give each of us more control over our choices.

> "By holding a positive and optimistic (word) in your mind, you stimulate frontal lobe activity. This area includes specific language centers that connect directly to the motor cortex responsible for moving you into action. And as our research has shown, the longer you concentrate on positive words, the more you begin to affect other areas of the brain.
>
> Functions in the parietal lobe start to change, which changes your perception of yourself and the people you interact with. A positive view of yourself will bias you toward seeing the good in others, whereas a negative self-image will include you toward suspicion and doubt. Over time, the structure of your thalamus will also change in response to your conscious words, thoughts, and feelings, and we believe that the thalamic changes affect the way in which you perceive reality." www.powerofpositivity.com

Words Carry Energy

The late Dr. Masaru Emoto revolutionized the idea that words have power in the book *The Hidden Messages in Water*. If you're not familiar with his work, I highly recommend reading one of his books. He scientifically validated that the molecular structure of water changes when exposed to emotional words, thought, sound, and intention.

Considering that our bodies are comprised of 60% to 80% water it would be reasonable to assume that that the molecular structure of our bodies would also be affected by emotionally charged words. It is said that love is the strongest, most powerful emotion that we can give and receive. It would be safe to say that the more we speak and feel love, the more we can affect change as it is the glue of the universe, the force that binds us.

The spoken word carries its own energetic vibration and, depending on the feeling infused into the word, it can create different responses. By becoming conscious of our words, we can be more in control of our destiny. Coincidentally, the words often used by optimistic people are more positive and uplifting compared to the words used by pessimists.

Empowering Emotions Release Happy Hormones

We can surmise then, that emotions are the thoughts you think that put the energy in motion creating the feeling of the thought.

Emotions can be either positive or not so positive. Empowering or uplifting emotions include love, appreciation, gratitude, happiness, joy, pride, excitement, peacefulness, enthusiasm, euphoria, altruism and optimism. I'm sure you can think of a few more.

When you experience elevated positive emotions, the brain sends an electrical signal, and hormones such as melatonin (the hormone that controls mood and sleep), are released into your physical body.

Dis-empowering Emotions Release Stress Hormones

Dis-empowering emotions include anger, fear, disappointment, disgust, sadness, anxiousness, contempt, shame, envy.

When you experience elevated negative emotions, the brain's system may release the stress hormone cortisol, which is a major contributor in the gaining of weight, especially around the mid-section.

Your brain and my brain could be considered the master chemist. It automatically prescribes and releases the right chemical combination for bodily functions based on the information that is being received, 'programmed into' the supercomputer.

There is new science to support the effects on our body relating to the emotions we feel, both empowering and dis-empowering.

Referencing this valuable subject:

"Human emotion literally shapes the world around us. Not just our perception of the world, but reality itself. The scientists concluded that "Human emotion produces effects which defy conventional laws of physics." *New Research Shocks Scientists: Human Emotion Physically Shapes Reality! Originally published on Life Coach Code, on February 26, 2017*

Everything we give emotional energy to, a positive or negative charge, will show up in our lives positively or negatively. The energy in motion, 'emotion,' is like the wind, the intangible effects that cause change to water, the tangible.

A is for Actions

T.E.A.R. (Thoughts + Emotions + Actions = Results)

Depending on your past experiences, beliefs, and programs, your brain will elicit either positive or not so positive emotions each time you are presented with a choice or decision in life—no matter how large or small.

Your ability to take action, and the level of action you take, is directly linked to the quality of your thoughts and emotions. Taking action is a forward or upward movement depending how you think about it. No action keeps you energetically stuck, and unable to move in any direction.

> "The law of gratitude is the natural principle that action and reaction are always equal and in opposite directions."
> Wallace D. Wattles

Remember how many thoughts you think in a day—the ones that could create a book? What would be the title of your book? What story would you tell?

"I Am Not Good Enough"
"'I Don't Care Anymore"
"I Am not Worthy to Receive You; Say the Word and I Shall be Healed"
"Everyone Is More Important Than Me"
"I'm Not Smart Enough"

Six – Mind Over Matter

"I don't Have Enough Money"
"Nothing Ever Works Out for Me"
"Poor Me: A Pity Party Near You"
"I Can Never Lose Weight"
"I'm Too Old"
"I Hate my Life"
"How Could I be so Stupid"
"Welcome To My world, Let Me Be Your Doormat"
"Everyone Hates Me"
"Play Low."
"What Other People Think is Important"

What story are you telling yourself every day? More importantly, what story do you believe to be true for you? What story has been controlling your life, defining your actions, how you participate in life?

"What the mind can conceive and believe, the mind can achieve."
Napoleon Hill

I have had the idea to write a book for many years, and the story that kept me from moving forward and realizing my dreams was: 'Who do You Think You Are?

It is a story deeply rooted in my subconscious thoughts coupled with the feeling of not being good enough. There are still lingering doubts that pop up in my mind. Bringing them to my conscious awareness, I am able to release and let go, replacing them with uplifting thoughts and the feeling of confidence, knowing that what I am sharing with you might have a huge impact in the way you live the rest of your life.

My story has played out in other areas of my life, particularly into the spaces of my home. The proverbial, 'Who do you think you are?' sneaking in. It's another way of saying you don't deserve to have nice things. Many times throughout my life, I have bought gently used furnishings and clothes when I had the financial means to buy new. Conscious thought was to save money when, in fact, the subconscious was in control, acting on 'my story.'

I have to consciously remind myself that I am worth it, that I don't always have to put the needs of my family and everyone else before my own. This story I have held on to likely comes from my upbringing, being the ninth in line to the throne, and having to wait my turn.

Ask yourself: What story is keeping me from having the life I dream of? Am I playing the role of victim? Am I unaware that I've been using that story over and over again?

Once you have identified your story, the one that has been holding you back, keeping you energetically stuck, recall how many times you have used that 'story' as an excuse of why you couldn't do something else, or chose not to do.

The underlying reason of why you do anything is how you do everything.

Do you have a conscious awareness of your 'story'? When 'your story' shows up in your awareness you can make a conscious effort, shifting your mindset, releasing and letting that sh__ go.

Making an energetic shift requires that you let go of that which no longer serves you, both seen and unseen (that includes your possessions), or you will continue being stuck in a loop, wondering why the same results keep showing up. You have likely heard that you cannot solve a problem with the same mind that created it—it requires a shift in your thinking.

There is a big difference between the word's activity and action. Activity is your subconscious keeping your conscious mind busy, so you don't have to participate fully in life.

Now that you have a conscious awareness, you can take 'action': acting-on releasing this story from controlling your life.

R is for Results

T.E.A.R. (Thoughts + Emotions + Actions = Results)

Have you ever heard or used this phrase? Repeated action over time equals your Results.

This is such an important statement, I encourage you to say it aloud right now.

Whatever has shown up in your life to date: a loving relationship, a nice house, a not so nice house, a reliable car, a crappy job, good or bad health, or the ability to have income from multiple sources—whatever it is for you—it is a direct result of the thoughts + emotion + action that has given you those results.

If there is an area in which you want to improve, or you want to create different results, then you must change one of the three components—T, E, or A—that is currently not working.

Your positive thoughts create your positive results. Your negative thoughts create your negative results… or more of the same.

Where your attention goes, your energy flows. What you continue to focus on expands. In Feng Shui we say: Where the eye goes, energy flows, where energy flows, attention goes.

What physical aspects in your home are you repeatedly putting your attention on? (Repeated action equals results.) When you walk through the doorway of your home are you greeted with a beautiful piece of art that was given to you by someone you deeply care about, or is there something that is anchoring a not-so-positive emotion?

Every space of your home is being occupied by some 'thing' that is sending energetic, subliminal messages to your heart/brain, and is either producing a state of coherence or incoherence. In the following chapters I will share with you some ideas and tools to live with what you love, and love where you live.

> *"Living with items that make your heart sing and evoke positive emotions will increase your personal vitality and health."*
> Anita Adrain.

Fixed ideas (thoughts) + feelings (energy in motion—emotion) + actions continually express until you make a new conscious choice. Making a new conscious choice involves awareness.

Considering that we spend approximately one third of our time in our home, or intimate environment, wouldn't it make sense to match the energy to the results that we desire?

I'm Not Worthy

Remember what we learned at the beginning of this chapter—how a thought moves from the conscious to the subconscious? You are not even aware that your environment has been reinforcing the thought or thoughts and keeping you stuck in the story you've been telling yourself.

Let's take the story 'I'm Not Worthy' and see how it might be reinforced in someone's environment.

Recently I was asked to do a Feng Shui home assessment for a lovely couple. One of their main concerns was a strained relationship with their son; specifically, with the son's wife. They were hoping that I would be able to see their space energetically, and perhaps make recommendations that would help them heal this relationship. There were many things that came to the surface, one of which was a reflection of self-love. As we went through the home, room by room, discussing specific enhancements for each area in relationship to the bagua (more details about the bagua later in the book), we came into one of the bedrooms used as a guest room. The room was spacious, and immediately gave a feeling of welcome and comfort; exactly how you would want your guests to feel.

It had what looked like a comfy bed, a reading area with a lovely chair, lamp, and bookcase. The walls were decorated with paintings that enhanced the color pallet chosen for the room. Overall, it was a great space in their home. I asked how often they had guests, and the answer was several times a year. What was interesting is that their own bedroom, the one that they both used every day—every night—lacked any aesthetic attention. It was what you would call boring or lackluster, acting more as a utilitarian space solely for the purpose of housing the bed.

When I pointed out the differences between these two rooms, and that energetically they were telling the story that they were not good enough—that their guests deserved more comfort and attention than they did—the realization was a true 'Aha!' moment for this couple.

> "How you do anything is how you do everything"
> T.Harv. Eker

The couple likely didn't make a conscious choice not to make their bedroom as comfortable and welcoming as the guest room. They merely were acting on the subconscious programs and beliefs that were running their lives.

Six – Mind Over Matter

They had been putting the needs of their son and daughter in-law and other people above their own.

There are many instances and examples that I could share with you—another book perhaps—when the energy of the home tells a non-supporting story. Even though you may change your thoughts, and the feelings leading you to take action in creating different results in your life, you must also make changes in your physical environment that support and reinforce your new view.

When your home environment supports positive **T**.hought and positive **E**.motions, you will be lead to take different **A**.ctions, ultimately producing different **R**.esults.

Are you now wondering what subliminal messages you are receiving every day from your home?

Life is an interactive experience.
This is your space.

T is for Thoughts / E is for Emotions

Becoming consciously aware of 'energy' begins with you and the thoughts that you think. What sabotaging self-talk or dis-empowering words have you used in the last day or so?
Please list 12 or more

-
-
-
-
-
-
-
-
-
-
-
-

In the next day or two, when you catch yourself saying one of the dis-empowering words that you wrote down, you can re-wire and fire new brain patterns by, saying 'cancel' 'clear' 'delete' and then immediately replace with an empowering thought.

OR

The practice of 'Ho'oponopono' (an ancient Hawaiian prayer and practice) is very effective: I'm sorry, forgive me, thank you, I love you.

Six – Mind Over Matter

What would your life look like, living in joy? What would be different?

A is for Action (act on)

What excuse have you or someone living with you used that has kept you or them from experiencing something great?

What story have you been holding on to?

What thoughts and/or emotions have reinforced that story?

R is for Results

Look around your home. If area(s) or item(s) have been reinforcing your story, please list them.

Next, please note what emotion comes up when you focus your attention on the area or item. Write that emotion beside the area or item.

Six – Mind Over Matter

Focus your attention in the area of your heart.
With the intention of breathing in gratitude and exhaling love:
Take a deep breath in for 5 seconds or more.
Hold for 5 seconds. Exhale for 5 seconds or more.
Bring your awareness and attention to each word and
or phrase in the Energetic Heart Code below.
Bringing them into your heart— feel the feeling of the
word or phrase radiating to every cell of your being.
Relax and repeat, while continuing to breathe,
to create heart-brain coherence.

ENERGETIC HEART CODES™

H.armonic **E**.nergy **A**.mplified
R.esults **T**.ransformation

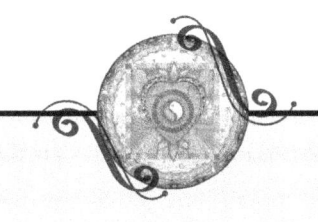

Seven – The Writing Is On The Wall

*"Your thoughts have created your current reality,
no one else is responsible for anything
that you are currently experiencing."*
Anita Adrain

Conscious Awareness

Have you ever wondered what lies dormant within a seed that determines its future, and distinguishes whether it will grow into a tree, a flower, or a weed? What wisdom is embedded in that tiny seed?

Characteristic potentials, designed by nature, signal the seed to grow into a mighty oak tree, expanding outward, expressing its life purpose. Every living thing on this planet carries the same wisdom of growth—and that includes humans.

From the time of our conception we are programmed to grow as a baby, a toddler, a child, a teenager, and into adulthood. Within our genetic program (our DNA) is an innate sense, a natural desire, to expand and grow, to experience life as a human being reaching our fullest potential, or creating the best version of self, not unlike that of a tree.

It is natural for us to seek growth—to expand, to evolve and express ourselves—but, in my opinion, we have mistaken this 'innate urge to grow' by accumulating possessions.

Somewhere in our psyche, the need to feel accepted, loved, and respected is satiated by accumulating more stuff; consuming for the sake of comfort, prestige, status, and/or satisfying the ego. It is my observation that the increase in consumerism is a contributing factor to the increase in STRESS in the general population, which parallels the increase in disease.

Stuffology

In a world that grows materially, we continually add, over time, to our collection of 'things.' Expert marketing of gadgets and gismos, media blitzes for 'new improved,' intrigue us and cloud our natural sense of growth—and misleads us into thinking that the purchase and accumulation of 'things' is itself growth. It is a profitable (for some) illusion that has created a generation of human doings measuring success and accomplishment by the perceived value of possessions.

The ability to purchase more stuff that is bigger, better, shinier, and can be delivered right to your door, is the world we live in. According to a national survey of 5000 shoppers by *The Wall Street Journal*, 51% of purchases were made online. The exchange of energy for these goods is largely purchased with invisible energy: credit cards, PayPal, and e-transfers, even in deferred payment—in some instances, adding financial stress.

> *"The natural state of seeking to expand and grow*
> *has been mistakenly interpreted by growing our possessions."*
> *Anita Adrain*

In one of my speaking presentations I ask the audience to raise their hands if they have a post-secondary degree. I ask a few people to share what degree or profession they're in. I then ask who did not attend college or university—usually more than 50% of the room.

I reassure them that everyone in the room has a degree… a degree in Stuffology. Of course, everyone laughs, and they agree that we live in a time where we have… a lot of stuff. I have never offended anyone by this statement. Why? Because they agree they have too much stuff.

It was at one of these presentations that I met a businesswoman with more than fifteen years of experience as an interior designer. She had recently partnered with a home builder, and shared that she is looking forward to designing homes to fit more stuff. Based on her experience, she thinks her clients need more space to organize their stuff.

In my experience and opinion, what people need is the conscious awareness of how 'the stuff' is impacting the well-beingness and quality of life. Quantity needs to become less important, as does the space required to house 'the stuff.'

There are several kinds of possessions that take up space in our home. There are functional, useful objects which enhance or make our lives easier—fridge, stove, furnace, microwave, couch, chair, pots and pans, dishes, vehicle, tools... these possessions are there to 'serve.'

Seasonal items, such as Christmas decorations, and garden tools like the lawnmower or snow shovel, need to be stored and easily accessed for their season. These items should be neatly organized and, if required, labeled for quick access to avoid any frustration when they are needed.

'POSSESS'ions

We then have items that have been specifically chosen as a form of self-expression, items that represent that innate sense of growth and expansion. As we are naturally drawn to environments that reflect beauty, just as Mother Nature shows us it makes sense that we would want to try and duplicate this feeling in our home. Quite often there are possessions that are primarily chosen for their aesthetic value, the ones that match the color pallet of the home.

These items usually have no apparent function, and often fall into the category of clutter. You will know if this is the case if you have to expend energy to maintain them. Possessions are here to make our lives easier, to enhance this experience known as life; they are not here to drain our life force energy or take control of how we live.

Functional, seasonal, aesthetically pleasing, and personal items all live together under one roof, contributing energetically to the visual triggers of all the home's occupants. The possessions that hold deep meaning: the painting on the wall, the sculpture on the coffee table, the family photos on the cabinet, the fridge art, the knick-knacks and trinkets that adorn the shelves—all of these possessions hold memories and emotions. All of

Seven – The Writing Is On The Wall

these items tell a story that is programmed in your subconscious. And here is the important part: the 'item' is either telling you an empowering story or a disempowering story.

It's easy to become complacent in our home environment, no longer aware or conscious of what thoughts and/or emotions are attached to any 'thing.' When in fact 'everything' that resides with you is constantly broadcasting a subliminal message.

Contemplate the word possession, the root word being POSSESS. Are your possessions controlling your thoughts, your emotions? Are you being possessed by some unseen energy source that dictates how you show up in the world?

> *"If thoughts become things,*
> *is it possible the things are in control of the thoughts that you think?"*
> *Anita Adrain*

Every single thing, every possession, is reflecting an outward image of your inner journey.

What deep emotional attachment are you holding on to in the form of a possession that is controlling or in charge of your Thoughts, Actions and Results? (T.E.A.R.)

> "The thoughts or images which you consciously choose and impress upon the subconscious (which is in every cell of your body) move your body into action. And the actions you take determine the results you get in life." Bob Proctor www.proctorgallagherinstitute.com

The Story Of The Trunk

When I first took my official training at The Western School of Feng Shui in 1999, many of the people closest to me were skeptical, and not very supportive of my new endeavour.

It was important at the time to validate what I had learned, not only for myself, but for all the naysayers in life.

I was eager to apply, in my own environment, the principles that I learned, and went to work transforming our home, consciously viewing every possession through my 'Feng Shui Eyes.'

I had started on the main floor and was ready to move into the basement. I asked my husband if there were any items that he specifically wanted to keep or let go of that had been taking up space in our basement. He replied that the old trunk gave him the creeps, and perhaps it was even haunted. The trunk had been lying in wait, threatening to unleash the spirits of the past, or at least that was my husband's perception. He confessed to me that this was the reason he didn't like going downstairs to the family room.

It was an amazing revelation to me; all this time, he hadn't been spending time with our children watching a movie or building with Lego, all because he felt the heebie jeebies. WOW!

You see, the trunk was something I had packed around for years; it belonged to my grandmother and likely held her treasured possessions. At one time I had used it to store the vacuum cleaner, while posing as a coffee table. In this house, however, it had taken up residence under the stairs, and could be seen when in the family room. I looked inside the trunk, and it was holding 'stuff.'

I used to love the old trunk, and now I just liked it. I had asked myself the important questions, do I love it? Do I need it? Is it serving a purpose in my current life? Knowing that it made my husband uncomfortable, I made the decision to release and let it go that day. I phoned a friend of mine who had an antique store, and she agreed to consign it. I liked antiques and had used quite a few pieces to decorate our home. A couple of days passed, and she phoned to let me know that the trunk had found a new owner. She had just received a new shipment, and it would be an opportune time to stop by, as I now had a nice credit at her store. I went to take a look and was amazed to find six elegant antique T-back oak chairs that would be perfect around my oak family heirloom table. They even had padded upholstered seats that were in the same color as my countertop—what a coincidence.

For years, whenever I visited an antique store or stopped at a garage sale, I was hopeful that I would find matching chairs to go with my table. The search was over, and I was elated. Finally, I had a matching dining

Seven – The Writing Is On The Wall

room set; the mismatched set of wooden chairs that we had been using went to my friend's antique store on consignment.

Several weeks passed and she called to let me know that I had another store credit—the chairs I'd taken in were gone. By this time I was putting the finishing touches on my Feng Shui home transformation and was in need of a lamp. I found exactly what I was looking for: a stunning upright antique lamp with a marble base. The color of the marble was rose, the same color as our rug in the living room. Another coincidence?

The moral of the story… Sometimes we hold on to possessions that **had** deep meaning for us in the past and are no longer serving a purpose. When I consciously assessed the trunk's value and usefulness in our home, I realized that it was taking up space, and giving a negative vibe to my husband.

By taking immediate action and releasing it, I made room for other possessions to come into our life that not only served functional purpose but were aesthetically pleasing—in alignment with our personal taste. An 'Aha!' moment: not only did I get some 'new to me' furniture, but my husband started spending more time in the family room, interacting with our children… all as a result of the willingness to release (letting go of) one piece of furniture, one item, one POSSESSion—all because I let go of the trunk

That was a huge validation for my family of the power of practicing Feng Shui.

"Home is where your heart lives."
Anita Adrain

The things that you buy, that you bring into your home, are meant to make your life easier. They are there to serve you, to provide comfort, generate the feeling of safety, create an environment that truly reflects the person you are today.

Over the years, in working with many clients, I have seen where aesthetically pleasing takes priority over safety and comfort. Take the metal dining table with a stylish glass top. The contrast at first glance is stunning and portrays a subtle elegance. The reality, however, is that the right-angled corners signal 'sha' energy similar to that of a poison arrow, and the metal legs are always competing with the knees or toes of the people sitting at the table. Over time, the table sits unattended as the home's occupants find other comfortable areas in the home to sit and eat their meals, often away from each other. The flat surface that was once inviting is now the catch-all for the other stuff that says, "I am just here to look good."

Have you ever wondered why the flat surface of a counter or dresser seems to be a magnet for the family's assortment of stuff—keys, papers, jackets, books and other items? I'd like to solve the mystery. Where the eye goes, energy flows, where energy flows attention goes. The flat surface is the first thing the 'eye' sees in the room and sends the signals to the brain that this would be a good landing space.

A very simple yet effective solution is to place some 'thing' at eye level that takes the attention away from the flat surface: a picture on the wall, a round, faceted crystal hanging from the ceiling. Use anything that lifts the chi.

If you have ever taken young children shopping, you might have noticed that all the goodies that they want are strategically placed at their eye level. Expert marketers of big box stores understand the subliminal messaging that leads to making more purchases. They know exactly what to place in your 'view' as well; usually the more expensive items.

You can use the same marketing techniques in your home, placing items—your possessions—at eye level or at strategic points of interest that will elicit positive emotions when viewed by you or others in the home. This will impress subliminal messages of empowerment upon the subconscious mind.

Are you aware that everything that physically shows up in your home is influencing how you show up in the world? Some of the subconscious programs that are running your life are a direct result of the environment in which you live. Each day you process information that you receive from your 'visual' environment that you act on.

Your Home – A Vision Board

Have you ever made a vision- or dream-board? The idea is to put together a visual reminder of what you want to materialize in your life—a

Seven – The Writing Is On The Wall

collage of inspirational pictures, words, phrases that represent your goals and deepest desires, a future image of your life. Ideally, when complete, you will place your vision board in a 'high visibility area,' some place where you will see it several times a day. By creating a vision-board, you are impressing a visual reminder on the subconscious mind which immediately goes to work to find a vibrational match. Visualization is considered one of the most powerful manifestation practices you can perform, especially when you can add the feeling, as if you already have obtained or achieved what it is you desire.

> "When we focus on the emotions of what we'd like to have in the present moment, as if what we want is already present, our brains get rewired, our bodies create new patterns, our behavior changes, and the experience of what we want finds us." Dr. Joe Dispenza
> https://www.facebook.com/DrJoeDispenza OfficialNewsFanPage/posts/d41d8cd9/1625460010812720/

Have you ever considered that the walls in your home are acting like the back-drop or canvas for a very large vision board?

Every picture, every knick-knack is anchoring a story, a belief, an emotion (feeling) from your life, visual reminders stored in the depths of your subconscious programs.

Where your eye goes, energy flows, where energy flows attention goes. That energy is being imprinted in your mind, either sending subliminal messages of empowerment or dis-empowerment, the very messages that move you to take action, to grow and expand as a human BE-ing. How expanded or contracted your energy is, in any given moment, determines the quality of your life.

> "Yet the subconscious mind, which processes some 20 million environmental stimuli per second versus forty environmental stimuli interpreted by the conscious mind in the same second, will cause the eye to blink."
> (Norretranders 1998)

> "The subconscious mind, the most powerful information processor known, specifically observes both the

surrounding world and the body's internal awareness, reads the environmental cues, and immediately engages previously acquired (learned) behaviors all without the help, supervision, or even awareness of the conscious mind."

The Biology of Belief, Bruce H. Lipton, PhD

When I came across the above paragraph, I had to read it more than once, to make sure I read the information correctly. The subconscious mind processes 20 million environmental stimuli per second! Staggering, almost incomprehensible information.

I have been teaching my clients and students for almost two decades the power of subliminal messages received from their home environment and how to activate positive ones.

A Picture Is Worth A Thousand Words

There are times when I have been asked to present or speak on the topic of Feng Shui for breakout sessions. My audiences have included women's business groups, educators, soul groups, holistic practitioners, and Indigenous groups. Sometimes I have an hour or less; sometimes up to two hours.

For these short sessions, I present this very simple, yet powerful exercise. I pass out two envelopes to each attendee. One envelope is labeled #1 and the other #2. Inside each envelope is an image—none of the images are the same.

The first envelope contains a picture of a completely cluttered environment. I'm talking total disarray in a bedroom, office, closet, living room, garage or other space.

I ask that all the participants open the envelopes marked #1 at the same time, and either write or shout out the first thought or thoughts that come to mind. Together, we discuss all the words that come from looking at the one image.

These are some of the words: **crazy, confusion,** busy, **disaster,** sloppy, **potential undiscovered, unclear, uncertainty,** clutter, lazy, too sharp, yuck, mess, hoarders, disorganized, **unrest, unworthy, angry,** scattered energy, lack of focus, **fatigue,** too **overwhelming,** no way out, messy, chaos, **uncomfortable,** not too productive, **claustrophobic.**

Seven – The Writing Is On The Wall

The words are then separated to discuss the emotions related to those words. As you can see by the highlighted ones, there are some very powerful words that are dis-empowering—words that can have an effect on a person's physiology and psyche. Potentially, the self-talk of someone who actually lives in this type of environment would be detrimental.

The general consensus from the participants in this exercise is that it would make sense to take action and remove the stress, by way of removing clutter?

We then have a drum roll... and open envelope #2. The envelope contains a random picture of someone's home environment that is in order, or pleasing to look at.

Again, I ask for participation in that they share the first words that come to mind. The following is a list: Oh, WOW, breathe, organized, nice, **soothing, inviting,** clean, **bright,** fresh, **beautiful,** structured, tidy, **illuminated, balanced,** colors, **warm** and **relaxing,** homey, **relief, inviting, welcoming, Zen, comforting, happy,** elegant, open, **confident, uplifting.**

"A picture is worth a thousand words, and has the power to transmit a deep emotional connection to the receiver, either eliciting a positive or not so positive response."
Anita Adrain

It's interesting, when doing this exercise, how the whole energy of the group shifts when they start to share the words from picture #2. Remember, there is no personal connection with any of these images, and no one has the same image, yet they start to get excited, talk louder, laugh, have a physical exhale, sigh of relief. You can see their physiology change in a dramatic way, all as a result of positive visual stimulation—a 'shift' in their energy that is clearly noted and felt.

The discussion that follows this simple, yet powerful, exercise reveals many 'Aha!' moments for the group, with the realization that living in a clutter free environment is in fact beneficial in living a healthier life.

Note these energetically charged words from participants, based on viewing picture #2 (the aesthetically pleasing, clean space): **soothing, inviting, bright, beautiful, illuminated, balanced, warm, relaxing, relief, inviting, welcoming, Zen, comforting, happy, confident, uplifting.**

The thoughts (**T**) charged with an emotion (**E**) move the person(s) into Action or inaction (**A**) creating the results (**R**) that are their current reality. The idea that your home environment could be acting like a vision board is valid.

What is manifesting in your life could be directly related to and connected to the place you call home?

This exercise also validates that 'The outer world is connected to, and reflected in, the inner world.'

Picture #1, the images of the cluttered room, or space, elicited the following emotional words, leaving me to believe that anyone living in a similar environment would also show up in the world as displaying some or all of the same traits: **crazy, confusion, disaster, potential undiscovered, unclear, uncertainty, unrest, unworthy, angry, scattered, fatigue, overwhelming, uncomfortable, claustrophobic**.

For people living in a cluttered, messy environment, the outer world would potentially show up in the inner world as being overwhelming—manifesting in a not knowing where to start and which direction to take.

The outer world chaos would likely affect the close family and or intimate relationships, as the person or people living in this environment would likely prefer being anywhere but home.

Chances are, their health would suffer as a result of being on the run and not having a nurturing environment in which they could prepare healthy meals to nourish their body.

Reflecting chaos in the inner world: anger, confusion, being scattered, feeling overwhelmed, discomfort, uncertainty, and fatigue are all emotional responses that result from living in a space that is filled with clutter.

> "Clutter can play a significant role in how we feel about our homes, our workplaces, and ourselves. Messy homes and workspaces leave us feeling anxious, helpless, and overwhelmed. Yet, rarely is clutter recognized as a significant source of stress in our lives." Sherrie Bourg Carter, Psychologist—Article in *Psychology Today*.
> https://parentingisnteasy.co/messy-home-anxiety/?fbclid=IwAR2sSyqA-K6WjsIrUg4I0tV7d5k3x-CKNmssnW0wBtePemXYhX6J_R3NdFs

'Rarely is clutter recognized as a significant source of stress in our lives.' This sentence surely caught my attention. Why is it that educators, teachers, scientists—the people we look up to for providing us information that will ultimately improve our situation—have not been addressing the 'messy environment' as a large contributing factor in experiencing stress? Perhaps it's because there isn't a 'pill' that can be prescribed for the situation, nor is there money to be made in telling people they'll feel better if they go home and clean up their mess.

Where Do You 'Spend' Your Energy? Why you are here? What is the purpose of your life? The purpose in your life has nothing to do with the stuff you are spending so much energy on accumulating and maintaining.

According to a study on clutter performed by UCLA (reported by Huffington Post) there are other ramifications of living with clutter.

Selections from UCLA studies on clutter as reported by Huffington Post:
"UCLA's Center on Everyday Lives of Families continues its fascinating study of contemporary suburban America with a book titled Life at Home in the 21st Century. Thirty-two Los Angeles families opened their doors to CELF's researchers. What they found: a staggering number of possessions and an array of spaces and furnishings that serve as the stage for multiple family activities—and tell us a lot about who we are as a society."

"The researchers found that 'cars have been banished from 75 percent of garages to make way for rejected furniture and cascading bins and boxes of mostly forgotten household goods.'"

"Thus, our excess becomes a visible sign of unaccomplished work that constantly challenges our deeply engrained notions of tidy homes and elicits substantial stress."

Life at Home notes that 'our data suggest that each new child in a household leads to a 30-percent increase in a family's inventory of possessions during the preschool years alone.'"

"Dual-income parents get to spend so very little time with their children on the average weekday, usually four or fewer waking hours. This becomes a source of guilt for many parents, and buying their children toys, clothes and other possessions is a way to achieve temporary happiness during this limited timespan."

"A lot has happened since the *Life at Home* study concluded in 2005. If invited into the same kinds of homes today, what do the researchers think they'd find? The same stuff, different year."

"If we were to study the same types of families in 2012, I don't think the results would be significantly different,' says Graesch, whose home refrigerator boasts 66 magnets on three vertical surfaces, most of them letters and numbers that his toddlers play with. 'We are still a child-centered society, we still have trouble managing our massive inventories of objects, and we still struggle to find a balance between work, school and family.'"
Sources for above:
UCLA's 'Life At Home In The Twenty-First Century' Study Reveals Just How Disorganized American Homes Are| HuffPost Canada https://www.huffingtonpost.ca/entry/life-at-home-in-the-twenty-firstcentury_us_659172 Life at Home in the Twenty-First Century: 32 Families Open Their Doors UCLA Cotsen Institute of Archaeology http://www.ioa.ucla.edu/press/life-at-home

Clutter can show up in other areas of life and cause inner chaos—mind environment clutter. Our computers and cell phones are sources of accumulated piles of messages, files, pictures, emails, and other electronic filler. It is important to free mental clutter regularly by purging electronic clutter. Make it a weekly 'best practice' to delete unwanted emails, texts, and similar things that 'pile up'.

Electronic clutter is an area of growing concern as the effects are as stressful as living in a physical environment of clutter. Added stress can be averted by simply becoming aware and taking action.

As interesting as the UCLA study was, it failed to offer solutions, actionable steps to reduce clutter in the home. Further to that, it failed to list the psychological reasons that we hold on to our stuff way too long, and it didn't report the energetic benefits of releasing all that stuff and letting it go.

Life is an interactive experience.
This is your space.

Where has clutter accumulated in your life? Your home (outer world)? Your mind (inner world)? What about your electronics?

Are there areas of your life in which you are feeling stuck or blocked? Please list them.

Seven – The Writing Is On The Wall

Where the eye goes, energy flows, where energy flows, your attention goes. Choose several areas in your home, your front entrance, the view from your desk, the favorite chair, or even the view when lying in your bed.

1. Where does your eye go?

2. What were the first thoughts that came to mind when looking at this particular area or thing?

3. Is the attention empowering or dis-empowering? What changes could you make to shift the energy in this area to support positive results?

Focus your attention in the area of your heart.
With the intention of breathing in gratitude and exhaling love:
Take a deep breath in for 5 seconds or more.
Hold for 5 seconds. Exhale for 5 seconds or more.
Bring your awareness and attention to each word and
or phrase in the Energetic Heart Code below.
Bringing them into your heart— feel the feeling of the
word or phrase radiating to every cell of your being.
Relax and repeat, while continuing to breathe,
to create heart-brain coherence.

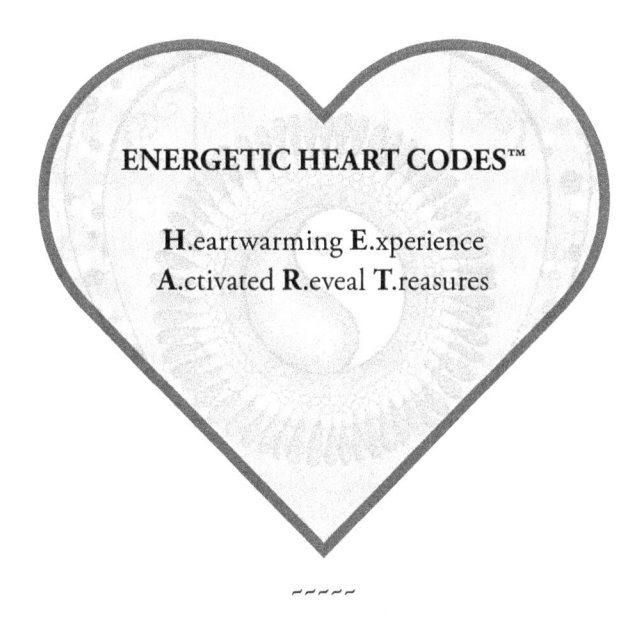

ENERGETIC HEART CODES™

H.eartwarming **E.**xperience
A.ctivated **R.**eveal **T.**reasures

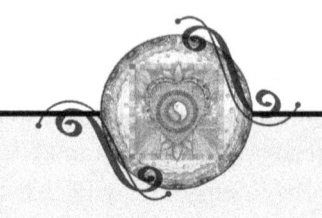

Eight – Live With What You Love: Out Of Chaos Comes Clarity

"Elevated positive emotions open the heart to a greater sense of well-being which translates to a healthy life."
Anita Adrain

Feng Shui teaches us that we are energetic beings living in an energetic universe, and that energy moves in a cycle.

When we are willing to release and let go of something, it creates an energetic space, a void which makes room for energetic potentials that you have been seeking (or praying for).

Personal growth is not growing your possessions, as chi is constantly moving and changing.

You cannot hold on to the old while affirming that you want something new. The only way to bring in the new is to make room for it. You must be continually making space for the good which you desire, releasing items back into energetic circulation allows for this exchange.

There are many reasons we hold on to stuff way too long, keeping us stuck in the energetic loop of the past. Would you like to learn why you hold on to 'stuff' and how to release some old beliefs, patterns and behaviors? Here are what I believe are the top three:

REASON #1- SENTIMENT and/or OBLIGATION

One of the main reasons for holding on to possessions—that 'stuff'—is for sentimental reasons. People hold an underlying belief that they must keep things—even if they don't like those things. The item and the mental burden both take up energetic space. Freedom is experienced by understanding that emotional attachment can be made to the person associated with the item, not the item.

Many people keep things because they believe they will feel guilty getting rid of those things. You may have burdened yourself with a deep sense of obligation—not because you love a thing, but because you feel obliged to its giver. Wouldn't it be easier to have a conversation with the person who gave you the thing? "John, I really appreciate the sentiment, and I love and appreciate you. The tea set is lovely. However, I do not drink tea. Would it be okay with you if I returned it or re-gifted it?" John's reply might be: "Of course, I bought it because I thought you would like it."

"For it is in giving that we receive." St. Francis of Assisi

It's interesting to observe people if they have given a gift freely from the heart. They will have no attachment to the outcome from the receiver. You will know when this is not the case, as you will feel obliged to take the 'thing' out of hiding when you know the person, the giver, might be coming to your home. As the recipient of an item, you should be able to have full control of what items you choose to reside in your home with you—without feeling guilt or remorse. Attaching an emotional outcome to a gift is a tricky situation, and usually ends up with a not so pleasant outcome. Either the giver or the receiver, or both, have hurt feelings. Having a conversation is the best way out of this scenario so you are not obliged to keep the thing that you don't like or use.

Then there are the items that we keep because someone has transitioned to the other side, and the 'stuff' reminds you of them; a natural and normal response. I would recommend that you create an area in your home in which you can honor that person or those people: an altar of sorts where you can circulate memorabilia in that one area. In doing that, you can

Eight – Live With What You Love: Out Of Chaos Comes Clarity

store all the other treasured memorabilia—the stuff that you absolutely are certain you want to keep—for changing up your alter in the future.

You must ask yourself what emotion is attached to the thing, and if it brings your personal energy up or down. Your feeling will be your cue whether to keep the 'thing' or not.

REASON #2 ~ VESTED INTEREST

There may be some items that you currently have in your garage, or on the shelf in the storage room, because you might need it someday. Perhaps you bought the newest, greatest model of 'something' and kept the previous one you had.

For years you hold on to the thing and then you take my Feng Shui workshop and realize the thing is taking up energetic space. You make the decision to release it, although you have some apprehension: "Well, I've kept it this long."

After going back and forth a few times, indecisively, you tell yourself it's going, and you put the thing in the give pile and off it goes. Several weeks go by and, wouldn't you know it, the thing that you just gave away you now need. You say: "I knew I should have kept…"

What just happened? The law of attraction is at work. You put a lot of energy and attention on deciding whether or not to keep the thing, and the universe heard your reluctance. The universe answered your reluctance by saying: "It's okay, Jane, I will help you create a situation where you need to have the thing that you didn't really, really want to let go of in the first place."

Sound familiar? The 'might need it someday' story sends a signal to the universe that 'some day' you may not have the financial means to replace the thing. In keeping the thing, you are attracting a situation to happen in the future that is not desirable. Be extremely clear and decisive in your action (inspired action) when you are releasing possessions that no longer are in service to you.

The more attention you put on what you want or don't want in your life, the more likely that it will show up. Where your attention goes, energy flows, as repeated action over time equals results.

What message(s) are you putting out there or broadcasting to the universe? Sending a message of lack transposes to a future when you will lack the resources or means to replace the one item you are currently reluctant to let go of.

You are blocking the abundant flow of energy that you are currently seeking, because you have been holding on to 'I might need it some day.'

REASON #3 ~ COST

There is 'the thing' you have been holding on to for no other reason than it cost you a lot of money. Those 'sexy' boots in your closet, oh they sure do feel nice and soft. And they look great from the outside. You know the ones that you only wore once because they were so uncomfortable and made your feet sore and blistered. Yet you still keep them as a reminder of the pain that, somehow, you were tricked into paying two hundred dollars for them. **REALLY!!!!**

What is really going on in your mind? What belief is keeping those boots on the shelf in your closet? Or the tool(s) in the garage that you have yet to use, the half price one that would come in handy some day. Meanwhile, you have other items that are competing for space, and every time you go to get ready for work or try and work in the garage, you encounter deep feelings of frustration and angst that you have no room; things are a mess.

Does any of this make sense? Freely let go of the boots. Freely let go of the tool(s), or whatever item that you have been holding on to because it cost a lot of money. Thank the universe for the lesson and move on. I challenge you to let go of something that you no longer need, no longer want, no longer serves a purpose; something that cost you a lot of money and is currently taking up prime real-estate in your home.

Sometimes we have to ask ourselves if there is an underlying reason for keeping a particular item or items, a subconscious belief that governs a particular behavior.

The outer world is connected to, and reflected in, the inner world, and sometimes we have to bring forth into our conscious awareness the thing that no longer serves us—to release it to the spam folder and hit delete. A willingness to find the weeds and dig up the deep roots, making room for the new seeds to be planted in our subconscious, is a necessary process when clearing the clutter from your physical environment.

Some possessions take up energetic space for no apparent reason. For some, I believe it is their past conditioning, and the fact that they were raised by people who experienced the great depression, a time when everything was saved, and nothing wasted.

Deep Roots

My amazing Mother, who is over eighty at the time of this writing, has some deep-rooted weeds that still control some aspects of her life. She has been known to hold on to and keep every plastic bag from everything, even going to the trouble to wash and air dry a few. I'm an advocate for reusing and recycling; it's a good habit to have. However, in her case, it is extreme to the point where she will never have a use for all the plastic bags she has stored. Where did this habit start? What deep rooted belief anchors her current behavior? Could it have something to do with being a child in the 'dirty thirties'?

A scarcity mindset can rule the subconscious—values and habits passed on and learned.

When I was young, growing up in a busy family with ten siblings, my Mother exhibited those 'waste not want not' traits and, as a result, stuff accumulated in every available crevice in our already crowded house.

I remember one particular time when my Mom had to go into hospital for over a week, and my older sister took it upon herself to completely do a spring purge of our house. She was on a mission. She had the pick-up truck backed up to the door and, with the help of a couple of my brothers, began filling it.

They did not consider whose possessions they were getting rid of, and did not take the time to ask for permission. They acted on what 'they' believed were items to keep and treasure, and made the decision based on what they regarded as junk.

When my Mother came home from hospital, the reaction my sister was hoping to get was not the one she received. Our Mother had some expressive words that clearly let us all know that she was not happy about losing her stuff. That experience affected decisions throughout my sister's life.

The silver lining was that my sister had uncovered love letters that our Father had written to our Mother when they were separated by provinces in the early days of their courtship. Likely those intimate letters were the reason they pursued one another, and eventually married, producing a family of eleven.

Interestingly, many years later, my Mother gave those letters to my sister for safe keeping. Funny how the mind works. Maybe it was her way of saying thanks for cleaning the house.

For every action there is a reaction; the big lesson here is for all of us to be aware of other people's possessions.

It was during this purge that all of my treasured school memories disappeared—many of my school photos. As a result of this one event, I have buried a weed in the subconscious too, one that has been a directive for many years while raising my own children. So, guess what? I saved everything from my children's lives. I mean everything: from their first haircut, then their first lost tooth, and including the remnants of a cast of a child's broken elbow in grade six.

I have three boys. Each one of them has a store of 'keepsake' boxes that outline the history of them growing up. Now I have to ask myself what I was thinking. Obviously, I was not. I was acting on the subconscious level of having my own treasured memories taken from me without permission all those years ago. I guess, for me, keeping all the stuff for my boys, was me saying that no one has the right to decide regarding my stuff, except for its rightful owner. My children's stuff is now in their adult hands, and they get to make the decisions of which items will be treasure and which items will be trash. It is totally up to them to decide.

The Law Of Reciprocity

The law of reciprocity cannot be engaged until you give, setting in motion the movement of energy. When starting on the de-cluttering journey, whether it is one item or a truckload, become aware that unseen forces may be at work.

Eight – Live With What You Love: Out Of Chaos Comes Clarity

Free yourself of any emotional attachment and/or outcome, and be mindful of what 'potential' the universe replaces it with. Let the law of reciprocity play out.

For example: you may be gifted with a pair of tickets to see a concert that you really wanted to attend—those particular tickets may have been out of your price range or they may have been sold out.

Trust that when you give, it always turns out that something that you have previously had a positive thought about, that went into the field of energy as a pure potential of conscious thought, will show up. That is the law.

Have faith and trust that when you give freely, with no expectation of the outcome, you will be rewarded—possibly tenfold—completing the energetic circle. Regardless of spiritual faith, most people have heard this:

"What you give freely returns tenfold." (LK.6:38)

That phrase is referred to as the biblical law of seed and multiplied harvest. Examples abound of how energy moves in a circle or cycle, or what you give out returns in an expanded form.

Also known as the law of circulation, transmutation, or the law of reciprocity, dictates that there always has to be an exchange of energy.

Mother Nature demonstrates this 'law' every day. The wisdom within a tree acts like the subconscious mind acting without specific instruction, exchanging carbon dioxide for oxygen. Perhaps, within the unseen part of our own DNA, is the same innate 'law,' a spiritual practice, 'when we give we receive.'

Bottle Depot Bonus

A while back, I tidied the garage. One large bag of bottles had accumulated, and demanded to be recycled. I put them in my car, planning to call into the bottle depot later that day. When I arrived, there was a line of people ahead of me. At the same time, two young children and their dad showed up with five bags of bottles.

As I stood waiting, I could hear the young boy—age nine or ten—talking with his older sister—about age twelve—as to how they would divide the proceeds. He was pointing out that they had an uneven number of bags.

I smiled to myself. As a young child, my sisters and I would collect bottles along the ditches in the summer, and there was always some kind of discussion of fairness, and further discussion on who collected the most bottles. When they were young, my sons had also collected bottles (not in the same manner), and trips to the bottle depot always included a conversation on how the money would be divided amongst them.

As the siblings were deep in their discussion, I started talking with the father of the children. I asked him if the kids were planning a trip to the local fair with their proceeds, or something else. He told me that they were going on a trip to a special farm with all kinds of activities. He said they'd be able to use their bottle money there.

I interrupted the children's conversation and asked them if they would like another bag of bottles as I didn't really feel the need to wait in the long line. They were thrilled; it helped even up the resources, as they now had six bags.

I smiled at the Dad, bid them all a great day, and left the building. Just before I was getting back into my car, someone I knew was pulling up with some bottles. I stopped to have a quick conversation. The Dad saw that I was still there and came outside then asked if he could have a moment of my time to share a story. I said goodbye to my friend, and the Dad (never did find out his name) proceeded to tell me a story that happened a week before.

Apparently, they had gone to the city as a family and along the way had encountered a homeless person. The homeless person approached the family and asked if they had any spare money. The Dad asked his wife, and all she had was a twenty-dollar bill. So, the Dad said to the man that he would take him to the McDonalds (that was close by) and buy him whatever he wanted.

The homeless person agreed, and the Dad asked his son to come along and bring the twenty dollars from his Mother. The Dad then asked his son to go up to the counter and pay for the stranger's meal, which he did. They left the man to his meal and returned to the car to continue on their shopping day with the rest of the family. Once in the car, the young son asked his Dad why they did that. He noted that the man stunk, and his appearance was unsettling. The Dad explained to his son that what they had just done was a 'good deed,' and that it is okay to do something nice for someone, in this case someone who was less fortunate and needed a hot meal. The Dad continued to teach his young son about the law of reciprocity even though he didn't call it that. When you do something nice for someone from the goodness or compassion of your heart, it will come back to you.

When I had given the young boy my bag of bottles, and then left the building, the son rushed up to his Dad and said, "Dad you were right, it worked! You said when you do something nice for someone that something good will come back to you." His eyes grew larger, and he was excited to share his insight with his Dad.

As the Dad was sharing this story with me, he had tears in his eyes, and mine started to well up. He thanked me for listening to his story, and again thanked me for the bottles.

I must say, I left the bottle depot more energetically charged, with a big bright smile on my face as I continued on my way to finish my errands. I had been totally unaware that one bag of bottles—eight or ten dollars' worth—would have such an impact on my day.

I could have chosen to continue waiting in the line at the bottle depot with the others and not participate in conversation that day. I could have chosen not to listen to my inner guidance that was prompting me with the warm memories of my own childhood, and that of my sons' first encounters with redeeming bottles. The young fellow would have surely been rewarded somewhere along his journey for his kind deed of feeding a stranger, a month or a year in the future. The fact that it happened on that day, one week after his Dad was teaching him about giving, allowed the young fellow to recognize it immediately. I can only imagine that this young man will continue to give freely his entire life, having learned the law of reciprocity firsthand.

What you put out there freely without expectation or judgement returns to you.

So, on that summer day I was like a pebble after being tossed in a pond, causing ripples to radiate outward in a circular rhythm. Who knows how far those ripples will go and how long they will continue?

My energy had shifted that day when the Dad took time to tell me the story. For the rest of that day the ripples continued outward, touching everyone in my path, whether it was a smile or a heartfelt thank you, as I felt truly grateful for the blessings of that day. That one unplanned act brought something else to my awareness. As I have said many times before, Mother Nature has been my best teacher, and it is only when we are in the flow that we become more aware of the messages and 'Aha!' moments that show up.

We've all heard the saying 'free as a bird.' What does that really mean? For me, it's about giving freely, giving without expectation or judgement—giving for the joy of it. The bird gets up in the morning and immediately begins singing. He gives freely of his gift, with no expectation in return. The bird knows that he has nothing to worry about; he is always provided food and shelter. Every day, his basic needs are met, and he can sing his song, bathe in the sunlight, rest on a tree branch, eat a bug—he can do whatever he wants. He is in harmony or symbiotic rhythm with Mother Earth. So, if we each were to be truly 'Free as a Bird,' we would wake up knowing that our daily needs will be taken care of and we are free to give of our talents, our gifts, our food, our love, our smile, our money, our bottles, whatever it is that we have to give.

Consider that all of your possessions have an energetic value and, when they no longer serve a purpose in your life, you can give them freely, knowing that there will always be an exchange of energy (by nature's laws), and that something good will come back to you.

Here's the thing that I have noticed in my personal life: when I give the 'thing' freely, with no expectation, I leave the space open and available for something better. Instead of selling an item at a price of twenty dollars, giving it away (without expectation) sets the energy for receiving—whether it is something that comes along that is valued at one hundred dollars, or the arrival of something more valuable than money.

Remember, how you do anything is how you do everything. Just as money is an 'energy system' and only has value when it is in circulation, so do your possessions.

How you respect, care for and value your money, is the same as how you respect, care for, and value your possessions. This is a pretty good

Eight – Live With What You Love: Out Of Chaos Comes Clarity

indication of how you respect, value, and care for yourself and other people.

Now that you know the top three reasons why you have held on to your stuff way too long, you might consider that the overall reason may have something to do with indecision. Not being able to make a decision for fear of making the wrong decision will keep a person stuck—render them unable to move in any direction. In this case there is always another 'story' running in the programs of the subconscious?

#1 Sentiment and/or Obligation
#2 Might need it some day
#3 Cost a lot of money…

…and now that you are aware of the energetic potentials of letting that stuff go, are you ready to release some of those old patterns, programs, and beliefs?

Clutter Affects Psychology

Many years ago, I did some personal development work with Peak Potentials Training and T.Harv Eker. He also teaches that the inner world is connected to the outer world in relationship to wealth-building principles.

I remember, during one of his seminars, doing a very powerful exercise to pull out the weeds (by the roots) that can grow in the subconscious garden of our mind. Perhaps, like my sister and I, there is an experience that has buried itself so deep that it governs how or why you keep certain possessions. Perhaps, like my Mother, that's why you have the need to fill every crevice with stuff.

Whatever it is for you, first you must identify the time when the weed's seed was planted. Close your eyes, take a few deep breaths, and take yourself back to that experience. Really feel into it. Get a clear image in your mind of what that experience looked like and felt like.

Once you have it clearly defined, imagine that experience is surrounded by a bubble, just like the one you produce from a toy bubble wand. Imagine that there is a very hot stove-top near you. Now take that bubble and gently carry it to the stove and release it. In your mind, listen as the bubble hits the hot surface...srrrrrr....srrr. Watch as the bubble disappears as the water molecules evaporate. As the bubble goes, so does the experience from your subconscious. Now you can replace that memory or experience with a visualization of how you would have liked the outcome to be different, or you can just release the memory and be grateful for the awareness of it. Plant a new seed in the garden of your mind. One that will flourish and grow.

There are other visualizations and exercises that you can do to accomplish the same result; whatever resonates for you to clear the clutter stored in your subconscious (the inner world). The important thing is to recognize whether there is an underlying cause for your relationship with the 'stuff' in your environment, and if it has had an effect on how you view your possessions.

You are intimately connected to your home and all its contents—your worldly possessions. Your inner journey, your personality traits, and your values show up in your environment.

Do you know someone who has lived in the same house for many years, with the same 'stuff' they moved in with? Has that person, in your observation, grown mentally or spiritually, or is she stuck in an energetic time warp, living in the past?

Imagine if that person were to be given notice of one week to live. She gathers her loved ones to disperse her worldly possessions before her departure; after all, that person has told herself that a lot of the accumulation was for these loved ones. But what this person might discover, at the end of her life, is that her treasured possessions have little value for the people she was keeping them for. The same might be true for you. Ask your loved ones (or yourself), what items they (or you) would keep if they (or you) were to transition next week.

Just as a pool of water reflects an image of the environment which surrounds it, your home reflects the image of the content and quality of your life.

How you participate in life as an energetic being in this energetic universe is a direct result of your environment: your mind environment and your physical environment.

Eight – Live With What You Love: Out Of Chaos Comes Clarity

When you work on the inner world, clearing the clutter of the old programs, you must also clear the clutter in the physical outer world. Clearing the clutter is the first step to enlightenment. Here is a clear guideline to help take actionable steps for de-cluttering so the task becomes less daunting.

Clearing Clutter

Note: It's important to ask permission when clearing clutter or items that do not belong to you. Everyone has their own emotional attachment or story for each item they own; it's not up to you to decide for them what that is

Any 'thing' only has value (meaning) based on the meaning that we give it.

Either bookmark this page, or take a separate piece of paper and write the following, so that you can have it in hand as you begin the de-cluttering process.

Choose one room, one area, one closet, one drawer at a time and, as you bring your attention to an item ask yourself:

- Do I love it?
- Does this item lift my energy or drain my energy?
- Do I need it?
- Does it serve a purpose in my current life? (You are the 'master' in your home; it is important to be certain that the possession is serving you.)
- Does this item add value, contributing and enhancing my life experiences?
- Does it need repair and, if so, am I willing to take the time and/ or spend the money to fix it?
- What 'story' is attached, and am I ready to let that 'Shi(f)t' go?

Consider enlisting the help of a family member or close friend if you feel completely overwhelmed and have no idea where to start. Share with them the above strategies and get started. A step in action holds many rewards.

Have three boxes or containers ready and labeled 'throwaway,' 'stowaway,' and 'giveaway.' If it's time to let it go, then you must take action immediately and remove the 'giveaways' from your home within a day or two of purging. Otherwise, you may have second thoughts and some of those POSSESSions may talk their way back into your house.

Everything is energy, and when you release and let go you are moving energy. 'What you put out there comes back to you' is an example of the energetic circulation that is evident in the physical laws of this universe. Nature is always demonstrating the exchange of energy, a universal law that dictates there always has to be an exchange of energy.

Giving freely with joy, no expectation, is living in the abundant flow, 'free as a bird.'

You may consider 'borrowing away' an item that you still have a deep positive emotional connection to, an item that doesn't currently match your décor and/or that is too nice to live it's life in a box. A close friend or relative may be thrilled to temporarily house the item for you.

The same guidelines apply when you are contemplating a new purchase. Ask yourself before a purchase: Do I love it? Do I need it? Does it serve a purpose in my current life?

Becoming consciously aware of why you hold on to possessions and why you purchase new ones could be an energetic game changer for you.

The quality of life that you are currently experiencing is a direct result of the thoughts that you think and your state of emotional wellness, both of which are intimately attached to the possessions that are taking up residence in your home.

I am not suggesting that you take on a minimalist existence. It's perfectly fine to have many possessions, so long as they are all loved and well cared for. Think of all your possessions as being 'alive' with chi supporting and serving you, so that you can create a life of ease.

I have encountered a few people that have home environments in perfect order: absolutely no clutter, everything has a place and space. The clothes in the closets are organized in color, the flat surfaces, counters, and tables are clean and clear, beautifully chosen pieces of art appear throughout. From the outside looking in, these people would appear to

Eight – Live With What You Love: Out Of Chaos Comes Clarity

be living a charmed life. However, that is not always the case, as their outer world displays the same rigidness, the need to be in control, and the inflexibility that they exhibit in the inner world.

Dis-empowering emotions can be triggered easily if someone else in the home does not have the same characteristic traits.

Maybe their significant other has been designated a space, and chooses to fill the garage with tools, unfinished projects, and a whole lot of other stuff. They don't notice, or are not cognizant of, the 'man cave' until the weather changes and it is necessary to park the car inside the garage. (Remember that UCLA study that reported 75% of garages no longer have room for the car?)

It is not unusual to have long periods of minus-twenty weather and, on a day when there is snow, one has to clear off a frozen car, a car which needs fifteen minutes to warm up—imagine, all because the garage was full of 'stuff.' Where I live, not being able to park in the garage would be very inconvenient, frustrating, and almost cause for divorce.

There are many things that could be going on in one's home; things that are no longer even noticed that can contribute to feelings of frustration. It's easy to become complacent in the home and accept things in slight disrepair. All the while, every day, little by little, the stress accumulates and, over time, puts the occupants out of ease or out of balance.

Some examples of items that could be adding subliminal stress:

- the toaster doesn't work properly and burns your toast;
- the closet door doesn't close properly—needs a new hinge;
- you go to use the bathroom and you have to jiggle the flusher thing otherwise the water keeps running;
- a room that was painted a year ago is still missing the baseboards or electrical covers;
- the clock in the dining room has stopped working—likely needs a new battery;
- the door on the pantry sticks just long enough for you to give it a big tug and lose your balance.

All of these little annoyances add up and contribute to the level of STRESS being experienced by the home's occupants—all the while with no cognizant awareness.

> "Ninety-five percent of all dis-ease is caused by STRESS and 100% of stress is caused by the wrong belief, and it's almost always subconscious."
> Bruce H. Lipton, PhD, Cellular Biologist

I have done many Feng Shui home evaluations for clients where there is often a burned-out light bulb, a squeak in the front step indicating a loose board, or perhaps an overgrown tree blocking the doorway—little things that are easily fixed and that may be causing some inconvenience or discomfort to the home's occupants. When I have asked about these little annoyances, the client usually acts surprised, as if they are finding out about it for the first time. They have accepted the dis-repair into the subconscious as they have patterned a new behavior that includes adjusting to the inconvenience. Repeated action over time equals results: just as water (energy) has the force, over time, to smooth a jagged rock, subtle annoyances can cause stress on some level.

Author Jack Canfield recommends a list of all the rooms in your house. Then, go through each room and list all the things in that room that irritate you or are in disrepair. He says: "If you are willing to settle in the small areas of your life, then you are likely to settle in the big areas of your life as well."

It's recommended that, after you've made your list, you put a completion date beside each thing that you need to accomplish in each room. Taking inspired action will lead to positive results!

Not replacing a burnt-out light bulb for a lengthy period of time, and not taking the time to repair a small item, is connected to a self-worth issue. There is likely a program running in the subconscious that says 'not deserving,' 'other people are more important,' 'I'm not worth it,' 'I have a fear of not doing it right.' Dis-repair in the outer world signals dis-repair in the inner world. Until the file (root) has been deleted and replaced with a more supportive file, the past will continue to dictate the future.

Eight – Live With What You Love: Out Of Chaos Comes Clarity

As I get older, I have come to the conclusion that, at the end of the day—that is, the end of my life, and that of my friends and relatives—we will be honored with a one-hour-or-so power point of pictures of our experiences, from birth to death. I have yet to see someone's entire life represented in pictures of all the 'stuff' that they accumulated, maintained, and possessed (or which possessed them) throughout life.

The tangible, seen energy in your home is having an effect on the unseen, intangible energy of your thoughts and emotions. Living a life on purpose is living a vibrant life whereby experiences and contribution take precedence over making room for more stuff—stuff filling the spaces of life, consuming and contracting the breath of chi around it—where quantity becomes less important.

Consciously arranging one's environment to create a healthy, peaceful, and dynamic flow of energy, including living with what you love, relaxes the nervous system, inspires the mind, and calms the emotions.

I love the song by Johnny Nash: 'I Can See Clearly Now.' I often play it to increase my vibration. It's a feel-good song, although I have a slightly revised version:

I can 'chi' clearly now, the clutter is gone, all obstacles out of the way. It's going to be a bright, (bright), bright (bright) sun shiny day!

As you begin to embrace the practices presented within, you may begin to 'chi' clearly and raise your vibration.

Life is an interactive experience.
This is your space.

Consider what possessions are currently taking up space—prime real-estate—in your home, that may be blocking or keeping you from receiving something better. Choose one item—the one that first entered into your conscious awareness. Ask yourself how you feel about this item.

Does it lift your energy or drain your energy?

Do you love it? Do you need it? Does it serve you? Explain your reasons.

Eight – Live With What You Love: Out Of Chaos Comes Clarity

What item(s) do you feel obligated to display or store that do not resonate with your personal tastes?

What expensive items are currently residing in your home, taking up energetic space?

What items in the category of 'might need it some day' are currently residing in your home?

What is the 'thing' that you do, learned behavior from a parent or past experience that extends into your possessions? (For example it is my past experience of losing my childhood keepsakes that caused me to make sure my children's keepsakes are safe.)

What have you been tolerating in your home? Burned-out light bulbs? Squeaky floorboards?

Eight – Live With What You Love: Out Of Chaos Comes Clarity

Focus your attention in the area of your heart.
With the intention of breathing in gratitude and exhaling love:
Take a deep breath in for 5 seconds or more.
Hold for 5 seconds. Exhale for 5 seconds or more.
Bring your awareness and attention to each word and
or phrase in the Energetic Heart Code below.
Bringing them into your heart— feel the feeling of the
word or phrase radiating to every cell of your being.
Relax and repeat, while continuing to breathe,
to create heart-brain coherence.

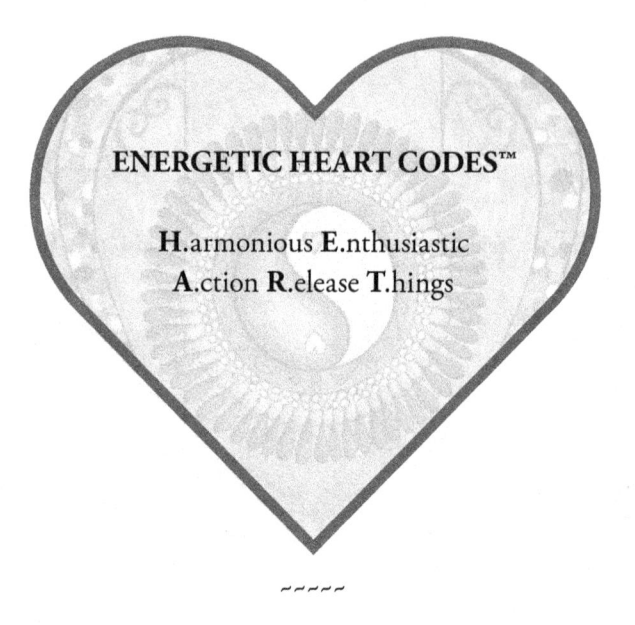

ENERGETIC HEART CODES™

H.armonious **E**.nthusiastic
A.ction **R**.elease **T**.hings

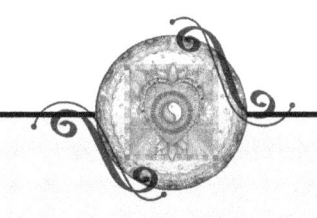

Nine – Change Your Frequency—Change Your Life

"Your energy (vibe) and action create a rhythmic vibration that is matched by the universe. This brings back to you the exact same energy vibration that you broadcast."
Anita Adrain

If you change your frequency, thereby increasing your personal vibration, you can change every area of your life.

> "According to the law of vibration, we postulate that everything vibrates or moves; nothing sits idle. Everything is in a constant state of motion, and therefore, there is no such thing as "inertia" or a state of rest. From the most ethereal to the most gross form of matter, everything is in a constant state of vibration."
>
> *You Were Born Rich*, Bob Proctor

When you start to practice and embrace the principles and exercises presented in this book, you are beginning to increase your frequency and personal vibration, and the vibration in your home.

Changing frequencies is like changing channels on your T.V. or radio. You have to be willing to turn the dial, tune in to a different channel, and learn something new.

Nine – Change Your Frequency—Change Your Life

Increased awareness—consciousness—enhances or heightens the electromagnetic waves (your heart in coherence is a powerful electromagnetic field) transferred through vibrations of other electromagnetic fields (your physical body).

The strength of the signal being transmitted, your signal, is what the universe hears and responds to.

The energy wave, which is a common term indicating energy is transferred, creates the frequency. Depending on the number of crests in the wave, the frequency is higher or lower.

Potential energy, or a higher energy state of consciousness, is achieved when the waves have a high frequency and a short wavelength.

'When you increase the frequency of your vibration you affect everything and everyone around you.' This might seem like an 'out there' statement, and yet it is a widely accepted by any Feng Shui practitioner or metaphysical teacher. It is the belief of many metaphysicists that raising human vibration is why we are here.

Dr. Joe Dispenza, along with a group of scientists, have measured the energy in a room at one of his advanced workshops that validates this statement.

> "Melissa waterman, BS, MSW, and Certified Advanced Level GDV User, measured the energy of the room, the energy around students' bodies, and the energy centers of their bodies using Gas Discharge Visualization (GDV) imaging, a breakthrough technology that measures the human energy field. Beyond people aligning and expanding their energy fields, the most interesting result was that when our students were doing a walking meditation 12 blocks away, they actually raised the energy in the hall where our lectures and mediations took place. We were pleased to see this phenomenon occur again after we discovered the same shift in energy last October at the Cabo San Lucas's Advanced retreat."
> http://drjoedispenza.net/blog/science/firing-up-the-networks-and-stepping-up-the-game/

What is significant about this is the person's energy field remains in a space after he or she is physically gone—an energy imprint. Compared to leaving your footprint in the sand, the energy of your physical feet is beyond or ahead of the energy impressions left in the sand.

You may have experienced this first-hand in a situation where perhaps you had a heated argument with someone and one of you left the room. The residual energy of the low energy vibration of your feelings and actions still lingered, and either you were stewing in the energy, or instinctively had to leave. In Feng Shui, practitioners often offer clients the service of space clearing the unseen, stuck, stagnant, or discordant energies in a space.

Ancient cultures practiced space clearing, some of which have been passed on and are relevant today. The Indigenous space clear by smudging as it is called, using a bundle of sage and/or sweet grass. Other cultures use incense, bells, chimes, music, and essential oils to clean and clear the unseen energy in a space. Some practitioners, today, change the energy of a space simply by their presence and what frequency they are broadcasting into the energy field.

On several occasions I have witnessed negative residual energy accumulate in a space—day in and day out—from the lower vibration of the home's occupants. I've seen it radiate outward, beyond the physical walls of the home. That energy is absorbed by the trees and any other plant life around the home as nature's way of balancing or space clearing the negative energy. But, over time, the overwhelmed flora and fauna begin to die from the prolonged negative energy force. (Repeated action over time equals results.) To a passerby it may look like the home is in disrepair—that maybe the owners don't care.

It's important to note that there may be other influences that contribute to a home's overall energy, besides that of the occupants. Contributing factors include geopathic stress and harmful EMF's created from electric and electronic equipment in the home. Note: there is a solution to clear these energies offered at the end of the book in 'resources.'

Have you ever listened to crickets or frogs chant on a summer's evening? I like to think this is nature's way of space clearing and restoring balance.

Nine – Change Your Frequency—Change Your Life

Energy expert, Dr. Eric Pearl, states in his book *The Reconnection* that: "Physics is just coming around to confirming the long-held belief that, ultimately, everything in the universe consists of vibration occurring at different frequencies. Change the frequency of that vibration and you change the nature of that particle that the vibration defines."

The Wonder Of It All

In the summer of 1989, my brother took me trail riding to one of his favorite spots in the Rocky Mountains.

The image is still etched in my memory. For several days, our home was a plateau several miles above the valley where we'd started our trail ride the day before. Large tents, the kind you see on the old western movies, were erected on the flat ground. One became a cook house and gathering spot; the other two were sleeping quarters.

The area appeared well protected, with towering evergreens and small shrubs creating the perimeter of our camp. I felt somewhat uneasy not knowing what might emerge from the forest at any given time, but my brother assured me we were in a safe location. He had chosen this spot away from any natural feeding grounds of local bears and mountain lions—and he explained he had several guns that would stop any intruder in their tracks (just in case).

It was from this base camp that we would explore several areas only accessible by foot or on horseback. Our first day was spent getting accustomed to our new surroundings and taking the horses for a few short rides.

The next day we were to be up early, taking advantage of the daylight for our ascent to the top of the mountain. The trail ride was expected to take three or four hours to reach the top. Provisions were packed for the full day adventure, strapped to one of the pack horses.

We saddled up and began our ascent at a leisurely pace, not really having to direct the horses, just sitting in the saddle, taking in the smells and sounds, and feeling the rhythm of the horse's body moving side to side—a slight rocking motion.

As we moved up the mountain it didn't seem that we were reaching a higher elevation, as the tall evergreens obscured any view of the valley below, yet there were certainly times when the incline could be felt through the horse—an upward and forward motion. I don't recall there being a clearly defined trail; my brother led the group of horses and riders.

There were moments when we would catch a glimpse of the mountain peaks, and times when we'd spot a bit of the valley below, but most often they were obscured from our view. We didn't realize how much ground had been gained on the vertical climb until we crested the mountain.

The landscape turned more barren with boulders; shorter trees revealed the sky. We had reached our destination. We dismounted, leaving the horses to graze on a small meadow as we took in the sense of time and place—it would be the spot where we would enjoy our lunch.

It was no wonder this was my one of my brother's favorite spots. We were blessed with a clear blue sky and a few puffs of white clouds in the distance.

The awe-inspiring, spectacular view from the top of that mountain was like no other I had seen before. If I had to estimate, I would say that we could see for a hundred miles or more in every direction. Beyond our peak was another beautiful snow-capped mountaintop, and another with hues of blue-grey.

There were no words to describe the feeling of being one with nature in that moment—the exhilarating feeling of being on top of the world. No thing to distract from absorbing all the energy of Mother Nature in her untouched, raw beauty.

In that moment, I had such an overwhelming feeling of accomplishment, and deep awareness, that I was completed supported.

I was not the only one. We all basked in the feeling of oneness and silent appreciation for being alive, for being able to witness the power of our mother Gaia.

My brother just smiled, the biggest smile I'd ever seen on him, as he knew he had touched my heart and soul by bringing me to this magical place.

Nine – Change Your Frequency—Change Your Life

This experience was before I discovered Feng Shui. I tell you this story here as a reminder that nature is reflective and holds clues to our continued survival and evolution.

If we were to look at just one wave pattern, joining several M's together—MMMMM—it might look like a natural formation that we see in the mountains, with valleys and peaks. If you have ever climbed a mountain by foot or by horse, you know the amount of effort it takes to get to the top. You are rewarded for your efforts by the panoramic, breathtaking views that await you, an accelerated level of energy that you can only experience firsthand by making the climb.

Perhaps you have made a metaphorical climb to the top of a mountain, having overcome some personal challenge or obstacle. You may have experienced that same euphoric feeling, that no one can touch you—the sense of being unstoppable.

The two views—one from starting off low in the valley, one from standing at the peak—registered two very different experiences for me. One was apprehension and caution, the other was exhilaration and freedom.

I believe we are designed to live closer to the energetic high that we feel when we are at the top of the mountain, on top of our game. The amount of energy it takes to get there is worth it. When you are in an energetic valley in the lowest part of the wave, you might feel closed in (like having a tall shelter of trees) and consumed by the barriers around you, unaware that there is something spectacular (potentials) waiting to be discovered.

As you start to ascend, you will get glimpses of what living in a higher state of vibration is like. The more you increase your vibration, the more of life's beauty will be revealed.

> "As we shift to a higher vibration, messages tend to flow more quickly. When we are using our gifts and abilities with right intention, things come to us."
> *The Celestine Prophecy*, James Redfield

Awakening, expanding knowledge, conscious thought, and inspired action will result in rising to a higher level, a higher vibration. It takes courage, physical, emotional and mental energy, to climb your mountain—a definiteness of purpose with a clear vision of the peak. Ascension is reaching your full potential.

Having clutter in the home is like being in the valley of the energy wave. Its walls close in and it's very difficult to see your way to the peak or to muster the energy it takes to get there.

When you remove clutter in your home, you are essentially removing the low energy that keeps you stuck in the valley. You are increasing your vibration that will elevate you to the peak of your mountain; living closer to, and in alignment with, your pure potential.

On page 422 of *Kryon Book VII Letters From Home,* a question was asked on what would help our vibrational levels. The answer included what hurts your vibrational growth, and included: "Holding on to portions of your life that you know very well are of low vibration because you can't think of a way to exist without them." What will assist your vibrational growth are the following things: "Casting away inappropriate energies in your life that at one time might have seemed 'sacred,' but which now you can indeed live without."

Clearing out the old programs, beliefs, and energetic stuff (clutter) is the first step to ascension, living heaven on Earth.

High and low vibrations cannot co-exist; it's one or the other. (Germs, disease, and negativity vibrate low.) Scientific studies at UCLA show that, when our vibrations are elevated, our intelligence, co-ordination, consciousness, happiness and levels of health can become elevated. Living a healthy, vibrant life in a healthy environment is supported when you choose to raise the vibration in your home.

Life is an interactive experience.
This is Your Space.

Have you ever climbed to the top of a mountain or perhaps a metaphorical mountain? Take a few moments here and recall that experience. How did you feel? (If you have difficulty recalling, then can you imagine how it might feel, and go through it in your mind.)

List the top 9 emotions that you associate with your climb.
-
-
-
-
-
-
-
-
-

Use this list as inspiration to clear clutter—the stuck energy in your home. By doing this you will likely elevate your frequency, experiencing similar or matching energies to the above words.

Nine – Change Your Frequency—Change Your Life

Think of experiences where you felt more energy, felt more alive, in tune or in-sync, on top of the world. What were you doing? Who were you with? List those experiences and do more of that! Increase your VIBE

Focus your attention in the area of your heart.
With the intention of breathing in gratitude and exhaling love:
Take a deep breath in for 5 seconds or more.
Hold for 5 seconds. Exhale for 5 seconds or more.
Bring your awareness and attention to each word and
or phrase in the Energetic Heart Code below.
Bringing them into your heart— feel the feeling of the
word or phrase radiating to every cell of your being.
Relax and repeat, while continuing to breathe,
to create heart-brain coherence.

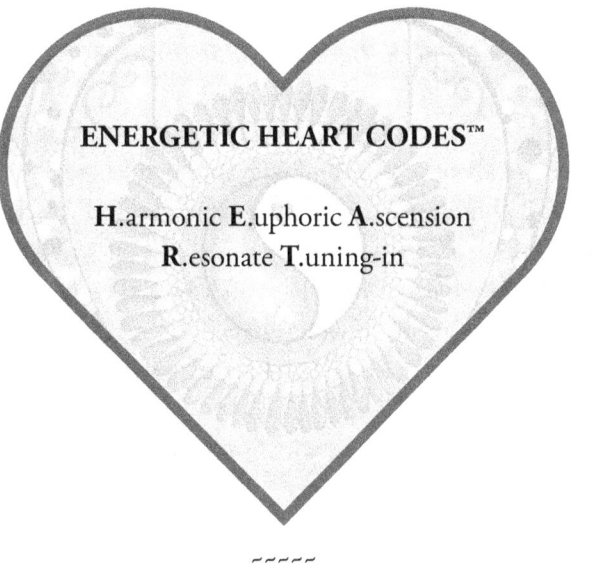

ENERGETIC HEART CODES™

H.armonic **E.**uphoric **A.**scension
R.esonate **T.**uning-in

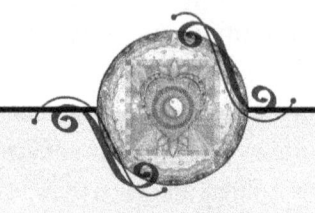

Ten – Nature's Building Blocks

*"The addition of live plants and flowers to your home is 'flower power';
it adds beauty and life to the environment and relaxes the nervous system."*
Anita Adrain

One of the goals of practicing Feng Shui is to increase your personal frequency—your vibration—so that you can become the rock in the pond, sending your energetic ripples out to positively affect all who come in contact. It's all about living with what you love and loving where you live.

As we discovered in the previous chapter, de-cluttering is the first step in Feng Shui'ing any environment. Achieving balance and harmony is the second step.

Feng Shui teaches us to look within our personal environment—our home—to create a harmonious space. One of the main principles or tools used to achieve this harmony is the use of the 5-elements chart as it relates to the tangible aspects of the space being occupied.

The five elements are the very building blocks of our natural environment from which all things take physical form. When all five elements: earth, metal, water, wood, and fire are present and in balance they have the power to affect every aspect of our life.

Are we connected energetically to everything in our home and beyond? I believe we are.

When we are aware of these energies, and we can recognize how they show up in the tangible results of our furniture, our stuff, our possessions, including the invisible energy field that surrounds them, it's like owning a magic wand.

All of a sudden one has the advantage of being able to cause change in an exact area where specific results are desired.

When I began to learn how to recognize the five elements within the parameter of the physical form—shapes and colors that manifest in our life and our home—I began to see another pattern emerge.

Magic Wand

What would you change in your life if you had a magic wand? Would you create a healthier body? Would you create more prosperity and abundance? Would you live in a different house? Perhaps a different part of the world?

Maybe you would choose to paint like the masters, play the guitar skilfully, or speak fluent Spanish. What would your life look like if you had more energy and more time to pursue your heart's desire? Perhaps you do have a magic wand at your fingertips and you just haven't been aware of it, up until now.

Success leaves clues, and so does Mother Nature. It would be safe to say that she is very successful. If the human population were to vanish tomorrow, she would continue quite nicely without us. So, what clues has she given us that we are not consciously aware of?

Have you ever gazed upwards on a wonderful summer's day to see the white clouds billow into recognizable shapes, only to blink your eyes and find them gone? Those same clouds can quickly gather ferociously, producing blinding strikes of lightening that connect the heavens and the Earth. Within the same day, and sometimes the same hour, with precision and purpose she can paint the sky with a brilliant rainbow that emerges from the darkness of a storm.

Seemingly overnight, she can transform the landscape of summer into a stunning canvas filled with vibrant autumn colors of deep reds and warm hues of orange and yellow.

Every season, she continues to express her brilliance with the breath and ease of her magic wand. Barren tree branches come to life with diamond sparkles from crystals of hoar frost as the sun wakes them up on a cold winter's day. Intricate patterns form on every surface available, making the long winter days more bearable.

Ten – Nature's Building Blocks

It doesn't matter on which continent you experience the change of seasons Mother Nature will always express herself outwardly in the environment. From repeating precise patterns placed in the sand, to the powerful waves of the sea, Mother Nature uses her magic wand every day.

5-element Theory

An in-depth study on its own, the 5-element theory has evolved over thousands of years in mind-body practices.

Traditional Chinese medicine, acupuncture, and Tai chi practitioners refer to the 'five' elements. They too have looked to Mother Nature as a way of understanding the inner world, to help their patients achieve balance in mind, body, and spirit.

The 5-element chart is used by the skilled Traditional Chinese Medicine practitioner (TCM) to decode the body's messages as a preventative health measure, or to treat an existing condition as there are five element influences associated with major organs, and with areas of the body. For example: the wood element governs the liver and gallbladder and may suggest a diet of green raw foods to bring balance and support to these vital organs.

Feng Shui, also uses the 5-element theory, as its principles apply to the physical environment of one's home. It's important to note the differences between the TCM practitioner's 5-element chart and the Feng Shui practitioner's chart. The original 5-element chart, used by TCM practitioners, is broken down into elements, seasons, Yin organs, Yang organs, directions, tastes, tissues, colors, and sense organs. Feng Shui has adapted and acquired this knowledge to achieve balance in the physical space of the home, using the 5-elements as they relate to the seasons and directions, the colors and shapes associated with them, and even an association with the '5' senses.

When you can start to recognize the interaction of the five elements and their application to strengthen your outer world, your home, you will also experience their power to enhance your personal energy vibration of mind, body, and spirit—the inner world sanctuary.

Elemental Discovery

Have you ever gone to someone's home or place of business for the first time and immediately felt totally uncomfortable? Perhaps your physical body responded as well: maybe you felt light- headed, nauseous, or your heart began to beat faster. Perhaps you had the feeling that you had to get out of that space, the quicker the better.

What about when you've gone into someone's home and felt totally comfortable, relaxed, calm and at ease?

Have you ever re-arranged all the furniture in a particular room in your home, the bedroom or the living room? You have a plan, and you enlist the help of your spouse or child and everything is turned upside down before it gets turned right side up. You finish the task, stand back to observe your genius plan unfold, forefinger resting lightly under your chin; you pan the entire space, the lip begins to pucker, the nose twitches from side to side… mmm, not quite right. Then you re-arrange and re-arrange until the helpful person disappears and you end up having the same arrangement, or close to, as when you started. You can't quite put your finger on it, but something doesn't feel right—something is missing.

In these instances, you were responding instinctively to the absence or presence of one of the five elements.

Though you may be unaware of this until now, your persona naturally strives for balance, and looks to shelter the mind, body, and spirit in a harmonious space that allows comfort, and elicits a sense of well-beingness or safety.

The five elements have taught me to look beyond the color of the walls and look within the person whose walls are painted. The reflection is always in sync with the mind and spirit or emotional state of the person: the inner world is connected to, and reflected in, the outer world. People reflect their inner self through their outer selves—be it their choice of words, style of dress, or décor of their home, in the same way as nature shows us the quiet reflection from still waters of the flora and fauna basking on its shores.

Ten – Nature's Building Blocks

Creating Harmony and Balance

When my three boys were eight, six, and four, I was a busy mom. Most days I was a referee, cook, entertainment coordinator, organizer of toys, teacher, and chauffeur. That was one of my full-time jobs. The other was running a demanding, fulltime, brick and mortar business that was open six days a week and nine hours a day.

My husband worked long hours: gone by six in the morning and not home until seven at night—and that's when he was working close to home; otherwise he was away for weeks at a time.

I do not know how I managed to take time away from all that to train as an Essential Feng Shui practitioner. Twice I had to travel to San Diego—once in the fall and once in the spring—to complete the training. It was after my second trip that I gained the knowledge and insight that opened my Feng Shui eyes to a new a view of my own home environment.

I had been reading Feng Shui books for years and had, with great results, applied many of the principles to our home. This time was different: I had a different set of lenses with which to view every room. With a new awareness and understanding, particularly of the five elements, their presence or absence, and the powerful influence on the home's occupants, I went to work.

Our middle son had an internal alarm clock that went off every day between five-thirty and six in the morning, regardless of the day of the week. He was the last one to go to sleep at night. Quite often he would wake up in the wee hours of the morning and find his way under the warm covers, snuggling between my husband and me.

One busy weekday morning, I awoke at my usual time and didn't notice that he was in his own bed still sleeping. I was getting myself ready, making lunches, planning dinner, putting a load of laundry in the washer—all the usual morning routine—when I noticed he was not up. I went into his room and there he was still sleeping. I woke him along with his brothers. A half hour or so passed and his brothers were fully dressed, in the kitchen having breakfast. I had to go into his room again and wake him for the second time. I continued my morning chores, getting ready to pack everyone up to head out the door at our scheduled time of eight-thirty, as I had three drop-offs before opening the store at nine. Twenty minutes before our departure, he was still not out of bed. I had to use the firm Mom voice. Finally, he appeared in the kitchen, rubbing his eyes, clearly disgruntled about getting out of bed. I again had to use the firm voice, 'Hurry up we need to leave soon.'

He put his hands on his hips, leaned forward, and replied, "It's your fault MOM, you Fung Shoo-weed my room!"

There are many times as a parent that you must hide your smile, knowing your child is right and, somehow, he has managed, in a split second, to change your mood and melt your heart. This was one of those days.

I had Feng Shui'ed his room three days earlier. His room had previously been decorated around the theme of Thomas the Train, popular at the time. The theme colors were bright, fire-engine red, shocking royal blue, and vibrant yellow.

Not knowing any better, as a parent you buy what's available in the stores, and decorate your children's rooms, matching the colors of the comforter with the color of the walls, trim, and anything else to make it look aesthetically pleasing.

That is, until you learn about the five elements (and the 5-element chart) and the power of their influence on the subconscious.

Three days earlier, I had removed all the 'active' energy influence from his room, along with all the toys that were constantly saying 'come play with me.' I'd repainted the walls in a comforting earth tone, the trim a nourishing matte blue, replaced the comforter with a warm, soft, creamy yellow one, and moved the bed away from the window, snugging it against the wall and ensuring it had a clear view of the doorway. All the active toys were moved downstairs to a designated playroom. All that remained were items that conveyed the sense of relaxation, comfort, and security: books and stuffed animals. With the help of the 5-elements chart I was able to minimize the active elements that would keep him awake, and introduce the elements that would make him feel totally at ease. I am so grateful that I gained the knowledge to make the beneficial changes to my son's room, creating a space that encouraged rest and relaxation, an opportunity for his little body to rejuvenate during a good night's sleep.

Maybe you know someone with a small child who is still not sleeping in his own bedroom, or not sleeping through the night. By removing the two extremely active and 'awake' elements of fire and metal from a bedroom, and adding the nourishing element of wood, the comforting, supportive element of earth, and the soothing, fluid energy of water, chances are the problem will be solved—you'll have sprinkled pixie dust with your magic wand.

Programmed

Taking a closer look at our own personal environment, we can better understand what energy influence from natures' five elements might be in a causality conflict within our body, our mind, or our spirit.

We respond to our environment in one of two ways: positively, or not so positively. The unfortunate part is that the response is almost always subliminal, as 90% of the thoughts we think are subconscious.

We can become aware of the vibrations that radiate from our living space by understanding the five elements. When we take time to follow the 'clues' and look back in history, we can 'clearly' see the reflection in the 'outer world' that came from the 'inner world' by how many of the five elements were present, and in what form they were represented.

We can ask ourselves: did this—the presence or lack of five elements—have an effect on the occupants of that space called home?

Another contemplation, as we take a step back in time, is to ask the questions: do we seek to express ourselves outwardly 'in' our environment, or do we respond or react, expressing outwardly as a result of our environment?

If we look back, decade by decade, we can see how outside influences—things happening in our economy and social climate—changed the intimate space of the home environment.

For example: in the 1950s, the general outlook was positive, and it showed up in the housing boom as post-war optimism. At that time, bold designs popped up everywhere—fabrics with fruit, flowers, abstract and geometric designs in vinyl table coverings and wallpaper. These bold designs showed up in many North American homes.

Some will remember the vibrantly colored wall-to-wall carpet, floors chequered with black and white tile, chrome chairs and tables with Formica tops. Perhaps there is a memory of the colorful set of Melmac dishes and the stainless-steel bread bin with matching canisters that your grandmother had. There were colored pink or yellow ceramic sinks in the bathrooms, complete with matching, bright ceramic tile.

The 50s were prosperous times for the middle class and more emphasis was spent on enjoying life, having fun with family. The interior design of this decade certainly reflected the playful vibrancy of the times.

The enthusiasm continued into the early 60s, and then shifted with the events of the world. We came close to a nuclear war, the first man landed on the moon, love and peace were the messages from the Hippie generation in response to the Vietnam War, and we were introduced to The Beatles and The Rolling Stones.

There was a lot going on in the world in the 1960s, technologically and socially, and the decorating schemes reflected that wholeheartedly. Everything became more dynamic, graphic, and colorful. Psychedelic combinations of fuchsia, pink, and tangerine looked great together—in the same room. This was the decade that introduced and popularized lava lamps.

Floral-decorated metal T.V. trays adorned the living room, so the family could gather around the television and comfortably eat dinner. If you didn't have a big, comfy couch to sit on, then the must-have shag rug was an alternative sitting place. The decade saw us bringing nature indoors, with potted plants and dried flowers. Beads and feathers were popular accents, as was vinyl wallpaper.

One word sums up the decorating style of the 60s: contrast. Life in the 60s was a time of 'self-expression'; home decor was the place for people to display their individualism, making a statement that reflected their 'inner world' feelings, emotions, and mental awareness.

The late 60s seemed to awaken the masses in the Western culture to higher dimensions of human life, turning the focus to unexplored potentials within. (Sure, it might have had something to do with the use of mind-altering drugs.)

Moving into the 70s, the interest of Eastern philosophies and practices like yoga, martial arts, meditation, and Feng Shui grew in popularity. The exploration and materialistic aspects of 'self' expanded to technology and economic advancement.

Ten – Nature's Building Blocks

We could continue to analyze each decade until the present time and interpret; so powerful are the influences that affect the relationship between the 'Outer' world and 'Inner' world—everything is connected.

When you feel you have a better understanding of five elements, return to the decade descriptions and see if you can identify what elements might have been in 'play' in each decade since the 1950s.

In each decade you might discover, as I did, that there were very similar characteristics and parallels of one or more of the five elements influences present in the home, and the person.

Inner Balance

When you achieve elemental balance in most rooms in your home, you will feel more connected and at ease. This inner balance has the potential to radiate, similar to the effects of throwing a pebble into a pond and witnessing the ripples expanding in a continuous, vibratory rhythm, touching everything in its path. By understanding how to use the five elements in your space, you become the pebble tossed into the pond, radiating your energy outward, affecting everyone in your path, either positively or not so positively.

Life is an interactive experience.
This is your space.

In which decade were you in your youth?

Do you remember specific decorating schemes either in your home or someone else's? Write down all of the things that you can remember. Be as specific as you can.

Later, you can come back to this space to identify what element could be associated with each thing (you'll be cued to do this). This practice will help you to better identify what elements are in your own space.

Ten – Nature's Building Blocks

Focus your attention in the area of your heart.
With the intention of breathing in gratitude and exhaling love:
Take a deep breath in for 5 seconds or more.
Hold for 5 seconds. Exhale for 5 seconds or more.
Bring your awareness and attention to each word and
or phrase in the Energetic Heart Code below.
Bringing them into your heart— feel the feeling of the
word or phrase radiating to every cell of your being.
Relax and repeat, while continuing to breathe,
to create heart-brain coherence.

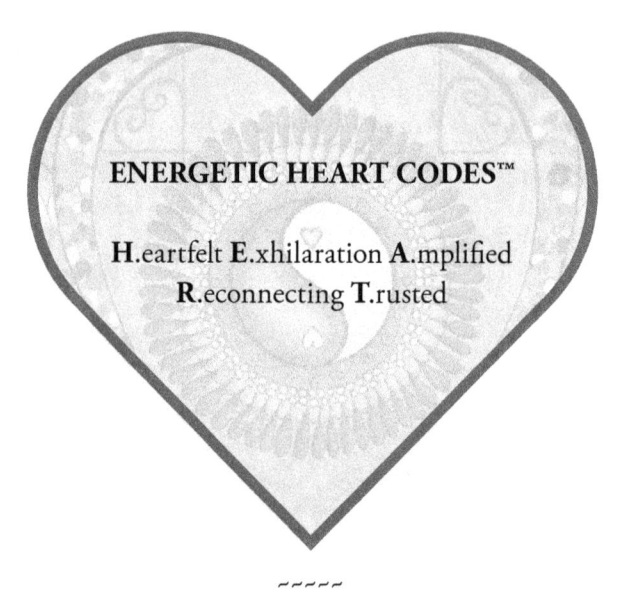

ENERGETIC HEART CODES™

H.eartfelt **E**.xhilaration **A**.mplified
R.econnecting **T**.rusted

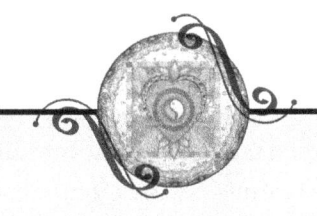

Eleven – Your Home, Your Sanctuary

"Your home reflects the results of conscious, seen energy—the Shui, and subconscious, unseen energy—the Feng."
Anita Adrain

The presence of each element in the home displays individual characteristics or influences that mimic the natural environment. Think of a time when you were out in nature—your favourite place to spend time outdoors, or the last vacation you were on. Did you feel at ease, relaxed, or calm? Did you find that after your experience you were invigorated?

Every year my family goes on a warm vacation to relax and rejuvenate the soul. We enjoy the feeling of the sand between our toes, the warmth of the sun penetrating every cell, the sound of the waves lapping the shore in a mesmerising tone, and the soft gentle breeze that rustles the leaves of the palm trees.

That feeling of my ideal outdoor environment stays with me all year; many times I recall memories of my ideal outdoor environment to help me relax and rejuvenate my soul. Recall serves me well, knowing I will get to go to that or a similar place again. It is in these ideal natural settings that all five elements are present. It is in these ideal places that the body, mind, and spirit are nourished positively. The heat from the sun and the bright sunny day represent the 'fire element.' The ocean or sound of water represents the soothing 'water element.' The rocks on the shoreline or in the distance represent the 'metal element.' The texture and feeling of being supported during a walk in the sand, represents the 'earth element.' All of the beauty of green palm trees and brightly blooming hibiscus and bougainvillaea represent the 'wood element.' All five elements are present and in balance: the nourishing cycle has the power to rebalance and nourish the soul so that, when me and my family return, we feel refreshed, revitalized, and ready to continue on life's journey, with the motivation and promise to return to that place to be re-filled again.

What if you didn't have to wait until the next vacation, or for the outside temperatures to warm, before experiencing similar feelings from your indoor space?

How we each decorate our homes, our 'visual' environments, is a determining factor that has the power to influence every aspect of each of our lives.

How does Mother Nature decorate her visual environment? Does her decorating style influence any aspect of your life?

Have you ever noticed that people are happier when 'she' decorates the sky with sun compared to grey rainclouds? Each of our homes has similar characteristics to Mother Nature's home, and the same effects can be a determining factor in how we live life. My observation is that Mother Nature works under the laws of the universe, consciously designing her space with all that is tangible and intangible. People today, on the other hand, unconsciously design their space with very little or no awareness of the effects their actions may have on living a more harmonious life.

Combining the five elements in your home has the potential of creating a space that nourishes you on all levels, revitalizing all of the home's occupants in mind, body, and spirit.

By learning how to recognize the five essential elements, quality of chi, in the physical environment of our home or office, we can increase our personal energy and vitality.

Five Elements

There are three attributes of the five elements that I will outline and focus on in the following paragraphs: color, substance/texture, shape. To keep it simple, I will list these attributes in the above order. However, please know that you may personally perceive them in a different order due to relevance.

As you become more aware of the elemental attributes of color, substance/texture, and shape within your personal space you may recognize a recurring theme.

There is an unseen attribute—the way you react to the presence of a dominant element or elements and how it impacts your spirit (your sensory perception). This dominant element becomes a part of your essence. You portray certain behavioral characteristics as a result of living in that particular energetic influence. This will be noted as 'elemental essence' under the description of each element.

Also paired with the five elements are the five senses which can be considered and engaged when creating balance in any space.

Visual information is most often received and processed first. Each elemental discovery will start with the color associated with that element. If you can 'think' in color, you will easily be able to identify elements in any space.

As we are all connected to the vastness of this planet, it would make sense that we would start our elemental discovery with earth. It is that which sustains our life and supports us in every way.

EARTH (engages the sense of hearing)

Earth energy is flat, and symbolizes the nurturing environment that enables seeds to grow, from which all living things emanate and to which they return. Earth nurtures, supports, and interacts with each of the other elements.

Color: yellow, browns, skin tones, and earthy colors.
Substance and/or texture: items made from earth elements such as terra-cotta, brick, ceramics, and soil-based substance.
Shape: square, rectangular, long and flat.

Recognize the earth element in your home:

The earth element can show up in our homes in many ways: materials made from the dirt of the earth like ceramics, pottery, and bricks. The earthy tones: shades of brown, beige, and/or skin-tones that may show up as the colors on the walls. Items: tables that are square or rectangular. Ceramic tile and/or flooring that mimics the shape and color of the earth are noted as earth elements.

Quite often we have a 'fusion' of elements, making it challenging to read the element of a particular item. A square table (the shape makes it earth) can be made of the element 'wood' and painted red—a 'fire' element. In this case the wood energy is no longer vital and has been diminished by the fire element. The fusion then would be of earth and fire.

Bring earth chi into your home or space when life appears hectic and/or chaotic. Restoring balance and stability, occupants will be receptive and feel nurtured. When earth energy is in balance with the other four elements, the emotional state of the home's occupants will reflect empowerment, support, fairness, wisdom, and instinct.

Elemental Essence

When earth energy is in balance in the home, each occupant will tend to take on the characteristics of a good listener: patient, and kind. Each person in the home is usually a dedicated individual.

Out of balance earth energy creates imbalance within each person—he or she may have difficulty setting boundaries and taking care of him or herself as the person is always putting the needs of others first.

Abundant or dominant earth energy in the space can affect the occupants' emotional state. Each person may express smothering and/or nervous energy, similar to the feeling of being shoulder deep in a mound of soil or sand.

Imagine the vastness of the prairies or a barren desert that can appear endless, with no hope of life.

Adding the element of wood, restores the helpless feeling, balancing the heavy earth energy, lifting the chi.

METAL (engages the sense of sight)

Metal is a conductor of energy, a precious commodity, a beautiful gemstone. It symbolizes strength and solidity, with the ability to contain objects. Metal is associated with autumn.

Color: light pastel colors, white, gold, silver, copper—the color of metal
Substance and/or texture: strong items made from metals such as: stainless steel, copper, brass, iron, silver, and gold.
Also: marble, granite, natural crystals, and gemstones.
Shape: circles, ovals, arches and scrolls.

Recognize the metal element in your home:

Metal shows up in homes as metal shelving, trophies, brass candle holders, and silver frames—anything that is made from metal. Marble or granite countertops, salt lamps, a collection of rocks or quartz crystals fall into the metal category. Items that are circular and/or pastel in color would be considered metal. An oval mirror framed in gold or silver would be a fusion of the metal and water element.

When metal energy is in balance with the other four elements, the emotional state will reflect the mental aspects of communication, brilliant ideas, and justice—think of the metal energy as being 'mental' energy.

Elemental Essence

Metal energy characteristics mirror the strength, adaptability, and endurance of metal itself. In balance, the expressions of metal energy people are organized, intellectual, and display traits of perfectionism. An over-abundance of metal energy reflects in the metal personality as being emotionally cold or detached. To balance the over-abundant metal energy, we would add fire to melt or control it.

When metal energy is dominant in the space, it can affect the occupants' emotional state, expressing as destruction, danger, and sadness, as metal can be made into the blades of weapons.

Add or activate metal chi in a space when tasks require a clear head, concentration and determination required to get things done.

WATER (engages the sense of taste)

Water energy is downward and symbolizes water in all forms as it shows up in our natural world: a gentle rain or a snow storm.
Color: dark colors—black like the depths of the ocean. Colors associated with water such as deep blues and turquoise greens.
Substance and/or texture: reflective surfaces, mirrors, glass. Water features like fountains, birdbaths, aquariums. Sinks, tubs, showers, and toilets.
Shape: free flowing asymmetrical shapes, wavy patterns.

Recognize the water element in your home:

The water element shows up in our homes primarily in bathrooms and kitchens, as a result of the modern-day convenience of indoor plumbing. We have all heard 'might as well have flushed that down the toilet.' It is important to note that the large receptacles in the home that hold water, such as toilets, be covered when not in use. Toilet seats down and shower curtains closed ensure the vital chi does not leave the home via the drain.

The water element, evident in any surface that is reflective—like still water—includes mirrors, shiny black surfaces, glass in any form (windows). Staircases resemble waterfalls and are therefore considered a water element; rushing water can move fast and sweep us off our feet. It is important, on a large staircase, not to accentuate the diagonal slope, rather to place items in horizontal view to slow the water energy down.

Elemental Essence

Water is vital to our existence in so many ways as we use it to nourish and clean our bodies from the inside out. Fluid in nature, water energy's mirrored characteristics remind us to go with or be in the flow.

When a space is dominated by water energy, the emotions of the occupants may reflect the feeling of being worn down or exhausted which, in turn, can create fear, nervousness, and stress. In nature, over time, water has the ability to wear down the rough surface of a stone. An overabundance of water energy reflects outward in the personality as being emotionally unstable. Likened to a stagnant pond in nature, they too can become stagnant, suffering from depression or procrastination.

Water escapes from our physical bodies in the form of tears which represent the emotions. In balance we can openly express those emotions with tears of joy. Out of balance and the tears of sadness naturally help to cleanse and release emotional blockages to return us to the state of ease.

When the water element is in control of a space, the earth element is required to damn the water.

When water in the environment is in balance with the other four elements, it has the ability to soothe, calm, and make us feel at ease. Occupants are more apt to be very resourceful, curious, often contemplative, dependable and, usually, spiritual.

Bring in water chi when you are feeling stuck, to get back in the flow. Adding the water element to an environment will help to improve communication, cash flow and opportunities. Adding a tabletop water fountain to a space is a great way to achieve this.

WOOD (engages the sense of smell)

In nature, wood energy expands upward, and symbolizes the nourishing growth of plant life in the spring. It can be sturdy as an oak tree and supple and pliable as bamboo.

Color: all shades of green—plants, and the blues of the sky.

Substance and/or texture: anything made from wood: wood furniture, paper, books, and paper money, flora, natural fibres that come from plants such as cotton.

Shape: columnar. Upright forms resembling trees.

Recognize the wood element in your home:

The wood element shows up in homes in its own form, depending where you live and what is readily available. Furniture and cabinetry are often made from oak, maple, or pine. All plants and flowers, either alive or artificial (silk), are wood elements, as is art depicting trees, or fabrics that have floral prints.

Elemental Essence

When wood energy is in balance with the other four elements, the home's occupants will feel alive, refreshed, uplifted, and supported, just as if they had taken a walk outdoors. People are often very bold and direct, with clear self-expression. They are self-driven, motivated, innovative, and strive to expand outward in their community.

When the wood energy is dominant in the space it can be overwhelming, with the sense of no clear direction—similar to the state of being amidst the tall trees in a forest. An over-abundance of wood energy can reflect in the body in carrying extra weight. Other expressions of too much wood energy in the environment can show up in stress, aggressiveness, an extremely competitive nature. Reduce the abundant wood energy by adding the cutting edge of the metal element.

Add wood energy to a space to support personal development, new beginnings, enhance growth, and expansion.

FIRE (engages the sense of touch)

In nature, fire energy expands outward and knows no boundaries, consuming and destroying all in its path. fire also has the ability to warm your body and cook your food.

Color: the colors you would find in flames—reds, oranges, all the way to purple.

Substance and/or texture: animals and people. Leather, feathers, and fur. Fire itself. Light and sunshine. Televisions, appliances—anything electronic.

Shape: triangles, pyramids, and cone shapes.

Recognize the fire element in your home:

We can recognize fire energy as we illuminate the darkness of night with the use of lamps, ceiling lights, candles, and fireplaces. A soft-colored leather sofa would be considered a blend (fusion) of fire and metal energy. Pictures of animals, and animals living or otherwise (trophies), add the fire element to the home. Today's modern family's and homes have and abundance of electronic equipment which fuel the fire element.

Elemental Essence

When fire energy is in balance with the other four elements, the home's occupants will feel vibrant, happy, and energetic. Think of the feeling you get sitting by a crackling fire, mesmerized by the flickering flames as it warms you from head to toe—body and soul. The fire essence can be associated with the lover and the fighter. In balance, fire's influence on the people occupying the space are often very compassionate and loving, wearing their heart on their sleeve. Enthusiastic like the flickering tendencies of the flame, they are fun, outgoing and, usually, the life of the party. They are self-driven, motivated, innovative, and strive to expand outward in their community.

When there is an abundance of the fire element the influence can be eruptive and explosive, and has the ability of destroying with great violence. It flits from task to task (jumping around like the fighter trying to outwit his opponent), with a tendency to take on too much, resulting in 'burn-out' or 'crash and burn.'

If you need to put out the fire, you can bring in the water element to douse the flames.

The addition of the fire element in a space will help to light a 'fire inspired action' and/or to ignite passion.

Bringing It All Together

As you read through each of the five elements and how they show up in your home, did you resonate with one or two more than the others? Take a look around where you are right now. Is there a predominant element? Are there items that are comprised of two or more elements—a fusion of elements?

I have two antique upright lamps in my living room that are a combination of elements. The stainless steel (metal) poles of the lamps resemble the upright nature of a tree (wood), supported by the weight of the marble (metal) base. The lights (fire) illuminate through the beige colored (earth) shades trimmed in oval, wooden beads. Although predominantly metal in the daytime, with a flick of a switch the soft glow of the lights melts the metal, accenting the earth and wood elements.

These five elements are the very building blocks of our natural environment. When they are present in our home and workplaces, we react to their presence on a subconscious level. The balance and interaction of these five elements has the strength to empower us naturally in mind, body and spirit, supporting us positively.

After de-cluttering a space, you can look at it 'elementally' and either add or subtract items that help to achieve balance depending on the room usage and the desired outcome. Once you have all five elements represented in the space you can take it another step further, by ensuring that there are Yin and Yang representations of each element. For example: earth may show up in a room as the color on the walls—which would be Yang, and Yin earth could be represented by a square table or picture hanging on the wall.

Practice… practice… working with the elements. Start with one room or area. What elements are present and what elements do you want to incorporate to achieve balance? How do you currently feel in that space and how would you like to feel?

The following will help to guide you in knowing which element(s) you need to incorporate into any given space to achieve balance and harmony.

In the nourishing cycle of five elements, each element feeds and sustains the other in perfect harmony in an endless, regenerating cycle. Use the nourishing cycle when you want to add or increase chi of one or more elements in a particular space.

In the Nourishing Cycle (also referred to as the Creative Cycle):

Earth creates metal
Metal holds water
Water nurtures wood
Wood feeds fire
Fire returns to earth

In the controlling cycle of the five elements, we see how the elements can dominate and control each other. The controlling cycle is not a negative influence, rather a way in which to recognize and balance an environment to achieve elemental harmony.

Example—What Would You Do?

Everywhere you look there is wood—furniture, plants, floral prints, bookshelves, books, floors, panelling—all sucking the life out of the room, leaving the occupants feeling overwhelmed and energetically stuck. What element(s) would you add to balance the space?

When one element is in control of a space, so too is the elemental essence that controls (influences) the occupants. The outer world environment is connected to, and reflected in, the inner world environment.

In the Controlling Cycle:

> Earth damns abundant water
> Metal cuts abundant wood
> Water puts out abundant fire
> Wood consumes abundant earth
> Fire melts abundant metal

A gentle way to bring an environment into balance is the use of the reducing cycle.

In the Reducing Cycle:

> Earth reduces fire
> Metal reduces earth
> Water reduces metal
> Wood reduces water
> Fire reduces wood

A home decorated in extremely dark colors: deep blues, blacks, with large windows, glass, mirrors and other reflective surfaces would be considered a very watery environment. Over time, the occupants of this environment would be affected, and the direct impact of living in the abundance of water would reflect emotional imbalance, feeling worn out and exhausted. They might be wishy washy in their thinking and have a difficult time being decisive.

As in nature, we can only sustain an abundance of a water feature energy (any of the five elements) for a short period of time.

An estimated 30 million people visit Niagara Falls in Canada each year. With over 3000 tons of water falling every second, that's a lot of water and a lot of noise. Anyone or anything in the path of this force would be swiftly washed away. The ocean is another example of an abundance of water that can dominate the psyche of a stranded sea traveler with no land in sight.

Inviting and adding the elements of earth and wood is recommended for a watery home environment. It offers the promise of 'land in sight' for stability, and the wood 'drinks' the abundant water. This would restore mind, body, spirit for the home's occupants.

There is so much more to discover about the five elements and in the 5-element theory. My goal was to give you a glimpse so that you can gain a new awareness, just as I did with my son's bedroom—the changes that made a huge impact on my life and his. The colors, textures, and shapes of the things that you put in your home are influencing the mind, body, and spirit.

Tree Hugger

Since the beginning of recorded history, man has been in tune with his personal space, the intimate environment of his home. Evidence of this relationship shows up on the walls of the caves visited by pre-historic man tens of thousands of years ago. Although it is not definitively known if caves, with art depicting the external environment of animals and such, were the dwellings of these people. I like to think they were—it helps me to validate my belief that humans evolving on this planet have always been connected to, and influenced by, their surroundings on a deeper level.

The more we can connect with the beauty and wonder of Nature, the more we can evolve and raise our own vibration. It's always possible to bring nature indoors—the 'wood' element is highly recommended. Having well-cared-for living plants, fresh-cut flowers in vibrant colors, and/or exhilarating fragrances engage our senses, thereby increasing our vibration.

In 1973, *The Secret Life of Plants* by Peter Thompkins was published. It documented experiments showing that plants have superpowers. Chemist Marcel Vogel worked extensively with plants and their sensitivity to humans and their ability to register human thoughts and emotions.
http://www.ebdir.net/enlighten/peter_tompkins.html

In one lecture he stated:

> "It is fact: man can and does communicate with plant life. Plants are extremely sensitive instruments for measuring man's emotions. They radiate energy forces beneficial to man. One can feel these forces! They feed into one's own force field, which in turn feeds back energy to the plant... The American Indians were keenly aware of these faculties. When in need, they would go into the woods. With their arms extended, they would place their backs to a pine tree in order to replenish themselves with its power." *The Celestine Prophecy: An Experiential Guide* by James Redfield and Carol Adrienne

There have been many studies since then, and other studies continue today, that explore the unseen energy plants have with each other and humankind. In the last twenty-five years-or-so more researchers have found that being near plants, even viewing them through a closed window, has therapeutic benefits—they make us happier and healthier. Even looking at pictures of landscapes with green space and water has similar results.

Having well-cared-for plants in your home is the key in reaping the benefits. Plants are extremely sensitive to environment and having living plants in your home can help to clean the air of harmful toxins, as well as add natural beauty to any space.

A lucky bamboo plant is not so lucky if its owner forgets to water it and all its leaves are turning yellow. Seeing plants that are barely surviving, a spindly trunk being propped up by a stick with a few leaves on top, tells me that someone, or some other situation, is also being propped up. It's the mirrored relationship in all things animate and inanimate. When I go into a client's home where there are thriving, healthy plants, it's a good indication of the health of the home.

Eleven – Your Home, Your Sanctuary

Adding the wood energy element in any area of your home is practicing good Feng Shui.

If you like plants, and have the time to care for them, great! If not, then it's time they go to plant heaven (compost) and are either replaced with easy-care plants or artificial ones. (My website has a guide to the top 9 Feng Shui recommended plants that are easy to care for).

If you choose not to have living plants in your home, then I encourage you to spend several hours a week in nature to absorb the energy trees have to offer.

Trees are the lungs of Gaia, constantly taking in carbon dioxide and giving us, in return, fresh oxygen to breathe.

New research suggests that trees communicate with each other, as well as share nutrients. Their intricately connected roots orchestrate an energy system considered a super-information highway. As the forest behaves as one single organism, demonstrating a social behavior, it suggests there is more to learn. The researchers at HeartMath Institute Interconnectivity Tree Research Project are doing just that.

> "There's a lot more to learn about trees especially how they may respond to human emotions, and how being in the presence of their Bio fields can have an uplifting effect on people."
> https://www.heartmath.org/resources/videos/interconnectivity-tree-research-project/

The ancients knew of the power of trees as a source of rejuvenation. The term 'tree hugger' comes from this exchange of energy, between man and tree, one bio-field connecting to another. Perhaps it's time for humanity to renew the connection with our benevolent Mother: Earth and her living landscapes (lungs).

Life is an interactive experience.
This is your space.

Return to the end of Chapter Ten 'This is your space.' Use or bring forward your item list from the end of Chapter Ten.
Beside each item, write down one of the five elements you've learned about. (return to page #143)

Notice if there were any parallels—influences—from the outer world to the inner world, and jot them down.

Which of the five elements did you resonate with?

Eleven – Your Home, Your Sanctuary

What element do you see predominantly in your home or a particular space?

What element(s) could you add to achieve elemental balance?

Did you notice any parallels in how your home is decorated 'elementally' with any behavioral characteristics? What are they?

Focus your attention in the area of your heart.
With the intention of breathing in gratitude and exhaling love:
Take a deep breath in for 5 seconds or more.
Hold for 5 seconds. Exhale for 5 seconds or more.
Bring your awareness and attention to each word and
or phrase in the Energetic Heart Code below.
Bringing them into your heart— feel the feeling of the
word or phrase radiating to every cell of your being.
Relax and repeat, while continuing to breathe,
to create heart-brain coherence.

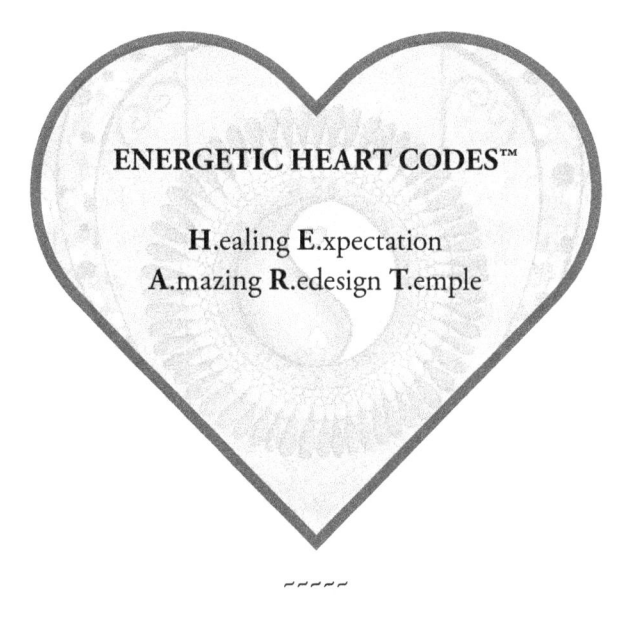

ENERGETIC HEART CODES™

H.ealing **E**.xpectation
A.mazing **R**.edesign **T**.emple

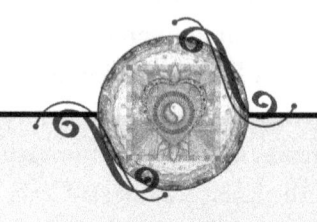

Twelve – Sacred Circle

"It is good 'medicine' to live with the heart, mind, body, and spirit in balance—all systems operating as one unit."
Anita Adrain

The Medicine Wheel recognizes the elements of the natural surroundings, and the goal to achieve balance. There are many similarities to the 5-element theory, and insights that can be gained in understanding our relationship with these elemental energies.

The Medicine Wheel, or Sacred Circle, is an example of knowledge passed down over thousands of years. The ancient Chinese and the original Indigenous tribes had no way of knowing each other and collaborating their stories, yet their cultural practices are mirrored in referencing the energies of the four directions and associating colors and symbols to express the teachings, some of which we will explore here.

Archeological evidence suggests that there were people in Alberta (the province in which I was born and raised) over twelve-thousand years ago, existing and surviving with only Mother Nature as their source. Before the settlers renamed the land in North America it was referred to as Turtle Island. One of the creation stories of the Indigenous describes a pregnant woman falling from the skies and landing on the back of a turtle—the turtle saved humanity from the great flood. Other native myths reference the turtle as having the world on its back as a symbol of life on Earth.

Turtle

The turtle is synonymous with the tortoise; both are often used in the same context. Note the difference: turtles are sea reptiles and the tortoise is a land lover. Both show up in artwork, myths, legends, folklore, and artifacts of other cultures around the globe such as the Mayans, Celts, and Indigenous people of Australia and of Africa.

Fossils of these ancient creatures reveal they have been on this planet for 120 to 200 million years. They are ancient keepers of the land and sea. The turtle carries its home on its back, its shelter providing protection and safety—a reminder that our Earthly body, although not physically attached, provides humans with shelter and all that is needed to sustain life. What other wisdom has been left for us to re-discover?

The Turtle Totem represents the sacred feminine: the peace maker—living in harmony with the Earth, with the ability to be on land/or in water. It is considered a symbol of good fortune and longevity.

The turtle even holds some deep meaning and symbolism in my own life. Somewhere in my pre-teens I wanted a turtle for a pet. Most kids ask for a dog or cat, possibly even a horse. Not me. I had to have a turtle, and I set about saving money so that I could have one, or several, shipped to my house from the USA.

It wasn't long before my mother found out about my plan and came up with all the reasons why I couldn't have a turtle for a pet, one of which was that she said they carried disease. My mom was, for the most part, what you would call strict. Of course, having eleven children means there had to be rules. I was extremely disappointed and gave up the thought of owning my own turtle.

And then my thirteenth birthday arrived, and I was surprised to receive 'a turtle.' It was the size of the palm of my hand and it was… plastic! I was thinking that it was a poor joke and, for a fleeting moment, thought it was my present. Then my mother instructed me to turn it over, and there, hidden in the belly of the turtle, was a new watch. It was then that I realized that, if she could have, she would have bought me a live turtle. It was her subtle way of telling me that she supported and loved me.

Fast forward more than thirty years…

Twelve – Sacred Circle

At thirteen years old, my youngest son had saved some money from collecting bottles and doing other chores. With two hundred dollars in hand, he was determined to buy a pet—and not just any pet. Specifically, he wanted a reptile, the slithering cold blooded kind that sheds its skin. Luckily for us he didn't have a driver's license, and was dependent on someone giving him a ride to the 'Reptile Show' to make his purchase.

His Father made some expressive comments; in no way was he allowing a snake in his house. I managed to be the voice of reason as well as the mediator, and the two of them agreed on a suitable family pet. Although it cost his Dad an additional two hundred dollars, a white fluff-ball with four legs and a cute black nose became the sixth member of our tribe. She—Meeka—stole our hearts. Two or three years passed, everyone grew, and the novelty and notability of having a dog as a pet diminished. Meeka became known as my dog. This left my teenage son without his own pet to love and care for.

He now had a part-time job after school, stocking shelves at the local grocery store, and his bank account was growing as were his thoughts of what kind of pet he could buy. Several of his friends had 'wheels,' and one particular weekend they set off to the annual 'Reptile Show.' Our son returned with a large, glass, rectangular tank, with a heat lamp and other accessories. It was to my great surprise that the newest resident in our home could fit in the palm of my hand and resembled the gift I had been given on my thirteenth birthday—a cute, baby red-footed tortoise.

Our son was counting on the fact that his Dad wouldn't be home for several weeks, and that I would be the voice of reason—after all, it wasn't a snake. His Dad eventually came to terms with the reptile that lived in the basement. 'Squirtle' grew in his new environment, and my heart was happy as I rekindled the memories of my youth—none of which our son had any previous knowledge.

The interesting thing is, the universe has a way of bringing things full circle. It whispers or gives us clues along our journey. In my youth I had no idea that the turtle would become a significant symbol in my life, and that within the markings of the shell, other ancient cultures also revered the turtle as a significant symbol of wisdom.

A valuable lesson is to remain open to the possibilities, listen and pay attention, as life may be giving you subtle, directional clues to a path of self-discovery, passion, and purpose.

The turtle and tortoise have great significance in the history of Feng Shui. The story goes: as the Chinese Emperor sat meditating on the banks of a great river, a giant tortoise emerged with patterns on his shell. The patterns were nine squares that represented the nine aspects of the life of man. The numbers 1-9 are the basis for Chinese Numerology and Astrology. The Feng Shui map, called the bagua, also has 9 squares. The shell of the tortoise, with its magic squares, is believed to have been the inspiration from which these three important teachings came to life, and then were passed down for thousands of years.

The term Feng Shui may have come to us from the Chinese, as stated earlier in this book, but I believe all Indigenous cultures have practiced Feng Shui and just call it something different. As by my definition, Feng Shui is the study of energy.

The Sacred Circle of the Medicine Wheel is symbolic in that it is a circle representing Mother Earth and all of creation. It is used to remind us of the cycles in nature, our connection to all our relations, ancestors, the life cycles of all human beings. It also reminds us of the law of reciprocity, a mutual exchange of energy with the creator and each other. Knowing that all life force 'chi' comes from the abundant resources of Earth, the keepers of the land, honored 'mother' in ceremony and dance with symbols of the circular energy.

The Medicine Wheel teaches of the sacred opportunity to walk in harmony and balance with Earth. When the four aspects of the human—mind, body, heart, or spirit—are broken, we are reminded to use the medicine of the wheel to regain balance and restore harmony.

A brief description of the four aspects of the Medicine Wheel have been noted here for you to see the similarities in the teachings of 5-element theory covered in the previous section.

The four aspects represent the four directions, the four seasons, the four stages of life: baby, youth, adult, elder. The four aspects also represent the four aspects of self: spiritual, physical, emotional, mental. The four colors associated with the Medicine Wheel may vary as to where they show up on the wheel, depending on teachings. The colors—white, yellow, red, and black— represent the skin of all the people on earth.

The Direction Of EAST

The red part of the circle is associated with the body, representing physical health. The vibrancy of the new day is reflected in the nourishment of the body.

The Direction Of SOUTH

The wellness of the heart is represented by the color yellow: the heart and soul of the person reflecting their emotional state of being, walking the path with love and compassion for each other and all things.

The Direction Of WEST

The part of the sacred circle that represents the mind is colored black: a reminder to keep the mind well by learning and understanding oneself and one's surroundings.

The Direction Of NORTH

Walking the path to wellness through the mind, the body, and the heart, the circle is completed at the white quadrant, associated with the spirit of the person.

There are many resemblances that surface in the teachings of Native Americans that are also taught in Feng Shui. The *Stories from the Bush* is a series of messages and wisdom from the Elders that convey our connection to all things—teachings that honor Mother Earth, our Creator, and each other. These stories can be found through www.circleteachings.ca. There is one story for each calendar month. *The Code of Life*, and *The Beauty Ways* represent two months.

In order to respect the wishes of the authorship and authenticity of *The Beauty Ways* and *The Code of Life,* it is recommended that the site be visited in order to witness the true word. It would not be honorable to attempt to paraphrase or re-tell such sacred stories.

I can, however, convey the following takeaways, wisdom from the Elders:

- Without the elements: earth, air, fire, and water, this Earth could not exist—it is vital that every person take responsibility for the way he or she interacts with each element. Doing this will allow Mother Earth to restore herself and heal—where necessary.
- The way we can take the best care of Mother Earth is to live in balance with her. We must be willing to enrich the environment. We must be willing to learn how to exist in harmony with our fellow humans and with all non-human entities.
- Each relationship with Mother Earth needs to be reciprocal—we see goodness in those who give an offering to Mother Earth each time something is taken from her. Gratitude for, and acknowledgement of, her gifts is paramount for nature and humans to thrive.
- We humans are not the only ones living on this planet—there are communities of animals and plants in co-habitation. There is no 'thing' that does not hold value. When we realize that harmonic living is dependent upon cooperation and reciprocal behavior, then all life cycles are improved.
- Our Earth Mother holds all the answers to our spiritual questions and to our inquiries as to how the planet—and all relationships on the planet—can thrive. We need to listen to our elders who relate stories that have been passed down from the very beginning of human life.
- Our knowledge of Mother Earth and her power are passed through birth—through our DNA. All that is known and has happened before us is in a chain of living memory and is available to all those who pause and listen. The songs and stories of Mother Earth's lifetime are passed orally, but also reside in our genetic makeup.
- Teaching our children to come from a place of kindness will pass on the responsibility to nurture and care for Mother Earth.

Circling back to the teachings of our ancestors—our Indigenous cultures—offers hope for our co-existence. As in *The Code of Life* teachings, we are our own ancestors. When we listen (or become consciously awake) to our physical bodies, our heart, our mind and spirit, we have the opportunity to co-exist as relatives. When we are truly aligned, we can walk in harmony with the natural law, in right relationship with Gaia, our Creator, Mother Earth.

The teachings of the Medicine Wheel is one way in which we can achieve this 'right' relationship. It is another example of a compass that gives direction and guidance to living consciously aware in balance and harmony with all energy systems present in our environment.

Life is an interactive experience.
This is your space.

Our ancestors, the Indigenous peoples of this nation, were acutely aware of the cycles of Mother Earth. Their life, in fact, depended on this awareness and their connection to all life forms in their environment.

Is there any energy system that you were taught growing up? What is it?

Are there any parallels with the teachings presented from the Medicine Wheel? Can you describe them?

Twelve – Sacred Circle

Have you already established that true health is a balance of mind, body, heart, and spirit?

Which area(s) do you feel need balancing, to be in right relationship with the teachings of the wheel?

Write down your current state beside each one, and then next to it write down your desired result. Contemplate how you can achieve balance walking your path of the sacred circle.

Mind

Body

Heart

Spirit

Focus your attention in the area of your heart.
With the intention of breathing in gratitude and exhaling love:
Take a deep breath in for 5 seconds or more.
Hold for 5 seconds. Exhale for 5 seconds or more.
Bring your awareness and attention to each word and
or phrase in the Energetic Heart Code below.
Bringing them into your heart— feel the feeling of the
word or phrase radiating to every cell of your being.
Relax and repeat, while continuing to breathe,
to create heart-brain coherence.

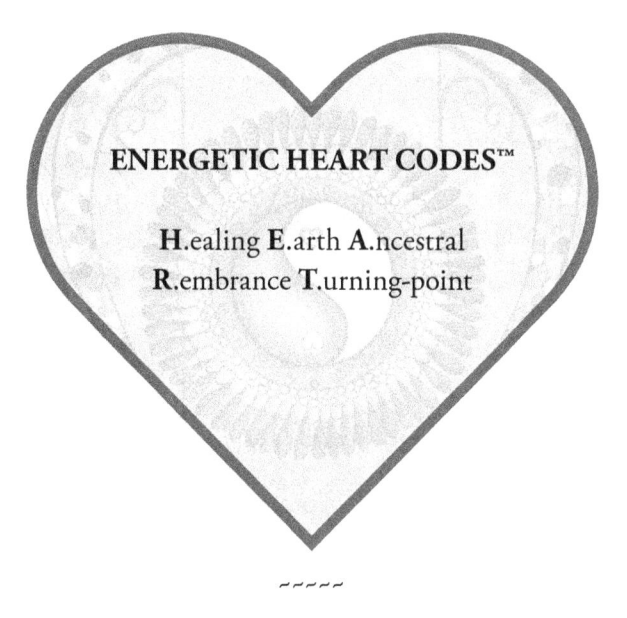

ENERGETIC HEART CODES™

H.ealing **E.**arth **A.**ncestral
R.embrance **T.**urning-point

~~~~~

Thirteen – Mirror, Mirror

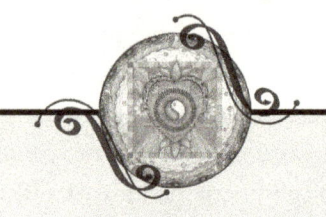

"The Earth's magnetic fields carry relevant information that connects all living systems."
Anita Adrain

Reconnecting to the Energy of Mother Earth in your personal environment can help to bring balance where there is imbalance, creating a space that is in harmony with you and your home's occupants.

Fractals And Symbiotic Systems

There are five predominant forces found in nature, from which ALL things are formed. You discovered this in the 5-element theory.

Is it a coincidence that there are five fractal patterns that repeat in nature, showing up in all things? The branching patterns that show up in a leaf, mimic the vascular patterns in our body.

In his book, *Fractal Time*, Gregg Braden brings awareness to the few and simple repeating patterns of nature, described as fractals, that make up or form everything in our universe, from the energy of the atom to the form of a tree.

When we look closely at these patterns in our natural environment, we can better understand the system of the universe. These are symbiotic systems (interdependent relationships) of the universe that connect us energetically to each other and to all things.

> "Nature uses a few simple, self-similar, and repeating patterns—fractals — to build energy and atoms into the familiar forms of everything from roots, rivers, and trees to rocks, mountains, and us. Seemingly overnight, it became possible to use fractals to replicate everything from the coastline of a continent to an alpine forest—and even the universe itself.
>
> Gregg Braden's blog on Fractal Time.

It's important to note that fractals are different than geometric forms such as triangles, squares, and circles.

These patterns that create everything that show up in our physical world, on a micro or macro scale, are present both in our visible and invisible space.

Under the umbrella of the study of energy, practicing Feng Shui is observing all elements in the environment that are relevant to improving the health of the home, thereby improving the health of its occupants.

Mother Nature's Mirror

Nature shows us mirrored relationships; clues left in patterns, in all things, all for the support of our existence and evolution. For example, if you slice a tomato in half it resembles the ventricle chambers of the heart. Guess what tomatoes are good for? Heart health. Cherries and strawberries look like miniature hearts and are rich in nutrients for the heart. Other fruits and vegetables that resemble body parts are, coincidentally, also good health for the body part they look like. If you cut a carrot it resembles the pattern that is found in the human eye. I'm sure you have heard that eating carrots will help you see better.

In the opening chapter, I introduced you to the *Guide to Indian Herbs* book which outlines how the Native Americans used plants as medicine for the body, mind, and spirit. Is it a coincidence that our Indigenous peoples had a close relationship with Mother Earth and recognized the patterns mirrored in the natural environment? How is it that they knew certain plants and herbs were good for certain ailments?

Thirteen – Mirror, Mirror

"But ask the beasts, and they will teach you; the birds of the heavens, and they will tell you; or the bushes of the Earth, and they will teach you; and the fish of the sea will declare to you. Who among all these does not know that the hand of the Lord has done this? In his hand is the life of every living thing and the breath of all mankind."

Job 12:7-10

Body Mirror

The body also offers some mirror or reflective images. If you were to draw a line down the center of your body, the right half would mirror or be a close replica of the other side. If you were to reach both of your arms out and measure from the tip of your middle finger on the right side of your hand to the tip of the middle finger on the left side of your hand, you might discover that the length is equal to the height of your entire body. Place the palms of your hands together as in prayer—the gesture of 'Namaste' representing: that which honors the place in you that is the place in me. Notice the mirrored image.

There are many practices that look for reflective clues to help their clients achieve optimum health—patterns and characteristics that show up in areas of the physical body that provide the practitioner information on the health systems of the client.

Iridology recognizes repeating patterns in the eyes, reflexology patterns in the feet, and ear reflexology in the outer part of the ear.

An acupuncturist places small needles in an energetic network of pathways, known as meridians, to increase the flow of chi, restoring balance in all areas of the body.

Mind Mirror

Louise Hay was a forerunner in introducing the world to the mirrored relationship of the mind, body—the mental causes for physical illness.

> "Dubbed 'the closest thing to a living saint' by the Australian media, Louise Hay is also known as one of the founders of the self-help movement. Her first book, *Heal Your body*, was published in 1976, long before it was fashionable to discuss the connection between the mind and body. Revised and expanded in 1988, this best-selling book introduced Louise's concepts to people in 33 different countries and has been translated into 25 languages throughout the world." www.louisehay.com

For example, pain or problems with the knee are:

> "Knee: Represents pride and ego. Stubborn ego and pride. Inability to bend. Fear. Inflexibility. Won't give in."
> https://alchemyofhealing.com/causes-of-symptoms-according-to-louise-hay/

The same energy of fear and stubbornness of not wanting to move forward or inability to be flexible could be anchored in the home as well, likely showing up as:

Pride – "I'm never getting rid of 'that'—it's part of our heritage."

Ego – "My kids are going to have all the things I didn't have when I was growing up."

Stubbornness – "What I choose to keep in my space is nobody else's business."

Perhaps you can think of a few other phrases that may be anchoring stuck energy resistance; other stories linked to self-worth, self-love?

Emotional blockages show up in the body as disease or discomfort. First, recognizing what emotion is unresolved, and removing the emotional blockage in your physical environment of your home, will help to release the emotional blockage in the body. Emotional baggage and physical baggage hold the same energy of past, trauma, drama and/or conflict.

Perhaps you already saw some repeating patterns in your home when you looked closer at your possessions. What story did you find was stuck in an energetic loop?

As within so without, is another way to say the inner world is connected to the outer world.

Reflections

Many other mind-body practices emerged and gained popularity in the 70s. Practices such as yoga, meditation, and massage therapy. The 70s ushered in awareness to women's rights, and the start of the digital revolution. Subtle water elements, such as waterbeds, were brought into the homes dousing the flames of the psychedelic 60s fire element.

The reflection of these experiences showed up in the decorating or style of the homes as well. Natural fibres, macramé wicker, rattan and wood paneling represented the wood element, the essence of which is to support and nourish, representing new growth and pioneering insights.

Earth tones, shag toilet seat covers, square patterns and bricks—all of the earth elements—offered stability and comfort.

The three predominant elements (from the 5-element theory) in the 70s were wood, earth, and water—elements that were definitely needed to help heal the hangover of the 60s.

What are some attributes of the 5-element energy that are showing up today? Are there any parallels—mirrored reflections—to what is happening in your life, your community, your Country?

Just as the many holistic practitioners look for reflective clues to help their clients restore balance and harmony to the body systems, practicing Feng Shui helps to restore balance and harmony in the environment.

As natural beings, we are instinctively moving toward restoring balance in all areas of our life, including our homes. A balanced mind-body connection is mirrored in the home.

Coincidence or Clues

The mind, body, spirit aspects of all humans reflect examples that can be considered hints in restoring balance to all three systems, creating a state of resonance—basically, all three operating systems in sync.

In ancient India, the palm reading was practiced to reveal a person's true character, life-path, and future challenges. It was believed that the lines on the hand told a story unique to that individual.

Face reading—physiognomy—is another practice that reveals to the trained reader the psychological meanings mirrored from facial characteristics.

Energetic beings living in an energetic universe: is it possible that there are other systems that mirror or reflect our relationship with the whole? Perhaps there are other clues that could improve our awareness which would lead to the better care of Planet Earth, and restoring its inhabitants to a state of balance.

The micro subatomic particle to the macro: The atom consists of three main parts, the nucleus (center) contains protons and neutrons; the electrons orbiting around the nucleus. Similar patterns may be observed from space within our solar system. The Earth has an electron, so to speak, orbiting around its perimeter—we call it the moon.

The moon's cycles have been observed by all ancient cultures and recorded with information passed on that is still used today.

Twelve moon cycles equal one calendar year divided into four distinct seasons. Coincidence, chance occurrence, or part of a divine plan to support life on Planet Earth?

There Are No Coincidences, Only Clues!

There are no coincidences, only clues. Let's take a closer, deeper look at other repeating patterns that may be offering clues, specifically numbers that show up in our natural world. Numbers are vibrational patterns. Repeating patterns are the fabric to our existence. Systems that we use every day—that we become complacent with, or not—in our conscious awareness, might hold messages for us.

Thirteen – Mirror, Mirror

Numerology, the science or metaphysical study of numbers, is another ancient practice with many authors—the Greeks, Hebrew, Babylonians, and Tibetans are some examples. Is there a mystical relationship between numbers?

As you begin your Feng Shui journey, you will be letting go of the old, and you will feel lighter and more energetic. Because of that, you will be vibrating at a higher frequency, connecting your self to the unseen forces, including the creative force. You may begin to notice number patterns on your clock, on a receipt, or while in your car. These numbers may be offering you clues as to your next best step, or in answer to a thought or question you have about a specific concern in your life.

Numerology can be used to learn more about a person, place, or situation, gaining deeper insight into the unseen energies at work. A numerologist assigns meaning to the numbers 0 to 9. Any numbers larger than 'nine' are reduced by adding the numbers together. For example, 22 becomes a 4, by adding 2+2, 144 becomes a 9, and so on.

The numerological meaning of subsequent numbers for the purpose of this book will be of the Tibetan and Chinese numerology systems. Note: I am not trained in either of these. I merely express my personal interest, and I invite you to discover your own method of numerology. As an aside, the simplest numerology to describe a system of defining numbers has been given by Kryon—see *Kryon Book Twelve, The Twelve Layers of DNA,* based on Tibetan Numerology.

Number -12-

There are 12 zodiac signs, 12 layers of DNA (according to Kryon). Jesus had 12 disciples, history references 12 tribes of Israel and 12 sons. Chinese astrology uses 12 animals as reference to the lunar cycles. There are 12 hours on the clock, 12 eggs in a dozen, 12 inches in a foot, and 12 ribs in the average human. The end of the Mayan calendar was December (12th month) 21st (12 reversed) 2012.

Number -1- & -2-

The number 12 is a combination of the energies of 1 and 2.

Tibetan numerology: 1 is new beginning, 2 is about duality, polarity.

Chinese numerology: 1 associated with honor, single and loneliness, 2 representing symmetry and steadfast.

Number -3-

When you add the numbers from 12—'one' and 'two'—using simple math we get 1+2=3.

There is great significance with the number 3; it reveals more energetic clues, most of which you are likely familiar but may not have interpreted any deeper meaning or relevance to your life, until now.

- Father, Son, and Holy Spirit sounds like mind, body, and spirit, or: mental, emotional, physical.
- The Yin Yang symbol shows 3 aspects, the 2 parts within the whole.
- Earth, moon, and sun.
- Noah had 3 sons.
- You have 3 layers of skin.
- Remember we can live without water for 3 days and oxygen for only 3 minutes?
- There are 3 attributes of each day, morning, noon and night.
- Earth is the 3rd rock from the sun.
- The word God has 3 letters and therefore the number 3 could be considered a master number.

Tibetan numerology: 3 is the catalyst, represents the inner child and joy.

Chinese numerology: 3 is considered a lucky number and sounds like the character used for 'birth,' symbolizing life and growth.

Number -4-

There are 4 seasons in the calendar year. 4 directions: east, south, west, north. The number 12 divided by 3 = 4

The ancient Greeks believed that the four elements of earth, water, air and fire that everything was made up of, all matter. Not to be confused with the 5-element theory (although similar representation), these 4 elements have been the foundation for science, medicine and philosophy

Thirteen – Mirror, Mirror

for thousands of years. Earth as the solid, water as the liquid, air as the gas, and fire as the plasma.

Tibetan numerology: 4 is Mother Earth energy; it stands for the physical structure and physical aspects of the world.

Chinese numerology: 4 is considered unlucky, as four translated to Cantonese sounds like the word death.

Number -5-
As Above So Below

Chemically, the Earth can be divided into 3 main parts, the crust, the mantle and the core. Further to that there is the upper mantle and the lower mantle, the inner core and the outer core, for a total of 5 layers.

The Earth's atmosphere has 5 layers as well, troposphere, stratosphere, mesosphere, thermosphere, and the exosphere.

The layers above equal the layers below: 5. Therefore: the natural world displays chemically and in substance 'as above so below.'

Interesting to me is the parallel between the seen and the unseen worlds as well, reflected in this example. Mother Nature has been mirroring deeper meaning and wisdom throughout the ages.

In Feng Shu we look at similar characteristics in the home and apply the same principles, as above so below.

Tibetan numerology: 5 represents change.

Chinese numerology: 5 is considered a lucky number as it is associated with the 5-elements; it symbolizes stability through balance, as well as the 5 blessings: wealth, happiness, longevity, luck, and prosperity.

Number -6-

Another layer, 2 x 3 = 6.

Tibetan numerology: 6 means communication, balance, and harmony. It is considered a sacred number. Perhaps of sacred spaces, creating harmony and balance in the home?

Chinese numerology: 6 is associated with ease and fortune.

Number -7-
Tibetan numerology: 7 represents divinity, wholeness, perfection and learning.

Chinese numerology: 7 associated with togetherness and connectivity.

Number -8-
As we learned earlier in the new version of the Yin Yang symbol, the number 8 (representing the 3 aspects of work, play, rest) is in the center of the whole.

Tibetan numerology: 8 represents responsibility, practicality, and manifestation.

Chinese numerology: 8 is considered the most auspicious number meaning wealth and prosperity.

Number -9-
More Clues The number 3 x 3 = 9

- There are many references in the bible to the number 9.
- Numerology and Feng Shui recognize the number 9.
- The average pregnancy is 9 months.

There are 9 planets in our solar system as we learned in school, however Pluto has since been demoted as a planet and it is considered in today's popular science that there are 8 planets in our solar system.

Tibetan numerology: 9 represents the completion of the cycle, sensitivity, and the psychic ability.

Chinese numerology: 9 represents everlasting, longevity and eternality.

I find numerology an interesting and enlightening study offering more insight into the study of energy; Feng Shui. The numbers assigned to the letters of Feng total 5, and the numbers assigned to the letters in Shui total 3.

My full name at birth calculated to the number 99 which reduces to a 9. (9+9=18 / 1+8=9) interesting I am the 9th child of 11.

Now that we have a deeper understanding of the energy of numbers, we may interpret the relationship of how it applies to your life and what the heck it has to do with Feng Shui.

In my understanding of how and why Feng Shui works, I had to look at all the energetic aspects of the whole. The reflective nature of this world shows up in all things animate and inanimate, seen and unseen, physical and esoteric.

Peeling back the onion another layer is a metaphor that refers to the exploration of many dimensions, as each layer is connected to the next and encompasses the whole. Maybe it's time to take a closer look at the onion? Its shape is a circle within a circle. The more green tops that show above the ground, the bigger the onion below the ground: as above so below.

Interesting that onions have been used as far back as the Egyptians. Touted to help balance the **mind** (it's considered high in vitamins and helps with depression), the onion helps to release toxins from the **body**, and helps to release toxins from the **spirit**, in the way of tears. When you slice an onion your eyes leak.

*"Considering we are energetic beings living in an energetic universe,
we too must have the same reflective rules of nature apply
to every area of our life, as there is no separation in energy."
Anita Adrain*

Exploring the layers, and gleaning insight from a closer look at the relationship of the numbers 3, 8, and 9, uncovers some hidden meaning behind energy systems that have been used for thousands of years.

Another Layer… The Energy of Three

Many metaphysical teachers reference that our planet has multidimensional fields of unseen energy; intangible energy systems that are connected to and interact with humanity, a transference of information between the mind, body and spirit. Here, I explore three of these energetic grid systems and how they may relate or apply to the study of Feng Shui.

You've already learned about the magnetic grid system that keeps us grounded. What if there were two other systems—an energetic grid connected to our consciousness (mind), and one connected to our esoteric or spiritual body.

The Magnetic Grid

The Earth's magnetic grid system is the navigation system used for migration of birds and animals. The ley lines of longitude and latitude follow the rules of the Earth's magnetic grid lines. The magnetic poles of North and South are the anchors for the magnetic grid. What we know about gravity, we have learned through science, and through our own experience.

The Gaia Grid

The Gaia grid energy system is what quantum study refers to as 'the field,' or 'the quantum field.' My understanding is that this field of energy is what connects our level of consciousness—our thoughts; the field of energy that our intuitive thoughts come from; the field of entanglement that connects our thoughts with the thoughts of someone close to us. It explains those instances when someone, located a great distance from a loved one, picks up a feeling that there is something wrong with that loved one, or encounters the feeling that they need to connect with that loved one for another reason. There is an electromagnetic field of energy around our planet (Torus field); science is starting to measure the human connection to this energy field.

> "The scientific community is just beginning to appreciate and understand the deeper level of how we are interconnected." https://www.heartMath.org/gci/

Thirteen – Mirror, Mirror

The Global Coherence Initiative measures the electromagnetic field of the Earth and has scientifically validated that the human consciousness is connected to this field of energy.

Basically, GCI have measured the increase in energy around the Earth coinciding with world events where humanity felt deep emotions of love, compassion, and caring. Events such as 9-11 / the 33 miners' rescue / death of Lady Dianna, and the passing of Mother Teresa, for example.

This field of energy changed significantly around these world events. As we are more technologically connected, more of the world's populations were aware of these events in real time. No matter where you were or what you were doing, you likely can remember how you felt and what you were thinking when you first heard the news of the 9/11 event. Collectively, these thoughts and emotions were measured by the GCI.

> "The Global Coherence Initiative (GCI) employs the Global Coherence Monitoring System to collect a variety of data, information about Earth's magnetic field and how it affects and is influenced by human emotions and behaviors." https://www.heartMath.org/gci/

There are many GSMS sensors monitoring resonant frequencies in the Earth's electromagnetic field, one of which is in my home province of Alberta, Canada.

The Crystalline Grid

The third grid or energy system that is speculation—yet to be validated by science—is the Crystalline Grid. Let's consider that this is a possibility and ask the questions: what do we know about crystal? What has science taught us? Do we currently use crystal to enhance our life?

There are many forms of natural crystals and variations used as essential components in your radio, televisions, cell phones, your watch, and your computer. Those crystals represent a transformer and energy exchanger.

What if we were to remove televisions, computers, and cell phones from every home? What if they were banned from use because they are of the unknown forces?

I'm pretty certain that there would be an uproar if this hypothetical scenario happened; we all rely on these devices to improve the quality of life, add convenience, and bring pleasure to our days. We take for granted that they will work instantly. Over time, what was seemingly magic isn't even in our conscious awareness. The example here, benefitting from the seemingly magical discoveries and applications of science and technology, shows us that: **just because we don't know exactly the intricate details of how something works, does not stop us from using the thing and benefitting from its use.**

I encourage you to keep an open mind and heart toward the future and further discovery. After all, what was once 'woo woo' is now your smartphone.

It makes sense to me that the layers of rocks, minerals, and crystals—between the ground we walk on through to the core of the Earth—act like the crystal in a radio, transmitting and receiving an energetic signal. This, to me and to many others, is an energetic crystalline grid that assists humanity in receiving information.

Let's consider the possibility that a Crystalline grid does exist and that it is acting like a recorder that has recorded, and continues to record, the residual energy of significant historical events, joyful and traumatic—all that this planet has ever carried over eons. What if it carried the energy of our story, the stories of our ancestors, the stories of all mankind?

All over the world there are historical and geological sites that are known as areas where great human sacrifice and trauma occurred. One of the memorial sites of the Holocaust, Auschwitz, is one of the most visited. It is estimated that over a million people lost their lives at this site between 1940 and 1945.

I have never visited this site, but people who have note that the energy can still be felt; people report experiencing deep emotional levels; feelings of emptiness, remorse, and sadness.

There are other historical and archeological sites of celebration or sacred joy in which visitors report feeling energized, uplifted, happy, and euphoric. These places include the Great Pyramids, Machu Picchu, and Stonehenge.

In my own backyard, a two- hour drive from my home, are pristine, crystal clear lakes flanked by the grandeur of the Rocky Mountains. Banff

National Park receives over four million visitors a year. People from all over the world come to experience the pure, clean air and stunning beauty. They leave feeling inspired, refreshed and with a deeper, amplified connection to Gaia.

If you have ever visited any of the aforementioned sites, or ones with equal significance, you may recall how you felt: empowered or disempowered. The energy of everyone who ever stepped foot upon the same land left an energetic foot- print.

The emotions generated by stories have been recorded by the multidimensional crystalline grid, which acts as a transformer and receiver. If emotion alters the state of a geographical site, then perhaps, in some cases, it might be possible to change the resonance on the sites that hold past trauma, have suffered complete destruction, and which represent great human sacrifice. Perhaps one could help clear the energies of the land by imbuing sincere love and compassion.

When we practice compassionate action, we activate the compass within. Maybe there are some clues in and with these words as well. COMPASS-ION the COMPASS is the gage which measures then provides a result such as feeling an elevated emotion based on the negative charge (ION) that comes from Gaia.

The energy of 'place' is especially relevant to Feng Shui. The land on which your house is built may hold some energetic memory in the crystalline grid from a previous trauma that you may not even be aware of. The negative energy of the land can impact those who decide to build a house upon it.

Friends of mine had a very successful business and decided to expand to a different part of the City where there was a recently constructed strip mall.

From the onset of signing a new lease, problems and delays began to surface, seemingly keeping their business from moving to the new location. They persevered only to be met with more costly challenges; it seemed that they were under a dark cloud. They consulted with several of their spiritual community members and discovered that the land had once been a native burial site. Following this, my friend hired someone to perform a ceremony, energetically clearing and blessing the land. The dark cloud lifted, and business prospered in this new location.

There are many things that can influence the energy of your home environment and many ways you can remedy negative energy. The first step is awareness, and being open to the possibility that you can, indeed, cause or effect change on an energetic level.

Consider the possibility that the electromagnetic field around Earth, the Gaia energy grid and the one beneath our feet, the Crystalline energy grid, are recording or keeping tabs on all your thoughts and feelings. The energetic imprint left by you is then connected to the energetic imprint of every other person connected to these unseen energy fields.

There is a new, proprietary quantum technology designed to create a high-consciousness environment for you to thrive in, consistently enveloping your home in positive energy. Directed at your home, it can help to clear energy of the land as well as mitigate harmful EMF's.

Think of it like wrapping your home in a bubble of pure energy. It works by activating and maintaining an energy field of 560 or higher on the Hawkins Map, and targeting your property.

The Map of Consciousness, also referred to as the Hawkins Map, was developed by the late Dr. David Hawkins, and first published in the book *Power vs. Force*. The map explains characteristics of energy fields, (the unseen) alongside measuring emotions on a scale from 100-1000. Measurement examples include: Fear - 100, acceptance - 350, love - 500 and peace - 600.

> "The Map of Consciousness identifies the fact that the more conscious we become, the more we contribute to the harmony and unfolding of the planet." https://veritaspub.com/

It is a theory of mine that this quantum technology, when directed at your home, creates a connection to both the Gaia and Crystalline grids, creating a field of energy similar to that of the torus. Based on what science has validated with other energy systems, it's quite plausible.

Some of the benefits of this consciousness technology have been the experience of an increase in personal energy and focus, and enhanced meditative practice and assisted healing, over time. More information can be found by following this link: www.flfe.net/chi Register your property for a complimentary 15-day trial. (No credit card or investment is required for the 15-day trial.)

Based on the above consideration, what goes on behind the closed doors of your home is relevant on many levels.

Life is an interactive experience.
This is your space.

What energy imprints are permeating the walls and spaces of your home?

Any 'Aha!' moments for you, reflective of the outer world - inner world relationship? Please note them.

Thirteen – Mirror, Mirror

Focus your attention in the area of your heart.
With the intention of breathing in gratitude and exhaling love:
Take a deep breath in for 5 seconds or more.
Hold for 5 seconds. Exhale for 5 seconds or more.
Bring your awareness and attention to each word and
or phrase in the Energetic Heart Code below.
Bringing them into your heart— feel the feeling of the
word or phrase radiating to every cell of your being.
Relax and repeat, while continuing to breathe,
to create heart-brain coherence.

ENERGETIC HEART CODES™

H.uman-consciousness **E**.volves
A.wakening **R**.adiant **T**.houghts

~~~~~

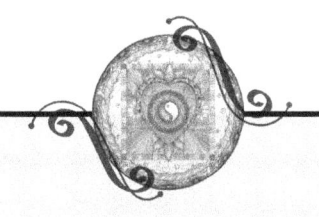

Fourteen – Science And Spirituality

*"How you decorate your environment
is a reflection of your vibration."*
Anita Adrain

Growing up, I remember that my Dad would comment many times to our Mom: "It's going to storm out later, you better get the clothes in off the line." My Mom would look at him and say, "I don't think so, it's a beautiful day." He would then tell her that he noticed the horses were frolicking—galloping up and down the field. They were sensing a change in the weather. Other times I would hear him say: "There must be a storm coming. You kids need to settle down." Of course, he was always right, and it wasn't that he had listened to a weather forecast.

Something was going on in the unseen energy of the natural environment for kids and horses to be acting rambunctiously. My Dad was an astute observer of nature, something he had learned over his lifetime working outdoors, just as his ancestors who had the same ability to predict the weather simply by observing nature. Horses, cows, rabbits, mice, insects, and other creatures all have a built-in barometer that lets them know when the air pressure falls or changes, signalling an impending storm.

Being in the state of awareness or living consciously, you too can become more in-tune with your environment.

Our bodies are finely tuned to work with the Earth in the sense there is a constant flow of energy between body and Earth—an invisible conduit that is the connection to the source of instincts.

Fourteen – Science And Spirituality

Have you heard of earthing? Or forest bathing? These are two practices that have hit mainstream in the past decade, all to clear or de-clutter the unseen energy fields of the body.

When you have your bare feet on the ground, touching the Earth with the bottoms of your feet, there is an energy transfer. Large amounts of negative electrons are being absorbed, and the effect is considered one of the most potent antioxidants known.

Just so you know, my Dad, wherever he is in the cosmos, is likely having a good laugh as I write this section.

My brothers, sisters and I rarely wore any footwear on the farm in the Summer months. It was normal for us to be barefoot, running through the barn yard, the garden, on the lawn, and even in the hayfield—how else would I know the feeling of a fresh cow pie squished between my toes? I truly believe our good health was a result of that—it was a rare occasion when any one of us was sick.

Positively charged ions are all around us in the air we breathe. Note: this is one of those confusing instances where positive really means not so good, and negative means good for you.

The positive ion is usually a carbon dioxide molecule that has been stripped of an electron. The positive ion has a negative effect on the human body and can significantly impact the immune system. The small ions can be absorbed into the blood stream from the air you breathe.

When there is an excess of positively charged ions in our environment it could be a contributing factor to the health of the home's occupants. Tiredness, depression, anxiety, lack of focus and energy may be clues to clean the unseen energy of the home.

There are many things you can do to clean the air, including smudging your home; wouldn't you know it, science has recently confirmed that smudging removes the positive ions from the air. Smudging: the thing the Indigenous people of North America—our brothers and sisters—have been doing forever!

Himalayan salt lamps are another natural way to put more healthy negative ions in your home. And, get ready for it, live plants in your home clean the air, or you can buy one of those expensive ionizer machines, your choice. All excellent ways to remove positive ions from the air, adding the charge of negative ion.

When you need an energy transfusion, go outside and stand barefoot on the grass, on the ground, in the dirt, on the sand—the Earth's slight negative charge will send healing power to every cell of your body.

Our ancestors spent a lot of time outdoors, 'earthing' and 'forest bathing.' We can equate that to today, when we hear someone say they are going on vacation to 'recharge their batteries.' This demonstrates that we instinctively recognize, when some of the body systems are out of balance, they need to be recharged and rebalanced.

When you connect to Earth and to the outside environment you can be in a better place to follow your own natural instincts—the innate system that is within you that interacts with the energies of Planet Earth.

Intuition

Instinctive behavior may also be the result of hard-wired genetic codes passed from generation to generation. The fight or flight response is a signal of instinctual behavior.

Today, it's no longer a part of our lives to be chased by sharp clawed predators, yet we still experience the instinctive response of fight or flight.

Currently, when we find ourselves in a state of fear or anger our immediate reaction is to run or defend ourselves. This affects the nervous system, sending a signal for the body to release adrenaline in response. Living in such a state for an extended period of time adversely affects the body and will eventually wear it down, putting it in a state of dis-ease.

Mankind naturally—instinctively—seeks safety and comfort in his immediate environment. We instinctively seek to add beauty to our home. In doing so, we often mimic what we see and feel in nature. Creating an environment that is aesthetically pleasing is another way of relaxing our nervous system, putting us in a state of ease.

One of the main reasons to learn about Feng Shui is to create an environment that feels safe and comfortable, thereby eliciting positive physiological responses. It is instinct or natural behavior to seek a greater existence, expanding and growing.

As a very young child, I felt the need to create a sacred space, to escape the sometimes hectic, chaotic, overwhelming environment. I was naturally seeking a place of safety and comfort.

Fourteen – Science And Spirituality

Instincts are unlearned behavior, inherent programs that are part of our system. It is possible that some of our instinctual behavior is passed down through the DNA memory—the multi-dimensional parts of our genetic codes that are not yet fully understood. (See the Medicine Wheel section.)

I have always said that, intuitively—instinctively—we all practice Feng Shui. Somewhere deep in the center of our beingness we are connected to all that is, ever was, and will be. The problem is we don't trust it—whatever 'it' is—the feeling or knowingness.

Have you ever done something, and then moments, days, or weeks later said, "I knew I shouldn't have done that?"

If we knew, and hadn't doubted our knowing, we would have trusted our guidance system. We would have led with our intuition—that fleeting thought, or feeling that guides us—the space between the doing and being.

You might recognize that an intuitive thought is that flash of a moment when you think of someone or of a situation, and then the phone rings and it's the very person you were thinking about.

Intuition is a cognitive process that elicits a psychological response, a thought within a thought producing another thought. The more you know about how that system works, and how to use it, the more intuitive you will become.

When you learn to trust your intuition, you are in the abundant energetic flow of the universe.

When I first began to learn to use my intuition, or as some people say: the 'sixth sense'—the esoteric part of the five senses plus one—I often asked my higher self to show me a sign. I wanted a physical sign that I would recognize anytime I had a thought or feeling that was in alignment with my highest good.

When I needed confirmation for a particular situation or personal matter, I would take a moment and listen to my body. Over time, I began to recognize a sensation that would go through my body, confirming that I was indeed on the right path.

Practice makes permanent. Repeated action over time equals results. Sometimes, I get a physical confirmation that comes in a specific feeling. Other times, I get validation through other signs; numbers that appear on the radio readout—3:33 or 11:11 get my attention. There are instances when I haven't seen someone for a long time, and then I bump into them two or three times in the same day. It happens in nature a well; animals crossing my path or a specific bird flying overhead, all carrying a message. Learning to listen, and being an observer in my own life, has helped me to trust my intuition and the 'signs' along the way. As everything is energy, and frequency carries information, this is the unseen communication that is happening every day.

Where does intuition come from? What is the source? My understanding is that we all have a built-in transmitter and receiver that is connected to the source energy that permeates all things (the Gaia grid, perhaps)—connected to that unknown, unseen place of nothing-ness that links us all and holds all the information of a collective consciousness of all that is, was, and ever will be.

Intuition is referred to as the sixth sense, and the sixth chakra is located center of the forehead: some cultures refer to it as the third eye area. The Hindus place a dot on the forehead to symbolize the third eye. As well, etched on many artifacts, the Eye of Ra was the symbol considered to represent the third eye to the ancient Egyptians.

In the middle of the brain, between the two hemispheres is small gland, known as the pineal gland. Typically referred to as a sleep modulator, there is currently believed to be much more to the pineal gland than originally thought.

Is it possible that ancient cultures knew about the pineal gland as a way of transmitting and receiving information from the esoteric or unseen energy?

> "Mainstream society has long suppressed the science behind the true nature of the pineal, but evidence of its multifaceted function and symbolic history is coming to light as the consciousness of the planet rises. The pineal gland serves as a symbol of spirituality, intuition, and clairvoyance in many religions and societies across the globe."
> https://awakeandempoweredexpo.com/magazine/pineal-gland-seat-soul

Intuition comes from connecting our conduit of energy to the ultimate energy Source: the field. When you increase your awareness, live consciously, your connection to this source is amplified.

Synchronicity

It has been my experience that, when I am in-tune and trust my intuition, life has a way of bringing the right people, at the right time, for the right reason, into my life, for my highest good. When the outer world environment of my home supports my energy instead of draining my energy and diverting attention away from that which I am seeking, incredible things begin to flow into my life.

Trusting the voice or the inner knowing regarding a specific situation, and then acting with faith (strong belief), always leads to synchronicity, seemingly chance events, or accidents by design.

I could share many stories where I have had 'coincidences' happen that have led me to something really great.

For example, the weekend that I met Jan Tober, I had a deep sense that I needed to go to Banff for the weekend for the first Kryon event in Canada. There were more reasons why I shouldn't go compared to why I should. For starters, my husband was not fully supportive of my reading and participating in any metaphysical work. You could say we were not on the same page at that point in our married lives—though that has since changed dramatically. I had three small children and I was the owner of a full-time business. I could have easily talked myself into staying home. I had no expectations of the weekend, just a deep knowingness that I needed to be there.

That was the weekend I was introduced to the term Feng Shui, and the first book of Terah Kathryn Collins. What has been my work, my passion for the last twenty years came as a result of following my inner-guidance system, my heart, and my intuition. In this instance, if I had stayed home that weekend, I believe that the universe would have continued to bring me opportunities that eventually I would have paid attention to, and led me on the same path. It just might have taken longer.

Definition of synchronicity:

"Synchronicity is defined by events that happen that are odd or unusual at unexpected times, which seem to strangely co-ordinate together. They are seeming coincidences that aren't, that will often surprise you. The occurrences you think will have the least promise, or the avenues you might have traveled down once that have brought no results, will often suddenly bring the most profound results."

https://www.monikamuranyi.com/glossary#comp-jf2z20b0

When you live in an environment that supports you, one that nourishes and uplifts you, one that makes you feel good, you are more apt to feel great, listen to, and follow your intuition. This will lead you to synchronistic events.

Another definition of synchronicity:

"…this was an idea that Karl Jung was terribly keen on. He suggested that as well as causality (the idea that every event occurs as the result of a specific cause) there is another reason why events occur – synchronicity. In some way's synchronicity is a posh way of saying 'by coincidence,' but the implication is that as well as events being shaped by random chance there are occasionally 'meaningful coincidences,' that is events that appear to happen purely by chance but carry some meaning for the person to whom they occur. So, by using an elaborate system like laying out a Tarot spread (Jung himself used to work extensively with the I-Ching), we are invoking synchronicity into our lives, and the cards will 'just happen' to have arranged themselves into an order which tells us something useful about ourselves, or the question we have asked."

http://www.weirdshitnotbullshit.com/articles/how-does-the-tarot-

Fourteen – Science And Spirituality

Divination

Carl Jung is best known for his work as founder of analytical psychology, and for his published works in 1912: *Psychology of the Unconscious*. He was also known to consult Tarot cards, and the *I Ching*: the book of divination. (Consulting the *I Ching* accesses the spiritual power of the subconscious.) The *I Ching* is synonymous with Feng Shui; key aspects of Feng Shui come from the observation and application of the wisdom from the book, *I Ching*.

Before we delve deeper into the *I Ching* and how it relates to Feng Shui, I would like to share with you some other divination tools. Some of which you have heard of, or perhaps used.

Divination: the word comes from the Latin divinare, meaning to 'foresee' or 'to be inspired by a god.' Sometimes viewed as a magical mystical practice, and other times considered as the occult, it used to be called fortune-telling. Given that, an image that may come to mind is a crystal ball.

Divination operates on the principle that, energetically, everything is connected to everything else. It supposes the ability to access the infinite energy grid (supernatural) to seek guidance on a current issue.

Many people of ancient cultures used some form of divination to gain knowledge of what the future might hold for an individual. Common questions might have been related to one's current or future relationships as well as the potentials of future prosperity.

The diviner or clairvoyant is someone who has a connection to the unseen energy. Today we might consider that unseen to be the quantum field, or the field of consciousness.

Popular divination tools that were used, and are still used today, include: tea leaves, tarot cards, stones, and runes, and pendulums. The all-controversial Ouija board, also known as the spirit board, is considered a divination tool.

Personally, I have used all the above divination tools, at different times, while guided by a diviner. I have many card decks that I consult or ask for clues and guidance to a particular issue or question. When I am quiet, take a few deep breaths, and focus on the question with the expectation of getting a definitive answer, I am accessing my energy field, ninety percent of the time receiving confirmation of my own previous intuitive thoughts.

We also have 'smart bodies' that may be smarter than smart phones. An alternative medicine practice called applied kinesiology, or muscle testing, can be used to access the information in the subconscious, the physical body, and the field. It might just be that we are considered a human pendulum.

For hundreds of years we have been taught that the power resides outside of us and how could we possibly know what's good for us. We have been conditioned and programmed to give our power to someone else or some outside source when, in fact, we have had access to this power all along, within.

North American Indigenous tribes had Medicine Men (and Women) who were the clairvoyants, the men of divination. Our North American society today considers people with these gifts as 'new age,' when history shows us it's 'old age.'

What is considered pseudoscience today might well become mainstream science in the future.

Fourteen – Science And Spirituality

Life is an interactive experience.
This is your space

Did any intuitive thoughts surface for you while reading this section? Please record them here. Hint: the first thought that came to mind is the one.

Can you recall a 'synchronistic' moment or event? Take note of how you were feeling energetically leading up to the moment.

What recognizable 'sign' have you received when you listened to your intuition?

Focus your attention in the area of your heart.
With the intention of breathing in gratitude and exhaling love:
Take a deep breath in for 5 seconds or more.
Hold for 5 seconds. Exhale for 5 seconds or more.
Bring your awareness and attention to each word and
or phrase in the Energetic Heart Code below.
Bringing them into your heart— feel the feeling of the
word or phrase radiating to every cell of your being.
Relax and repeat, while continuing to breathe,
to create heart-brain coherence.

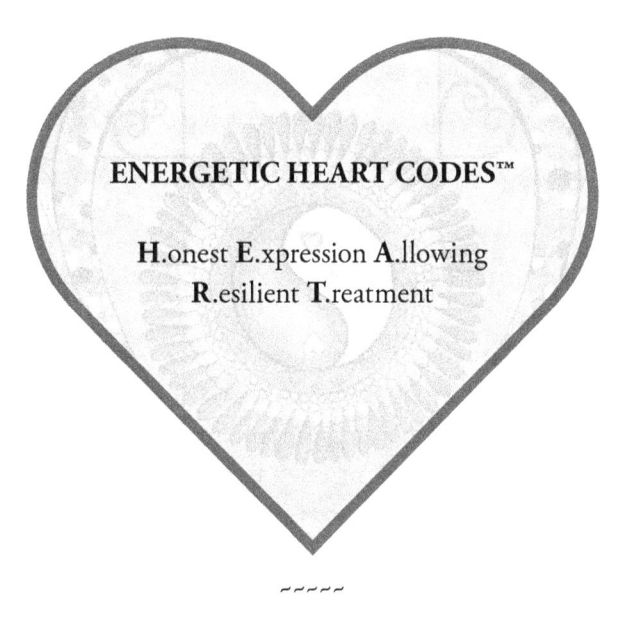

ENERGETIC HEART CODES™

H.onest **E.**xpression **A.**llowing
R.esilient **T.**reatment

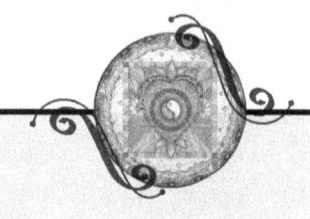

Fifteen – Awakening To A New View

"The mind, body, spirit connection is a divine system.
Anita Adrain

The Triad Of Consciousness

The Triad of Human Consciousness referred to is the brain, heart, and pineal gland. More than parts of our bodies, these three systems were designed to work together in harmony (resonance). The result of this 'together work' increases the connection to the field of energy. The result is compassionate action and enhanced intuition; similar characteristics to what the masters had—those masters who walked the planet thousands of years ago.

> "The Triad of Human Consciousness is the beginning of the realization of mastery."
> This is how Kryon, through Lee Carrol, describes the Triad of Consciousness on page 72 of *Book 14 – The New Human: The Evolution of Humanity*.

So powerful is the description, this bears examination: 'the beginning of the realization of mastery.'

My Feng Shui interpretation of The Triad of Human Consciousness is that there are three attributes of the mind, body, spirit of our intimate home (physicality): the home that sustains all life forms, Gaia and our home (the place you hang your hat).

It is my goal to help you embark on the journey of mastering your own life.

Consider the three whole aspects as being interconnected—and accept that they are alive with chi.

Our mind, body, spirit is in constant vibratory flux in an effort to align itself with the three forces of energy, chi, Yin Yang, and five elements—always seeking balance and harmony.

The mind, body, spirit connection is a divine system. There are plenty of teachers, fitness coaches, life coaches, and trained professionals that can help you achieve physical and mental health. There are spiritual teachers, such as Louise Hay, Lee Carroll, Marilyn Harper, Deepak Chopra, along with plenty of programs to help you understand your esoteric connection that of spirit.

I think we could all agree that there is a lot of information available, some of which is covered in this book, to help you understand how to restore harmony and balance to the three aspects of self.

The other two parts of the triad in your awareness to consciousness are the home as a body, and the planet body, Gaia.

Planet Body: An Energetic View

Nature knows only success in all things. It makes sense to me that the planet body has the same three aspects of the human—a mind, body, and spirit.

Two thirds of this planet consist of water, and two thirds of the human body consists of water. One third of the planet's body consists of matter, one third of the human body consists of matter. By this reflection, we could surmise that the esoteric or spiritual aspect of both these living examples reside outside or beyond our perspective.

In the planet body, water could be considered the mind aspect as it is fluid and has the ability to conform to the space in which it is held. The matter aspect is the body. The esoteric part the spirit is the unseen: the electromagnetic field and/or energetic grids of the Earth—the part that connects to the unseen energy, the quantum field, the god source, the universal energy, whatever you want to call it. Understanding this invisible force and source of energy will, in my opinion, be the subject of coming decades of study from which great realizations and discoveries will be made in the scientific community.

The Planet Earth body produces a toroidal field, as does the sun, and all other planets and stars in the solar system. Each toroidal field touches or bumps into the other fields, hence the connection to all things energetically.

The water (Feng) also produces torus, as does the air (Shui, wind), and can be manifesting visually as vortexes—hurricanes and tornadoes.

According to physicists, the torus is the fundamental form of balanced energy flow found in all sustainable systems. Plants, animals, humans, down to the sub-atomic particles, exhibit this torus flow dynamics and are directly influenced by the larger torus systems of the ocean, Earth's atmosphere, and the entire cosmos. This dynamic exchange of energy and information is directly impacted by our conscious awareness or level of energetic vibratory flux.

We are energetic beings living in an energetic universe: all things connected. When we live consciously aware of all these systems, we can create a better life, with more meaning and purpose, ultimately affecting the whole existence of mankind. It brings new meaning to "do unto others as you would have them do unto you."

Home body: An Energetic View

We can look at our home as being alive with chi—alive with energy—as everything that shows up in material form was at one time a rock, a piece of Earth, a dinosaur, or some other living organism. There is no thing that shows up in our physical reality that was not once something else.

Our home body is alive with life force energy—chi! And because it is alive, it must mirror or have similar characteristics of our mind, body, spirit connection—that of our physical body and the Planet Earth body.

The three characteristics also show up in our home environment, and we could even consider the possibility that our home has an energy, similar to the torus of all other living organisms.

When we treat our homes, as we do our bodies, as being holistic, recognizing that there is a mind, body, spirit aspect, then we are capable of achieving mastery in our life.

In Feng Shui we use a tool to enhance this triad of energy to help create flow, balance, and harmony in all areas of life.

There are many interpretations on this tool, depending on the Feng Shui school of thought. I would like to present my own interpretation of how and why it works. In my search to understand energy systems, I discovered what I believe is a NEW understanding of why and how this powerful tool can offer profound insights into improving your life.

If you have done some reading on the subject of Feng Shui, you may already be somewhat familiar with the bagua (pronounced bä ʹgwä). Whether you are or not makes no difference, as you will gain a deeper understanding of its application for you personally, in your intimate space, your home.

Fifteen – Awakening To A New View

Life is an interactive experience.
This is your space.

Make a list of contributions, enhancements or actions that you can take to synchronize the relationship of your 3-bodies.

The Physical body

The Planet Earth body

The Home body

Focus your attention in the area of your heart.
With the intention of breathing in gratitude and exhaling love:
Take a deep breath in for 5 seconds or more.
Hold for 5 seconds. Exhale for 5 seconds or more.
Bring your awareness and attention to each word and
or phrase in the Energetic Heart Code below.
Bringing them into your heart— feel the feeling of the
word or phrase radiating to every cell of your being.
Relax and repeat, while continuing to breathe,
to create heart-brain coherence.

ENERGETIC HEART CODES™

H.eaven **E**.arth **A**.s above so below **R**.econnect **T**.ranquility

Sixteen – Intentional Living

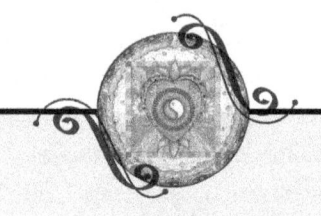

"With the right environment, you can grow a seed into a beautiful plant. It's the same for growing a beautiful human."
Anita Adrain

In Feng Shui, the bagua that is used to chart the home is based on the book of divination: *I Ching*.

> "The *I Ching* is the oldest of all the classical divination systems. It is also one of the oldest books in the world. Its first interpretive text was composed around 1000 B.C. The *I Ching's* actual discovery and much of its early history are the stuff of legends.
>
> There are a number of myths surrounding the origins of the eight trigrams and the development of the *I Ching* divination system. In one tale, Fu Hsi, the first emperor of china (2852–2737 B.C.), is said to have observed a turtle emerging from the Yellow River. <u>Knowing that true wisdom came from the direct and close observation of nature</u>, he had a sudden realization of the significance of eight symbols he saw on the turtle's back. He saw how the sets of three solid or broken lines, the trigrams, <u>reflected the movement of energy in life on Earth</u>.
>
> A similar myth describes Fu Hsi's contemplation of <u>other patterns in nature, including animals, plants,</u>

meteorological phenomena, and even his own body. These myths describe how he identified the trigrams that arose from his understanding of the connection of all things, through the interplay of yin and yang."
https://divination.com/history-of-the-i-ching/

The *I Ching*, also known as *The Book of Changes*, is comprised of 64 points of knowledge, or hexagrams, six lines either solid or broken. Each symbol conveys a specific message that relates to all areas of one's life.

Trigrams, as described above, each consist of three broken (Yin) or unbroken (Yang) lines. These trigrams represent the fundamental principles of reality.

Feng Shui has borrowed the wisdom from the *I Ching* and adapted it for use in the physical environment of the home.

In Feng Shui, bagua is regarded as a pattern that determines the significance and positive qualities of spacial relationships—bagua means 8 trigrams. The bagua is an energy system, or energy map, used to analyze the energy of any given space. Comprised of 8 squares around the center square of Earth, it is a powerful tool used by the Feng Shui practitioner.

Through the understanding and use of the bagua, we can redirect the energy flow to focus on the things we want to improve on by increasing the positive chi, and correcting not so positive chi, in any space.

The Treasure Map

As an Essential Feng Shui trained practitioner, the use of the bagua to map the home for each client is used in the same way—a non-directional approach. Every Feng Shui school of thought and teaching uses the bagua to assess the energy centers of the home. The only difference is how it is applied.

The bagua—Treasure Map as I like to call it and will refer to it as that from this point—will help you assess, improve, and enrich every aspect of your life and assist in your self-discovery.

What I have observed by using the Treasure Map with my clients is that it never lies. It always reflects the inner world of the home's occupants, and clearly illuminates areas that are not fully supported or are in need of improvement.

It was this mystery that kept me searching for more clues as to how and why the bagua works.

Sixteen – Intentional Living

Before I divulge my findings, which I believe have never been written about in any other Feng Shui book, I will share with you what the Treasure Map looks like, and how to use it.

The 8 fundamental areas of one's life circulate around the physical center of the home—the center square referred to as Earth energy. (Note the number 8 from the Yin Yang symbol.)

The 8 areas (also referred to as guas) of the map representing the fundamental aspects of life are:

- Knowledge & Self-development
- Health & Family
- Wealth & Prosperity
- Career
- Fame & Recognition
- Helpful people & Travel
- Children & Creativity
- Love & Marriage

The Treasure Map shows up like this:

Wealth & Prosperity	Fame & Recognition Fire	Love & Marriage
Health & Family Wood	Earth Center Earth	Children & Creativity Metal
Knowledge & Self-development	Career Water	Helpful People & Travel

Note: that the Treasure map shows the five elements from the 5-element theory that are associated with the areas of the map.

When assessing any space, we recommend using a holistic approach. The goal is to anchor the energy in your home in correlation with the 8 areas of your life. Whatever your current results in any area of your life, you will most likely see a parallel in that specific area of your home. If you want to create something better than what you are currently experiencing, you can activate and enhance the chi to the corresponding area of your home to match the energy of your desires and wishes. Using the Treasure Map is one of the ways you can achieve your desired results.

A client purchased a home—the third owner in a period of 18 months. The first owners—who were a young, newly married couple—had purchased it as a show home and, within six months, went their own way and sold the house. The second owners were a couple who ended up separating and dividing assets.

The third owner of the house became my client. She was a single mother of two. Whether we call it luck or synchronicity, we quickly became friends when she moved into the neighborhood. I shared the history of the house along with what I deemed as Feng Shui challenges. She was totally open to assessing her home as she was ready for positive changes in her life.

When we looked at the home as being a 'whole'—energetically 'alive'—we discovered that the Love & Marriage area of the home was not being supported, and the energy in the Wealth & Prosperity area was being drained. After making some enhancements, and anchoring the energy of these two important areas (guas), her relationships and finances flourished.

It was interesting that she also had possessions that were mirroring her previous life which, of course, she was quick to replace once she recognized how these items were reinforcing her thoughts of being single. Pictures in the home tell a story every day, impressing an image upon the subconscious mind and anchoring that energy as if it is in fact reality. We have all heard of the power of visualization when athletes see themselves at the finish line. Well, this—the images in the home telling a story and impressing upon the subconscious mind—is pretty much the same process; it's just that it's unintentional.

One of the artworks that she had on the wall in the staircase, an area that was very visible and that she passed by several times a day, was a picture of a tree: a single, lonely tree, with no leaves or blossoms. It was a very large print in black and white. Along with being desolate-looking, it was reinforcing her programmed beliefs that she wasn't good enough, beautiful enough, and that her love life, like the tree, was in a period of rest. The picture was also purchased when she was newly single, further anchoring her emotional experience in the subconscious. Upon realizing the impact of this one picture, she was quick to replace it with an image full of vibrant color that mirrored her deepest desires.

As she learned to use the Treasure Map in her home, she was empowered to find her true inner-beauty and worthiness. The universe quickly matched her elevated energy level—vibration—and opened her up to receiving many blessings in all areas of her life.

I have worked with many clients over the years, and all have had some profound shift after looking at their home with the Treasure Map as their guide.

I remember one client, a couple who had called me to come and assess their home as they were struggling financially and were eager to rectify the situation. They had heard that the energy of their home might be a factor, so they asked me to evaluate their wealth and prosperity areas as being the focus.

What was interesting to me about this particular consultation, was that in every room I looked I could see with my Feng Shui eyes that the Love & Marriage or relationship area of the home was not being fully supported. It was a consultation that opened my own eyes to the full power of the Treasure Map and ignited my curiosity to learn more about the energies of the home.

As I was hired to enhance and help them anchor the energy of the Wealth & Prosperity area of the home, and their lives, that is what I did. In my follow-up report, I gave them many recommendations on how to achieve this, along with subtle recommendations for the whole home, including the relationship areas. Several months after the consultation, I learned, through another source, that this couple had separated, as one of them had been secretly having an affair.

Although their inner world was truly being reflected in their outer world, it wasn't my place to fully disclose what I felt and saw. When the energy shifted, there was no place to hide; whatever needed to come to the forefront in their life did. This consultation taught me that the Treasure Map never lies, 'the writing is on the wall.'

There have been many clients since this particular one where I saw energetically the potentials of something brewing that may not be conceived as being positive.

The opportunity to grow and evolve sometimes comes in ways in which we are not expecting, yet ultimately serve for our highest good.

Helping my clients to vibrate at a higher frequency or energetic level puts them in a position to shift their own life. In doing so they may see or feel things differently and may have, for the first time, let go of energy from the past that was holding them stuck in their current life situation.

Remember the story of the client who lived with his girlfriend in the basement suite of his own house? After embracing the practice of Feng Shui and shifting their own vibration, this couple came to the realization that they didn't make a great couple. When they became aware of how they were living, and looking at everything as being alive with chi, they quickly became masters of their own lives and went on to create their deepest desires and wishes. They eventually went their separate ways, remaining great friends, and the universe matched their new vibration and brought to each of them the perfect partner in alignment with their true inner being.

'Aha!' Are the light bulbs coming on? As you begin to use YOUR Feng Shui eyes, you may have many 'Aha!' light bulb moments; observations of the inner world expressing outward, that are being mirrored into the spaces of your home.

Now you might understand why I wanted to let you know about the mirrored relationships that show up in all things natural. It is the reason I created the T.E.A.R. section. I wanted to explain how life force energy—chi—is evident in all things seen and unseen. It is essential to be clear about the workings of the conscious and subconscious mind, the Triad of Consciousness, and clear about the importance of being aware and awake in your own life. Your connectedness to the energy of Gaia, to our mother the Planet Earth, is especially relevant as we uncover the inner workings of the Treasure Map and how you can use it to enhance your own life situation.

By delivering the information to you in this thorough and detailed way, you will have been able to discover and uncover some energy systems that you may not have previously been aware of. Hopefully, the dots are connecting, and you are able to start to see how you can change your life by changing your frequency—starting with the flow of energy in your personal environment.

Bird's Eye View

Are you ready to use the Treasure Map to enhance your life? It's not difficult to learn to recognize which areas of your life are being fully supported and which ones are not.

Imagine your current home is roofless, and you are a bird flying over it. What is the floor plan of your house? Keep in mind that anything structurally attached to your house, such as garages and decks or patios, are included in your bird's eye view.

Now, take that image and lay the Treasure Map over it, ensuring the entrance to your home is at the bottom of the map.

Another way you can view this is to draw a footprint of your home by sketching the outside walls and anything structural that is connected to your house. Once you have this footprint: square up/rectangle up the floor plan to include areas outside the house—like a patio or the front steps—and then include the undeveloped areas that are in the same 'line' as that patio or those steps, that fall into the overall square or rectangle. Make sure those empty areas are taken into consideration—included in the footprint—for when you apply the Treasure Map. You can also take your map and divide it into nine equal squares.

Example

In this example, we could lay the Treasure Map over the floorplan and discover several things that may be mirroring or energetically showing up for the homeowners.

Energetically, this home is not whole, and not being fully supported in the areas of Career, Fame & Recognition, and Love & Marriage.

How did I come to this conclusion? Using the front entrance as the cue in which to lay the Treasure Map, and including all attached structures, we can see that the areas to the right of the patio are not being supported energetically or structurally when we are looking at a complete energetic whole. As well, the front of the house is indented, therefore the area of Career and Knowledge & Self-development is affected—falls outside the physical boundary of the house.

Sixteen – Intentional Living

At the back of the house, imagine drawing a line to complete the outside space of the bird's eye view. The line would be made from the outside of the patio to the right where the outside wall on the right-hand-side of the house would square up.

A line from the outside of the garage to the outside of the front of the house would create a complete rectangle to illustrate the house's entire energetic footprint.

Once the rectangle is created, the space can be divided into 9 equal squares to reflect the 9 areas of the Treasure Map. At this point it would be clear to see that there are specific areas of the Treasure Map that reside outside the physical structure of the home. These are areas that are not being fully supported.

In our example:

The Left Area Of Our Example

Knowledge & Self-development is the living room, foyer and entrance, including the area that is outside. Health & Family is the dining room, closet, hallway, and part of the kitchen.
Wealth & Prosperity is the kitchen and the patio.

The Middle Area Of Our Example

Career would be the den, and all the area outside from the covered entry to the left-hand-side of part of the garage. 'Earth' or the 'Center' of the home would be part of the den and the bathroom. Fame & Recognition would be the staircase off the kitchen, bedroom number two, as well as the space outside, to the right of the patio.

The Right Area Of Our Example

Helpful People & Travel is totally in the garage. Children & Creativity would be partly in the garage, the hallway, and some of the master bedroom. Love & Marriage is half in the master bedroom and the half the outside area.

In this example, there are a couple of recommendations that would help the occupants of this home experience a more holistic, balanced life.

An exact measurement is not required to divide the home equally, inch for inch, into 9 areas. To obtain the energy for a room, use the largest portion of the corresponding area of the Treasure Map. Even though the 3 guas might show up in one room or one area of the home, I would suggest activating the area that is predominant. It is not always possible to assign a room to a specific area of the Treasure Map, as there are doorways, hallways, and utility rooms that break up the map.

In this example, the people living in this house may not be feeling fully supported in their intimate, deep relationship as part of the Love & Marriage is residing outside. The good thing is that the master bedroom takes up half of this area. Without consulting with clients, and actually being able to see the contents of all of the rooms within the home, following are some general enhancements to anchor the energy of Love & Marriage.

Sixteen – Intentional Living

- Plant a quartz crystal, tree, or area of interest outside the master bedroom that aligns with the unseen energy of the outside of the patio as it would travel to the right, top of the house, connecting with the unseen energy if the right of the outside of the house extended to meet an unseen corner.
- Create a master bedroom that shows equality, signified by pairs of items: two end tables, two-night lamps, equal—or close to equal—space in the closets and drawers. Basically, give each person the feeling that they are sharing and are equal partners. Using the 5-element chart, you could add some fire energy to the bedroom to spark or ignite the romance.

The areas of Knowledge & Self-development and Career could be enhanced in this example. As the recessed front entrance and covered doorway may be sheltering and protecting the homes owners, the energy of the home could be reflecting the dispositions of its occupants. In this case it's quite possible that they would be somewhat introverted and not very sociable. The doorway to the home is the 'mouth of chi' or where the energy enters to circulate and nourish the home's residents. This is likened to our physical body, where our life force energy, the breath, the unseen energy of air, enters through our nose or mouth. Welcoming in the chi, or calling the chi, to the entrance of the home ensures that the life-giving energy nourishes all the home's occupants, creating a healthy home.

The den in this home is ideally situated to be a home office as it is at the front of the home where the chi is active, compared to the passive chi at the rear of the home. General enhancements for this area of our hypothetical home might include.

- Moving the office from a bedroom to the den area.
- Creating an entrance to the home that gives the illusion of starting slightly beyond the front of the garage and the outside wall of the living room.

- Painting the doorway, a bright color, adding planters with seasonal color.
- Suggesting the homeowners regularly use their front entrance instead of the doorway or entrance from the garage, encouraging chi to follow.

Every home is as individual as the people who live there. What works for one may not work for everyone. General Feng Shui tips should be used with your own discernment, using your intuition—your inner-compass.

The popularity of Feng Shui has increased in the last several decades as have the Feng Shui cures used to remedy disharmonic chi. There is a wide range: laughing Buddha's, golden frogs, coins hanging from a red string, money plants, mandarin ducks, and dragons. All are marketed to improve 'luck' and 'prosperity.' Remember, Feng Shui comes to the Western world from an Eastern culture steeped in history, cultural beliefs, and practices. If these items hold deep meaning for you, and you believe they will help, by all means use them as a 'cure.'

The reason I like to refer to the bagua as 'The Treasure Map' is for you to use your own treasured possessions to enhance and activate the chi in all 9 areas of the bagua. When you have a personal connection and attach deep emotional meaning to something—an item that makes your heart sing and elevates your personal chi—the item has a better chance to increase your luck and improve your situation. Any 'thing' only has the meaning that you give it. There may be items that you own that hold deep symbolism for you from your heritage and cultural practices. Symbols impact our subconscious mind, invoking memories from the past and stimulate present experiences. As we are operating ninety percent of the time from the subconscious, symbols hold an infinitely strong influence in our lives.

You could take a moment here, to draw a bird's-eye view of your home. Don't get too specific in your first attempt. The important thing is to draw the outside walls of your structure, being sure to include anything that is physically attached, with a rough sketch as to where the individual rooms are.

Now use a different color pen to complete the energy of your holistic home creating a square, rectangle, or grid.

Your House

Remember, in the non-directional application of the Treasure Map, you always use the map with the entrance to your home as your guide. Use it from bottom to top, no matter which compass direction the home is facing or how it is situated—hillside or valley. In addition, do not deviate from the instructions of overlaying the Treasure Map, no matter which compass direction that you resonate with, or which compass direction you personally associate with.

Note: if you are currently living in an apartment building or condominium, draw your personal unit, not the entire building.

Ancient cultures built their homes in a circular form that was more holistic than what we see in our modern architecture (another clue that the ancient cultures recognized the flow of energy). Energy moves in a cycle—circular—and I would have you draw a circle of your home, except most homes are built using right angles (squares and rectangles).

Another important discovery is that the three aspects of mind, body, and spirit that show up in the environment, the planet body, and the human body. (Note: the importance of the number three as it relates to the physical space.) These three aspects show up in our physical home environment as well.

If a person's physical body is out of balance (sick or diseased), would that cause stress, emotionally and mentally influencing how they show up or express themselves in the world? Yes, absolutely.

Chances are, there would be areas in the home that reflect this out-of-balance dis-ease of the physical body. Similarly, if the person was having challenges or issues emotionally or mentally, it would be reflected in the home environment. The inner world is connected to, and reflected in, the outer world.

Left Areas of The Treasure Map That Correlate with The Physical Aspects. (body)

- Knowledge & Self-development
- Health & Family
- Wealth & Prosperity

Center Areas of The Treasure Map That Correlate with Mental Aspects. (mind)

- Career
- Earth
- Fame & Recognition

Right Areas of The Treasure Map That Correlate with The Emotions. (spirit)

- Helpful people & Travel
- Children & Creativity
- Love & Marriage

What area of your Treasure Map are you wanting to improve upon? Perhaps you are currently looking to enhance your life-work, and looking for new employment opportunities. Maybe someone in your home is having some health challenges. Whatever it is, take a good look at the area of your home that correlates with the area of the Treasure Map. Now, look at the space with your Feng Shui eyes open, looking at everything energetically, as being alive with chi.

Are there possessions that are no longer serving you? Are there plants that are on their last legs? Are some things in disrepair, including small items? Is there a large amount of clutter in that specific area? What is being reflected to you? What story is being anchored energetically?

Once you have identified which area you want to start in, realize that everything is connected, and it's a good idea to make the complete circle and do some enhancements in all 9 areas of the map.

If you had poor health, would that effect your ability to go to work, would that have an effect on your finances, would being sick take a toll on your intimate personal relationships? Yes, being in poor health would ultimately affect every area of your life in a not-so-positive way. Starting in the health area of the home and moving throughout the other 8 areas is most beneficial for someone having health challenges.

What treasures did you find when you de-cluttered? Which ones are still serving you? Of course, they will be the ones to which you have a deep emotional connection—which hold symbolism for you in accordance with your values.

Now you have an energetic map in which you can amplify or magnetize that energy by displaying those items in a corresponding room or area in your home that matches the energy. That beautiful sculpture that you were given by the love of your life would help to anchor the continued feeling of deep, intimate relationship and could be displayed either in the Love & Marriage area of the home, or the Love & Marriage area of an individual room.

Remember: all your possessions are telling a story. Here is a quick guide to help you determine what could ultimately go where to enhance that energy imprint.

Physical Aspects. (body)

Knowledge & Self-development

- Enhance with items that support your personal journey of learning and discovery.
- Books, quotes, and affirmations that empower you to greatness.
- Enhance and/or activate with colors of black, dark blues and greens.

Health & Family

- Enhance with living plants, fish aquarium or other examples of life.
- Family photos of happy, healthy people.
- Other artworks that hold meaning of healthy family relationships.
- Any item of personal, emotional value relating to health and family.
- Enhance and/or activate with colors of green and light blue.

Wealth & Prosperity

- Enhance with items that symbolize wealth for you.

- Any items of value, such as crystals, collectibles, heirlooms, antiques or artwork.
- A water fountain or water feature is recommended in this area to have a constant flow of abundance in many forms in your life.
- Important to note here: bathrooms and sinks, even though water features, can drain away the family's wealth. If you have one of these draining features in the Wealth & Prosperity area of your home, you will need to balance the water energy with the earth and wood elements (refer to the 5-element theory). Round, faceted crystals can be hung from the ceiling in these challenging areas to lift the chi.
- Enhance and/or activate with the colors red and purple.

"Wealth is not just money. For most people, wealth includes an abundance of money, free time, loving relationships, inner peace, and having a sense of meaning and fulfillment."

T.Harv Eker, *Speed Wealth*

The left side of your home is associated with your physical attributes. If you are wanting to support, enhance, or improve areas of your physical body, these areas of your home are a great place to start. When you see the space energetically, you can decide if it is supporting your desired physical outcome. Example: weight management, nutrition program, learning and/or gaining new wisdom and understanding.

Mental aspects. (mind)

Career

- Enhance with achievements, certificates relating to career.
- Items in the water element, such as mirrors and artwork with water scenes.
- Any personal items that represent your current and/or future career.

- Enhance and/or activate with the colors associated with the water element, dark tones and black.

Earth

- This is the center of your home where all the energy circulates and pools.
- Ensure this area is free from obstructions to allow the free flow energy.
- Enhance this area when you are not feeling connected or grounded.
- Enhance with earth related items: rocks and crystals.
- Enhance and/or activate with earthy colors, shades of beige and brown, terra-cotta and earthy tones.
- Artworks that depict the colors and patterns of the soil of the earth.

Fame & Recognition

- How do you want others to see you in the world? What do you want to be famed for?
- Personally, or professionally, you can choose items that give you the feeling of recognition and raise your self-worth.
- Use quotes or affirmations that identify the personal attributes you are working towards.
- Enhance and/or activate with the colors red and orange, associated with fire.

The middle of your home is associated with your mental attributes. Does anyone in the home, suffer from anxiety, stress, or burn out? If you are wanting to support, enhance, or improve on areas of your mental health, these areas of your home are a great place to start. See the space elementally: there may be too much mental energy, too many to-do's, an overwhelming number of tasks to complete, many projects on the go, or too many irons in the fire.

Sixteen – Intentional Living

Emotions. (spirit)

Helpful people & Travel

- Enhance with items that represent travel for you personally.
- Anything to do with the esoteric world, angels, or other spiritual or religious representations.
- Pictures of people of another ethnicity, or representation of other cultures.
- This area is associated with synchronicity, having the right people show up at the right time, for the right reason.
- Opportunities usually show up in the way of helpful people.
- Enhance and/or activate with white-greys and blacks.

Children & Creativity

- Enhance this area to create more JOY in your life.
- Children bring us joy, laughter and the opportunity to play. This is the area to bring out creativity; get the juices flowing, create a place to let the inner child out to experience life in the moment.
- Enhance with items that are whimsical, playful, fun and creative.
- Enhance and/or activate with pastel colors and white.

Love & Marriage

- Enhance with items that represent LOVE to you.
- Pictures and/or artwork that convey deep emotions of togetherness.
- Pairs of items that represent two people or a couple.
- Decorate or accentuate with any of the sensual colors of red, pink, and/or burgundy.
- Any possessions and/or actions that support self-love could also be anchored in this area.

  "You, yourself, as much as anybody in the entire universe, deserve your love and affection."

  Buddha

The right side of your home is associated with the spiritual attributes. Do you feel loved? Supported by your 'tribe'? Do you take time for self-care? Are you happy? How are your 'spirits'? What are you passionate about? What brings you joy? Seeing the space energetically: is the outer world mirroring your desired outcome?

There is still much to be learned from the Treasure Map.

As Above So Below, As within So without

As we have learned, Mother Nature shows us there is a relationship between the macro and micro, often reflecting the same patterns in both. The Treasure Map brings our attention to those relationships.

As you begin mapping your own home, start with the main floor if you have more than one.

From there you can map the individual rooms within the home, using the doorway as your guide to lay the map. A bedroom may have a large walk-in closet and an en-suite. These areas would be included just as you included any decks or structural additions in the macro version.

Example

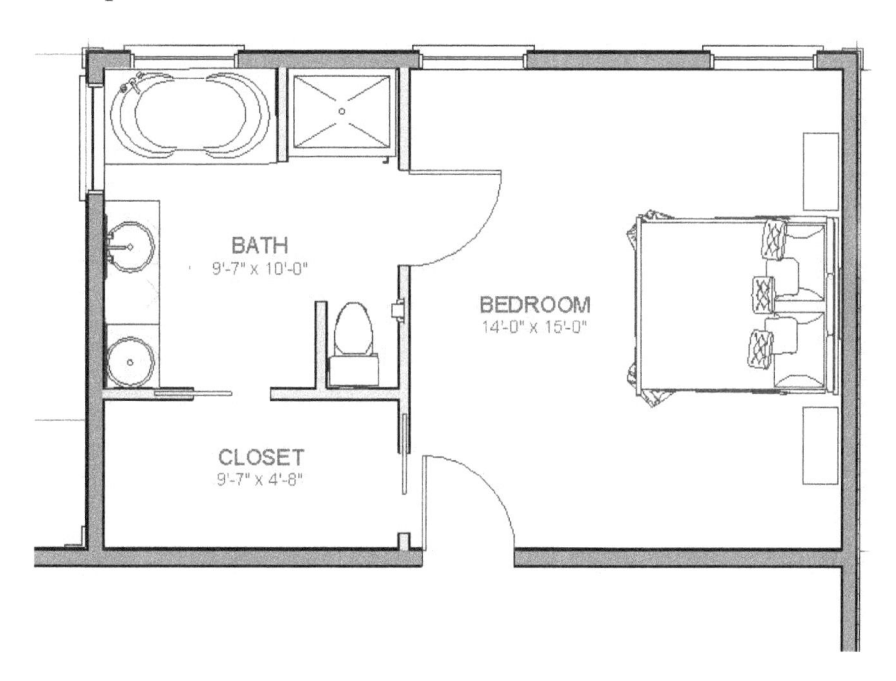

In this example you cannot get to the bathroom or the closet without first entering through the door to the bedroom, hence it is treated as a whole space.

The doorway to this bedroom would be entering in the Career area of the map, with Knowledge & Self-development to the left, and Helpful People & Travel to the right. Dividing the room into 9 equal areas would then give you a good idea of the position of each of the 'guas.'

This bedroom might show up in the macro Treasure Map of the home as being in, let's say, the Wealth & Prosperity area. First you would address the macro 'gua' and make enhancements suited to the environment of a master bedroom by creating a luxurious, grand oasis; a version similar to what one might find in a magnificent hotel. Of course, this would entail working within the individual's personal tastes, personal treasures, and budget. Within the micro space, wherever possible, use items that match the meaning for each 'gua' within the room.

Recommendations might include:

- Pictures symbolizing 'Career' framed in gold or metal frames to the right of the doorway. Anything from a beautiful water landscape to something that supports the feeling of success.
- A stunning black soapstone carving of a couple—one that was purchased while on vacation in a tropical paradise—placed on the nightstand in the Helpful People & Travel area of the bedroom.
- Matching night lamps with shades adorned with beads or crystals—something fun and whimsical for the Children & Creativity area.
- On the wall between the windows: a picture that represents a loving couple, or one that denotes attributes of sharing, kindness, honesty, or integrity. All of these are qualities in alignment with the Fame & Recognition area of a bedroom.
- A pair of candles, or a symbol of love, on the other nightstand in the Love & Marriage area of the room. A small picture on the wall above the nightstand with an affirmational quote on love.
- Silk or satin curtains in tones to match the room's décor in fire tones. (5-element theory.)

- Opulent bed covering and matching pillows—not too many pillows. You always want to leave room for a partner.
- Antique dresser on the wall between the bathroom and closet doorways. Items that symbolize stability, grounding, and being secure in the earth area of the room. A great place for a handmade clay container to collect money from pockets, or other small treasures that show up from time to time in a bedroom. Other personal items that represent wealth, that are suitable in a bedroom, could also be displayed here.
- Most of the closet area resides in the Knowledge & Self-development area of the bedroom. It is a room of function and not an easy space to make enhancements, to support learning and personal self-development, other than keeping all items organized, and area clear of clutter.
- The remaining area of the bedroom is the bathroom. Its nature is a very watery room, and the Wealth & Prosperity of the hypothetical homeowners could be going down the drain. It is amplified in this example: the bathtub and shower area are in the micro Wealth & Prosperity area of the bedroom. Remember the bedroom is the macro of Wealth & Prosperity—doubling the energy that may be draining the bank account.

One solution to soak up the abundance of water is to add live plants, as there is adequate light from the two windows flanking the tub area. Plants that have rounded leaves are best (no sharp, pointy ones). A Jade plant has leaves similar to the shape of coins and is considered a great choice for a Wealth & Prosperity area enhancement. The addition of plants, or the colors associated with the wood element, would be beneficial in absorbing the abundant water energy in the room. An important factor in this example is to not accentuate the water element, rather to balance with wood and earth elements. Of course, choosing items to enhance this area that are functional for a bathroom could include earthy colored towels and accessories that convey the feeling of wealth, floral patterns in shower curtain, and related accessories. Think luxurious spa retreat, as that would surely anchor the feeling of being wealthy and prosperous.

Sixteen – Intentional Living

The subliminal messages of wealth, success, partnership, and self-love would now be anchored in this bedroom by having made a few enhancements to support the Wealth & Prosperity area of the home. Remember, where the eye goes, energy flows and attention also goes. Where attention flows, intention goes. Having the 'intention' to improve the wealth and prosperity activated in the unseen and the seen world sends a vibration out that the universe has to match. The images that are being impressed on the subconscious mind would now be in alignment with the desired results.

The inner world results of having made changes to the outer world in this example might show up as:

- Feeling like the 'King and Queen of the castle'
- Self-respect, self-love
- Confident, I'm worth it
- Gratitude, blessings
- Feeling of comfort and safety knowing all needs are met
- Less financial stress equates to better sleeps

Now that you have an idea of how to use the macro and micro version of the Treasure Map, go for it. Feel into it: the journey of Feng Shui is a personal one, as your home is your intimate space. The best way to use the Treasure Map and Feng Shui your space is to use your intuition and work with the principle foundational tools that all Essential Feng Shui practitioners use: The Treasure Map, 5-element theory and the flow of chi (energy).

As above so below...

If you have more than one floor in your home, 'double' your enhancement by treating the rooms that are directly above or below. The previous master bedroom example was in the Wealth & Prosperity area of the home. If below this bedroom there was a basement storage room or another bedroom, this area would also be in the Wealth & Prosperity 'gua' of the home. If there happened to be a home-office or family sitting area above this bedroom, the room usage may be better suited to display the family's treasured possessions anchoring the Wealth & Prosperity energy.

Over the years, an interesting observation has surfaced from mapping the homes of many clients and students. Quite often, when an area—gua—is energetically outside the holistic home and not being fully supported, the same 'gua' shows up inside the home as not being fully supported. The pattern repeats from the outside to the inside.

If Helpful People & Travel is residing outside, it may be challenging to make enhancements within the individual rooms inside the home in the Helpful People & Travel area. These spaces may be a closet, a doorway, a furnace room, or other space typically void of any aesthetic enhancement.

The inner world result may be that the client is experiencing instances of not having helpful people in her life. She may experience trouble when traveling, such as delayed flights or vehicle problems, being turned down for a mortgage, and/or difficulty finding qualified helpers such as babysitters or handymen. This is a reflection of not having the right helpful people show up in the right place at the right time.

The use of the micro version of the Treasure Map then becomes very important, applying it in all rooms within the home and energetically enhancing all the 'guas' wherever possible.

The Treasure Map can be used in layers, from the macro to the micro. You can map the town or city in which you live, the area (crescent, street, village), the property or land your house sits on, the structural home, the individual rooms, the rooms within the rooms, the surface areas of desks and shelves. I encourage you to have fun with it and see what you discover. Always use the Treasure Map with the bottom of the map aligning with the 'mouth of chi' or entrance to the space you are mapping.

It is beneficial to map the property that the home sits on, as well as mapping the home (it's not always the same as the house). Feng Shui for the landscape is a broad subject taking into consideration many variables. Natural and man-made features play an important role in the flow of energy of the landscape, as does climate, therefore the flora and fauna supported by the area.

Note: If this is the start of your Feng Shui journey, you have the right book, because, as its title suggests by containing 'The Heart,' it is a loving overview on Feng Shui. The topic of Feng Shui landscape is specific to the area in which you live, thereby too large to address in this work. If you want to dive deeply into the topic, there are many great resources that address landscape.

Sixteen – Intentional Living

Life is an interactive experience.
This is Your Space.

Which area(s) of the Treasure Map will you work on first?

What are some of the changes you plan to incorporate? Write them out while they are fresh in your mind.

What were the areas (guas) that reflected your current inner world results? For example: if your inner world results were 'not being recognized for your true worth,' the area(s) that reflected this in your space (outer world)

And what changes can you make in your physical environment to support different inner world results?

Sixteen – Intentional Living

Focus your attention in the area of your heart.
With the intention of breathing in gratitude and exhaling love:
Take a deep breath in for 5 seconds or more.
Hold for 5 seconds. Exhale for 5 seconds or more.
Bring your awareness and attention to each word and
or phrase in the Energetic Heart Code below.
Bringing them into your heart— feel the feeling of the
word or phrase radiating to every cell of your being.
Relax and repeat, while continuing to breathe,
to create heart-brain coherence.

ENERGETIC HEART CODES™

H.ealthful **E.**mpowerment **A.**wakening
R.eality **T.**ransformational

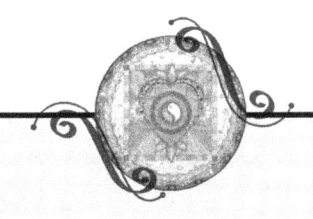

Seventeen – Using Your Inner Compass

*It's your turn, your time to shine your light,
to activate the piece of the puzzle that you are,
for it is that light which impacts future generations."*
Anita Adrain

There is one more layer that I want to share with you: specifically, when mapping certain rooms in the house, such as a bedroom or a home office, the optimum placement of furniture will take into consideration your personal power direction as well as the 'gua' that it sits in.

Using The Inner Compass: Your Best Direction

Even though the application of the Treasure Map as presented here is non-directional, meaning it does not take into account the compass direction in which your house or property is facing or how your house is positioned on the landscape (or the terrain of that landscape), does not mean that we do not acknowledge the four directions.

Specifically, the four directions add another layer or dimension in which you can achieve a state of harmony, relaxing the nervous system and all areas of your physiology.

You could consult a Chinese astrological chart and calculate, based on the date and time of your birth, your Feng Shui KUA number which will determine which directions are best for you, indicating whether you

Seventeen – Using Your Inner Compass

belong in the east or west group. Or you could try my method, or both, and see which resonates with your core-essence.

The best way I have found to honor the four directions with my clients is to teach them how to go within and use their own personal compass to determine the direction of influence that aligns for them.

Seat yourself in a quiet room. Take a moment to become aware of your surroundings and note which direction you are currently facing. Close your eyes, take a few deep breaths, holding each one for five or six seconds before exhaling for that same count.

Bring your awareness into your body; feel and sense the air around you. Tune in and note any feelings: physical discomfort or ease.

With your feet flat on the ground, take a quarter turn. Again, take some deep breaths and check in with all your senses. Take a few minutes or longer. Trust the information that's coming in.

Then do another quarter turn and repeat the process until you are back where you started.

Open your eyes and record your findings about each position. In which position did you feel the most comfortable? In which position did you feel the most uncomfortable? Now take note of which compass direction you were facing and match each to your feelings in each position. You may have to repeat this process a few times until you trust your inner feelings.

We all have an innate compass that lets us know which direction we prefer to face. Individually, we resonate with a certain direction—one that is better suited to each of us personally. It makes sense that, as natural beings, we respond to the magnetics of the Earth. (Animals, particularly birds, rely on the magnetics as their GPS compass.)

The direction of east, the direction in which the sun rises to a new day, might match the energy of feeling more alive, awakened, and vibrant, similar to how Mother Nature approaches a new day.

When the sun is in full display, warming the entire land, the direction is South, and the most active position of the day. You might discover that you feel more invigorated when you are soaking up the sun and facing the direct energy of South.

The westerly sky is where the sun starts to dim and finally settle into sleep for the night, giving way to the energy of the moon. You might feel more relaxed, at ease, and experience a feeling of connectedness in this direction.

The north sky is devoid of sun; it is there that she sleeps and is still. You might feel inner stillness, quiet, and calm facing this direction.

You may want to be mindful and mind-full for one whole day, checking on how you feel when the sun is in different compass directions.

What energy of the day matches your personal energy vibration? Are you an early morning person? Perhaps you feel supercharged by mid-day and start to fade as the day proceeds. Maybe you get your engine started after six in the evening and can go until midnight or later? These are all clues for you in which direction to place specific pieces of furniture, depending on your desired results, and depending on the use of the room.

Directional Sleeping / Facing and Supporting / Power Directions

All schools of Feng Shui recognize the importance of furniture placement within the flow of chi. Regardless of whether you are sleeping, awake on personal time, or working, when you do so in a power position, it is said that you will be blessed with good fortune.

Good fortune might be defined as 'simply amazing energy generated by the organization of positive conscious intent.'

When your eyes are open, the receptors (part of the eye that receives information) sends a signal to the neurotransmitters in brain. Your 'best vision' is facing the direction that empowers and supports your individuality.

When you are energetically aligned, whether at sleep or sitting at a desk at work in a power position, you are improving your performance, enhancing your happiness, and promoting personal positivity.

Chances are you already have instinctively placed your desk or bed in the most suitable position for you. Checking in by doing the 'test' will allow you to make some adjustments.

Feng Shui Eyes: Desk Placement

For example; when you are sitting at a desk in an office chair you may find your mind wandering or having an inability to focus on tasks at hand. Simply by repositioning the furniture to be in alignment with the direction that feels most comfortable for you to be facing, will improve the situation.

Size and shapes of rooms—including windows and walls—may keep you from taking full advantage of 'your power direction,' in which case you will have to go with the flow and make other enhancements. Be creative, think outside the box, and use your Feng Shui eyes—for example, when moving a desk is not an option, try adding a mirror behind it to reflect movement behind the office chair.

Desk placement is extremely important, be it your home-office or your work-office. It is recommended that you have support behind your office chair, be it a wall, divider or plant—something that energetically offers support.

When I came home from my first Feng Shui training, eager to practice and share my new energetic views, I remember giving a friend some advice on adjustments that could be made to his office. He had a busy alternative healthcare office with many treatment rooms, and a personal office space. His desk was up against a wall; when sitting in his office chair he had no clear view of the doorway or anything behind him. Energetically, he was in a vulnerable position. There was also a large metal filing cabinet that was against the other wall.

With my Feng Shui eyes I could see that the filing cabinet was pointing 'sha' or negative energy right at his back. To demonstrate, I remember taking my hand as if I held a knife, telling him that his current furniture placement was likened to being stabbed in the back.

Like many of my other close friends and family he didn't resonate with Feng Shui as it was a relatively new concept at the time (in Alberta) and, for the most part, he shrugged it off as another woo-woo thing that I was doing.

One week later, he came to my business clearly distraught. When I asked what was wrong, he informed me that he had just found out some devastating news. The other holistic practitioner that worked in his office, that he was grooming to one day become his partner, had just informed him that he was opening his own office. There were no immediate warning signs that came to mind, no indications that his intentions were to leave and subsequently take some clients with him. Metaphorically and figuratively, my friend had been stabbed in the back.

Did the furniture placement have something to do with what actually transpired? Yes, absolutely. Having no visual awareness to what is happening behind 'our back' sends a signal to the nervous system to be 'out of ease'. When the body's systems are compromised or out of balance the person is not in tune with everything going on around them. It is likely, in this case that, when my friend was at his desk, he had a hard time focusing on tasks at hand, and his attention was all over the place. There were probably some indicators—that his colleague was considering venturing out on his own—he missed as a result of not being fully present. His furniture placement was not supporting him to be in the command position of his office, and in command of his practice.

Think about how you feel when, let's say, you are seated in a restaurant in the middle of the room. Is it an uncomfortable position? Do you find yourself constantly looking over your shoulder? Are you able to relax fully and engage in conversation with other guests sharing your table? If you had the choice of all the seats in the restaurant, which would you choose? The one at the back of the room that gives you the clearest view of the entrance or the doorway, with the comings and goings?

Repeated Action Over Time Equals Results

Sitting in a vulnerable position, day after day, will eventually take its toll on the body's physiology, and will adversely impact all the body's systems—mind and spirit.

Instinctively we each want to feel safe and comfortable, fully supported, and in command of our own life—no surprises. Consider your personal inner-compass direction when placing furniture, as well as having a peripheral view of the room and support behind a chair, especially a chair that you spend a great deal of time in.

The command position is also known as the armchair position. Think about sitting in a comfortable armchair where your upper body is fully supported by the chair, your arms open, with hands resting comfortably

Seventeen – Using Your Inner Compass

on the arm rests. Imagine the feeling as if you were sitting in one now. An armchair is usually placed in a corner of a room and therefore gives a commanding view.

Similarly, make the same considerations when placing bedroom furniture, importantly your bed. What are your current results? Are you sleeping not so well? Do you have support behind your head, in the way of a headboard or wall? Is there a clear view of the doorway and windows? What is hanging above, or over your bed, over your head?

When working with clients I always note the position of the bed and which compass direction the head of the bed is being supported by. I then ask the clients how they are sleeping.

The very active energy of the south can sometimes keep people awake; keep some people from entering a deep, restful sleep. Asking the question: 'how do you sleep in this room?' lets me know if I need to suggest a different placement of furniture.

What other furniture in your home is supporting, or not supporting you, when you are sitting? What direction are you facing? What direction are you being supported by?

Being aware of your innate, optimum compass direction is extremely helpful when buying a new home or building one. For example, if east is your personal power direction, having a kitchen, office, or other active room in the home facing east would be most beneficial for you.

In working with the Treasure Map, it has been my observation and my experience that it never lies; it is always mirroring the inner world journey. As I gather the clues for the last chapter of this book, I will reveal my theory of why this is.

Your personality, the essence of who you are, resides and shows up in the intimate space you call home. It holds all your memories and your treasured possessions. The practice and application of Feng Shui is a journey, as unique as the individuals who occupy the space. It's important that you cultivate your own chi and use discernment when making enhancements to your space—the space in which you spend one third or more of your life. What feels good for you? What works for you?

Life is an interactive experience.
This is Your Space.

What resonated with you from this chapter, and what changes are you willing to make in your home?

What key points will you share with a close friend or loved one?

Seventeen – Using Your Inner Compass

Focus your attention in the area of your heart.
With the intention of breathing in gratitude and exhaling love:
Take a deep breath in for 5 seconds or more.
Hold for 5 seconds. Exhale for 5 seconds or more.
Bring your awareness and attention to each word and
or phrase in the Energetic Heart Code below.
Bringing them into your heart— feel the feeling of the
word or phrase radiating to every cell of your being.
Relax and repeat, while continuing to breathe,
to create heart-brain coherence.

ENERGETIC HEART CODES™

H.abit of mind **E**.xpansive
A.ppreciation **R**.eceptive **T**.alent

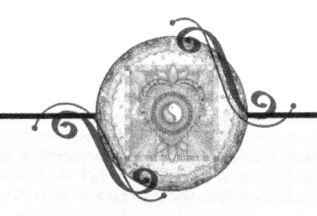

Eighteen – Success Leaves Clues

"How you visually present the entrance to your home dictates the health of the home, either attracting or repelling the life force energy chi."
Anita Adrain

Mother Nature shows us success in all that she does—from the tiniest sea creatures that live and survive in the vast oceans, to the largest animals roaming the African plains. There is an orderly system among all life forms on this beautiful Planet Earth; this includes the human life form which is on a journey of re-discovering these truths.

Who or what created this benevolent system, the one universe (uni/one verse/voice) that we all call home? There have been many clues left for us to unravel the mystery.

Success Clue #1

The study of sacred geometry shares the flower of life symbol, which represents the divine creation pattern encoded in our cells. Sacred geometry is recognized as an ancient science—subtle structures (that appear in nature), patterns, and codes symbolic of our own inner realm.

The most common form of the 'Flower of Life' symbol is a hexagonal pattern (where the center of each circle is on the circumference of six surrounding circles of the same diameter), made up of 19 complete circles and 36 partial circular arcs, enclosed by a large circle.
https://www.tokenrock.com/explain-flower-of-life-46.html

The number 19 reduces to a 1; the number 36 reduces to a 9—new beginnings and completion represented in one pattern.

The mind, body, spirit aspects of the home, as discovered in the Treasure Map, show up in 3 sets of 3, which equals 9. There is no coincidence that it consists of 9 squares including the center Earth. Completing an energetic circle or connection, a whole, holistic or holy unit, as the number 9 represents completion.

Is it possible then, that our Creator, God, the one unifying force (or whomever you believe to be the one), was the master mathematician? Could it be that a numbers system is the foundational concept from which all things unseen—Feng, and seen—Shui, have been created?

Success Clue #2

Perhaps one of the most famous mathematicians, the Greek philosopher Pythagoras, known for the Pythagorean Theorem, considered numbers necessary for understanding everything. Pythagoras described music and nature in terms of arithmetical relationships.

> Sacred Mathematics, by way of definition, refers to the concepts which, according to ancient (and a few modern) scholars, encompassed all of creation in mathematical terms. It includes numerical ratios of the most profound significance (literally <u>Transcendental Numbers</u>), the nature of numbers themselves (<u>Numerology</u>), their mutual relationship (<u>Astrology</u>), strange beasts such as <u>Magic Squares</u> and <u>Infinite Series</u>, those astounding aspects of geometrical relationships in <u>Sacred Geometry</u> which seem to defy logical or rational explanation, and the manner in which all of these aspects describe the universe.
> <u>http://www.halexandria.org</u>

The Power Of 8

Numbers hold energy—mathematical formulae and repeating patterns that might offer clues as to how we are connected to our environment, especially that of our homes.

In numerology, there is no 'coincidence.' Every number has an underlying energetic value as we discovered in the numerology section. The number 8 represents structure, (of the home, perhaps), responsibility, practicality, and manifestation. For this reason, it is considered a 'lucky' number, and is the most auspicious number in the Chinese culture.

My new view of the Yin Yang symbol offers the number 8 as a source of achieving balance within the 24 hours of the day. The number 8 on its side is the symbol used by the Metis, as it represents infinity.

The 8 'guas' or areas of the home that represent the 8 trigrams of the bagua, connect the fundamental aspects of our inner world to the outer world environment of our home.

If in fact the 'creator' of this universe was a master mathematician and left energy signatures in numbers for us to re-discover, then the teachings of the bagua are valid under this assumption. That said, the number 8, by way of the definition of the sacred mathematics, as offered in the preceding paragraph, may well be the 'magic square' pattern that we use in Feng Shui to map the energy of the home.

You have already learned the 'how' to use this powerful tool to map the energies of your home. Now we are brought back to the 'why' the Treasure Map works. I have a theory…

Why and How Feng Shui Works

The question had been a mystery to me early in my Feng Shui journey. The more I worked with clients, empowering them to see their homes energetically, using the Treasure Map and the other tools in my Feng Shui bag, the more I started to get reports back of all the amazing opportunities, events, and blessings that were happening in their lives.

I remember coming to a conclusion; the 'Aha!' moment. Of course, the reason the Treasure Map works is because as they (my clients) began decluttering room by room, and began noticing what emotions were attached to their possessions, they were able to clear emotional blockages, along with their stuff. They began living with the items that they loved, enhancing areas of their homes, anchoring the energy in each of the areas that they wanted to improve upon.

This clearing elevated their personal vibration—they were happier, felt lighter, and overall radiated more positive energy.

Their state of elevated emotion (feeling more personal energy) was a determining factor in the results they were achieving. Having possessions in each area of the Treasure Map that was in alignment with their positive, elevated emotions put them on a different wavelength. The universe was just matching their vibration. These results allowed me to explain why the Treasure Map works…

I remember thinking: *so that must be it. After all, emotions are energy in motion.*

As time went on and my own level of awareness and consciousness increased, I came to the conclusion that there was another force at work. It certainly had something to do with the emotional state of the client. Could it be that, when they focused their actions with pure 'INTENT,' their experience matched their deepest desires and wishes?

My inquisitive mind wanted to learn more. I wanted to learn what 'INTENT' meant. I went to the source, my spiritual mentor Lee Carroll. What did Kryon have to say about intent? Used as a noun, it means intention of purpose. Used as an adjective, it means resolved or determined to do something or showing earnest and eager attention. Kryon's use of the word intent is generally in reference to spiritual change. Pure Intent is an intent that is not casual, which holds a desire to continue or follow through, no matter what. https://www.monikamuranyi.com/glossary

With passion and an earnest desire to create different results, my clients were using the Treasure Map to make positive changes. They were using pure intent and, as a result, were experiencing a 'shift' and 'awakening' to spiritual wisdom that they may not have previously been open to.

As there is a direct correlation between high energy (elevated emotions) and rapid manifestation, when energy levels vibrate at the same level as our Intentions, what we most desire comes to us quickly.

Elevated emotion plus intention. That was it! Yes, of course that made sense, that's why Feng Shui works, specifically the application of the Treasure Map. I could relax, I had solved the mysteryand could share with my students and clients.

James Redfield's quote bears repeating.
"Where attention goes, energy flows.
Where intention goes, energy flows."

I came to the realization that the Treasure Map never lies. I wondered to myself: How is it that whatever issue the client or student is currently experiencing in their inner world, it shows up in the same 'gua' or area of their house, the outer world? If there was a health issue, sure as heck the Health & Family area of the house was not reflecting a healthy home. If it was finances, usually the Wealth & Prosperity area was not within the energetic walls of the home, and not being supported and residing outside the holistic home. On and on it went; I kept observing these parallels.

It has only been the last four of five years that I believe I have discovered the answer to this—yet another layer of the mystery. This answer has not been validated by science… yet. As far as I know, there is nobody else (noted authors and teachers) who has presented this idea—my theory.

With every clue that I have gathered, everything that I feel to be true for me, everything that resonates for and in me, I think my theory might be valid, or at least it offers a plausible explanation. It might make sense to you as well.

My Theory of Why the Treasure Map Never Lies

When you build your home, or your business, you are connecting to the energy of the earth. The foundation of your home, the supports, go into the soil and the energy of your home becomes one with the energy of the subtle electrical currents and magnetic forces of the Earth. The energetic grid of Mother Earth connects to the grid of your physical home.
The Treasure Map as presented here, is a pattern, a grid of divine design.

The circuit of energy 'chi' moves through the home, influencing the person or people living within. This unseen energy, the Feng, interacts with the seen—the Shui—increasing or affecting the vibrational resonance of the home.

Eighteen – Success Leaves Clues

The tree in your front yard is connected to the earth, its foundation of roots holding it firmly in place. At first glance it may appear to be standing alone, separate from the other trees planted in your yard, but it is exchanging energy above the ground as well as below the ground—a circuit of energy connected to the Earth's energetic grids. All around and within are vast fields of frequency and vibrational energies interconnecting with all other energy systems.

The fundamental pattern of life energy, the torus, is nature's way of creating and sustaining life.

The tree has a toroidal energy field. Does that mean your house has a toroidal energy field as well? It is my belief, therefore theory, that it does—or it at least has the potential.

If the tree is planted and your house is planted in the earth, then it too must reflect or have similar energetic characteristics that mirror the natural environment. In the case of a structure being built on the ground—a home, for example—once connected to the earth through the foundation, it is a case of: 'as below so above.'

So, there you have it: the reason I believe the Treasure Map never lies is because this toroidal field around your home is disrupted, and energetic patterns are weaker in the areas where there is no physical connection—no structure. As energy—chi—moves in a circular pattern, connecting to the circuit of Mother Earth in a natural flow of energy, it's important for it to have something to direct the rhythmic flow.

When the structure of your home is incomplete or not whole-listic, energetically it is, in parts, disconnected from the energetic grid of the Earth. This dis-connect puts the home's energetic field off balance (incoherence). You know the feeling of standing on one leg—you can only sustain the position for so long and then you have the potential of falling over if you are not quick enough to put your other leg down for support.

Just as you can rebalance yourself by planting your other leg (if you were standing on one), the incoherence in your home's energy system can be corrected and supported to complete the energetic grid, creating a holistic environment, a toroidal environment, a frequency converter.

Being in the 'flow' with this pattern of life energy means creating balance or coherence of your home.

Directing the 'chi' to circulate around the home is to include all aspects of the Treasure Map. It's like opening your arms in anticipation of a hug—you have prepared a space to bring the energy of the other person closer to you for a deeper connection.

Using the home blueprint example from a previous chapter, the energetic structure is incomplete—it is not a whole unit. The key word is 'plant.' Planting a crystal or a tree was recommended in our evaluation of this example. This created a holistic home that completed the energetic circuit connecting all outside structure with the energy of the Earth. I believe that all Feng Shui practitioners are aware of having a complete energetic flow around a home or building, and many recommend the planting of crystals to remedy specific situations. I also believe, for the most part, they are not aware that the important factor is connecting to the energy grids below the surface of the ground.

I always carry Quartz crystals with me when doing a Feng Shui home assessment. It helps to correct the irregular shapes we find in our modern architecture. Planting crystals are great energetic cures for balancing a home's energy, completing the circuit, enveloping the home and all its occupants in a constant flow of chi. This creates coherence.

> Resonating at the level of an individual's needs, Clear Quartz also amplifies whatever energy or intent is programmed into it, and continues to broadcast that energy throughout the world and into the etheric realms. This may accelerate the fulfillment of one's prayers, intensify healing or spiritual growth, or simply <u>allow the crystal to hold a pattern of energy long enough and strongly enough for the manifestation of a goal to occur.</u>
> [Hall II, 22][Eason, 133][Simmons, 318][Ahsian, 319]

Once you have determined which areas of your structural home need support (maybe more than 1), you can bury a medium-small quartz crystal, point up, anywhere from 3 to 6 inches below the surface.

It is not always possible to plant a crystal or anything in the ground. Placing some 'thing' on top of the ground, in the general area, will also direct the flow of chi, and connect the energy circuit from the Earth, ensuring a continuous flow around your home. (Occasionally I have recommended to clients to place large rocks, water features, birdfeeders, or other chi enhancers. Each home is unique as is the situation and challenges.)

- Based on our floor plan example: plant a quartz crystal, tree, or area of interest outside the master bedroom that aligns with the unseen energy of the outside of the patio. Note how this would complete 'the space'— outside of the house.
- Mirrors, considered the Feng Shui Aspirin, can also be used to 'cure' a structural deficiency. By placing a mirror on the inside wall of an area that is not being fully supported, it can energetically expand/or push the energy outward. Mirrors are very powerful and have the ability to enhance the chi or deplete it. It's best to consult with your 'intuition,' or contact a Feng Shui practitioner for optimum results.

The unseen is far more powerful than that which can be seen and touched. Connecting your home to the unseen attributes: energies of the Earth's energetic grids (crystalline grid and magnetic grid), combined with the power of connecting your intentions to each area of the map representing the aspects of your mind, body, and spirit, is a powerful and positive practice.

Living a holistic life, one that reflects your true inner aspirations bringing forth the potentials of living in joy, can only be realized when you see your home as being 'alive.'

Incorporating and practicing some or all of the Feng Shui insights presented in this book offers you a continuation of your journey

Putting On The Red Dress

Have you ever noticed someone, perhaps at a social function, who is wearing a red dress? The energy of the person appears to be more animated or energetic than the people around them, unless, of course, they too are wearing a red dress. They command the attention of everyone else in the room, as the eye is naturally drawn to the vibrant color of red. If you're a man reading this, maybe there has been a time when you were driving and happened to catch a glimpse of 'the red dress' walking down the street. The immediate reaction is to pause for a second, shifting your attention to the energy of the red dress.

I invite you to keep this analogy in your mindfulness as you embark on your Feng Shui journey. Putting the 'red dress' on your home means inviting the chi, the positive energy, the uplifting vibes, into the space of your energetic home.

Starting at the front entrance, 'the mouth of chi,' you want to attract the attention of passersby in a positive, uplifting way.

What can you do to make your home stand out? What can you do to make guests feel immediately welcomed, at ease, and in a positive state before they enter your home (bringing that good chi in with them)? You do not necessarily have to paint your front door red, as some Feng Shui books might suggest. Do whatever feels good or resonates with you; create the front of the home so it commands attention.

Everything is energy, and the positive thoughts (energy) of everyone who views your home from the outside will leave a residual energy imprint that will affect the overall well-beingness of your home. This will ensure a steady flow of positive vibes to your home, whether you are there or not, whether you know the people sending you good thoughts or not, whether those people ever enter your home or not. The care and attention you give the front of your home will ripple into the other spaces of your home as well as out into your neighborhood.

Eighteen – Success Leaves Clues

Life is an interactive experience.
This is your space.

And it truly is a blank canvas for you to 'freefall' all your thoughts and feelings. No prompts, just space for you to be you.

Focus your attention in the area of your heart.
With the intention of breathing in gratitude and exhaling love:
Take a deep breath in for 5 seconds or more.
Hold for 5 seconds. Exhale for 5 seconds or more.
Bring your awareness and attention to each word and
or phrase in the Energetic Heart Code below.
Bringing them into your heart— feel the feeling of the
word or phrase radiating to every cell of your being.
Relax and repeat, while continuing to breathe,
to create heart-brain coherence.

ENERGETIC HEART CODES™

H.eartwarming **E.**xperience **A.**spiring
R.esonance **T.**ranscendent

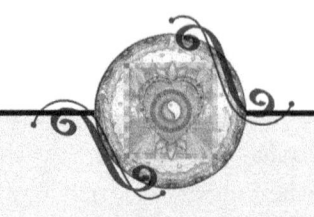

The Journey Continues From Here In Your Home And Heart

*"Beautiful, loving soul: you are fully supported on this journey.
The path you have chosen is yours."*
Anita Adrain

You are an energetic being living in an energetic world. By now you should see your home, and all its contents, as being 'alive' with life-force energy.

Nourishing the home's occupants with vibrant, uplifting, empowering chi equates to living a happy, healthier, and more joyful life.

Feng Shui is not a destination. It is a continuous voyage of wonder that invites you to embark on mastering your own life with the awareness of all energy systems.

Feng Shui being 'the study of energy,' takes into consideration that, because everything is alive with chi, you are connected to everyone and everything. With the realization that we are all connected, we can evolve toward living a peaceful existence, and perhaps experience a greater love for one another.

When we change the way, we look at 'the world'—our perception of it—the view through our Feng Shui eyes brings change to our beliefs and our experiences.

Imagine, once again, how one positive thought about your 'space' (your future, your present, your life, your family, your home, your work) can alter the course of many thoughts.

So, start with your home—for it is where the heart lives—and is the intimate space that holds all the physical attributes of your life's journey. Consider how much time you spend in your home environment—quite a lot of time. Wouldn't it make sense then to focus some positive attention to ensure the energetic flow of the home is in alignment with your goals and aspirations? When you view your environment 'energetically' you will become aware of all the areas—in body, mind, and spirit—that have been the cause of blocking the flow of abundant energy; areas of possible stress.

To experience lasting change, personal growth and ultimately more JOY in one's life, it is imperative that the outer world environment energetically matches the desires of the inner world environment of your thoughts and emotions. You've been learning this from page one of this book. You've literally been on a journey of self-discovery and empowerment, learning how to reduce stress by living a heart-filled, abundant life.

From now on, applying what you have learned here in *The HeART of Feng Shui… Simply Put*, will change your frequency, removing the blocks causing stress—ultimately, creating a healthy abundant life.

When you Feng Shui your space to support rich thoughts and creative ideas, your life will reflect the same. It will be graced with abundant resources to sustain life itself. We live in a spectacular universe filled with unlimited supply and abundance.

Your personal vibration, or the desired vibration, has to be in alignment with the vibration in your environment for you to achieve growth—for expansion in whichever area you desire.

The home body IS alive with energy. Balance and harmony are achievable in all areas of your life when you view your home from this energetic approach. Is it time to become the Master of your home, your destiny?

I re-invite you to take what resonates with you personally and use this book as a platform in your study of energy: the study of Feng Shui. Whatever that looks like for you, I encourage you to become energetically aware and consciously awakened to the possibilities: 'as within so without'.

Let's change the world, starting with our own space. Ultimately, all the positive changes that we make creates a ripple that affects all of humanity.

From my Heart to Yours
Anita Adrain

H.E.A.R.T. CLUES

Home is where the heart lives, and the clues that were left throughout the pages of this book are summarized here for your future reference. They are quick reminders to reinforce the principles, ideas, and new views discovered as you embark on your Feng Shui journey.

H.ome E.nergy A.wareness R.esults T.uning in

H.OME

- One of the main reasons to learn about Feng Shui is to create an environment that is safe, comfortable, and aesthetically pleasing, thereby eliciting positive physiological responses, positively affecting the nervous system.
- When we truly approach living with what we love, and loving where we live, we have established the heart of Feng Shui.
- Our mind and emotions are in resonance with our core values. Our homes reflect the same—energy/emotion is attached to possessions that we value.
- Living with items that make your heart sing and evoke positive emotions will increase your personal vitality and health.
- Feng Shui teaches us to look within our personal environment—our home—to create a harmonious space. One of the main principles used to achieve this harmony is the use of the 5-element chart as it relates to the tangible aspects of the space being occupied.
- Feng Shui is observing elements in the environment that are relevant to improving the health of the home, thereby improving the health of its occupants. 'To strive instead of survive.'
- When there is an excess of positively charged ions in your environment it could be a contributing factor to the health of the home's occupants. Tiredness, depression, anxiety, lack of focus and/or energy may be clues to clean the unseen energy of your home.

- The left side of your home is associated with your physical attributes. If you are wanting to support, enhance, or improve on areas of your physical body, these areas of your home are a great place to start. Seeing the space energetically, is it supporting your desired physical outcome?
- The middle of your home is associated with your mental attributes. Does anyone in the home suffer from anxiety, stress or burn out? If you are wanting to support, enhance, or improve on areas of your mental health, these areas of your home are a great place to start. Seeing the space energetically, there may be too much mental energy, too many to-do's, overwhelming tasks to complete, many projects on the go, or too many irons in the fire?
- The right side of your home is associated with the spiritual attributes. Do you feel loved, supported by your 'tribe,' do you take time for self-care, and are you happy? How are your 'spirits'? What are you passionate about, what brings you joy? Seeing the space energetically: is the outer world mirroring your desired outcome?
- We each have an innate compass that lets us know what direction we prefer to face.
- All schools of Feng Shui recognize the importance of furniture placement to honor the individual's personal directions. When you sleep, sit, or work, facing your direction, it is said you will be blessed with good fortune.
- What I have observed by using the Treasure Map with my clients is that it never lies. It always reflects the inner world of the home's occupants and clearly illuminates areas that are not fully supported or in need of improvement.
- When the outer world environment of my home supports my energy, instead of draining my energy and diverting attention away from that which I am seeking, incredible things begin to flow into my life.
- Where your eye goes, energy flows, where energy flows your attention goes. What physical aspects in your home are you repeatedly putting your attention on?

The Journey Continues From Here In Your Home And Heart

E.NERGY

- The fact is, there is NO-thing that we are not connected to energetically.
- Improving your life and, in turn, the lives of others, is about ELEVATING your awareness of ENERGY.
- If you change your vibration, thereby increasing your personal frequency, you can change every area of your life.
- One of the goals of Feng Shui is to raise your vibration. That is done by raising the vibration in your home.
- You are an energetic being living in an energetic universe. If you allow yourself to become consciously aware of this truth, you have the opportunity to live an empowered life in abundant flow.
- Words carry energy. Possess-Possession / universe-Uni-voice / Compassion-Compass-Ion / Conduit-Can do it.
- It is said that love is the strongest, most powerful emotion that we can give and receive. It is the glue of the universe, the force that binds us.
- When you can learn to sustain positive emotions, your heart becomes coherent, in harmony with all of your other biological systems.
- If coherence implies order, structure, harmony, and being in alignment within, then incoherence would imply the opposite: chaos, dis-harmony, and out-of-balance.
- When your nervous system is relaxed, it means that the heart-brain connection is coherent.
- Increased awareness—consciousness—enhances or heightens the electromagnetic waves (your heart in coherence is a powerful electromagnetic field) transferred through vibrations of other electric magnetic fields (your physical body).
- According to physicists, the torus is the fundamental form of balanced energy flow found in all sustainable systems.
- The mind, body, spirit aspects of all humans reflect examples that can be considered clues in restoring balance to all three systems,

creating a state of resonance; basically, all three operating systems in sync.
- My Feng Shui interpretation reflects that the mind, body, spirit show up in our physical form, our home, and our planet, Gaia. Our mind, body, spirit is in constant vibratory flux to align itself with the three forces of energy, chi, Yin Yang, and five elements. It is always seeking balance and harmony.

A.WARENESS (or Attention)

- Take a conscious breath and imagine the sweet scent of your favorite flower. Notice your body. Do you feel in a state of ease? Maybe it reminds you of the start of a meditation exercise? If not, then certainly a state of moving toward calm. Could this be another clue from Mother Nature?
- Inner world and outer world are intricately connected, and so it is that you can 'not' work on your inner world without also working on the outer world, or the other way around.
- Any 'thing' only has the meaning that you give it. There may be items that you own that hold deep symbolism for you personally from your heritage and cultural practices.
- It is wise to have a 'definiteness' of purpose with a clear vision of the peak. Clearing out the old programs, beliefs, and energetic stuff (clutter) is the first step to ascension, living heaven on Earth.
- Emotional blockages show up in the body as disease or discomfort. Recognizing what emotion is unresolved, and removing the emotional blockage in the physical environment of your home, will help to release the emotional blockage in the body.
- Just because we don't know exactly the intricate details of how something works does not stop us from using the thing and/or benefitting from its use.
- The study and application of five elements in your home has the potential of creating a space that nourishes you on all levels, revitalizing all of the home's occupants.

R.ESONANCE (or results)

- The natural state of seeking to expand and grow has been mistakenly interpreted—misinterpreted—by growing our possessions.
- Yin Yang shows us that energy is always flowing, moving like the seasons. It also shows us the benefit of a balanced lifestyle; creating a quality of life that can be extraordinary.
- If thoughts become things, then can the things be controlling and influencing the quality of your thoughts?
- Of the approximately 60,000 thoughts a day that you think, only 10% are in your cognitive or conscious awareness. The other 90 % of the approximately 60,000 thoughts a day are subconscious or subliminal messages that determine how you show up in the world today, tomorrow, and the next day.
- Repeated action over time equals your results.
- When you increase your vibration—your frequency—you affect everything and everyone around you.
- The five elements are the building blocks of our natural environment. When they are present in our home and work places, we react to their presence on a subconscious, intuitive level. The balance and interaction of these five elements has the strength to empower us naturally in mind, body, and spirit—they either support us positively, in balance in the nourishing cycle, or not so positively in the controlling cycle.
- The pineal gland was once called the third eye. Intuition is referred to as the sixth sense, and the sixth chakra is located center of the forehead: the third eye area.
- Our ancestors spent a lot of time outdoors, 'earthing' and 'Forest Bathing.' A new awareness and understanding exists when you hear someone say she is going on vacation to 'recharge her batteries.' This is an instinctive recognition that some of the body systems are out of balance, hence needing to be recharged, rebalanced.
- For hundreds of years we have been taught that the power resides outside of us—a 'how could we possibly know what's good for us?' We have been conditioned and programmed to give our power to someone else, or some outside source, when, in fact, we have had access to this power all along, within.

The Journey Continues From Here In Your Home And Heart

T.UNING IN

- We have an innate, smart body system already in place that is in alignment and full agreement with what we want.
- Even though Feng Shui has been defined as an Eastern philosophy, with deep roots in Chinese culture, I am certain that all the Indigenous cultures practiced Feng Shui. They may have called it something else, but they, too, looked for clues to their existence, and sought continued survival from the natural surroundings of Earth, the heavens, and stars above. They, too, recognized the natural rhythms and cycles of the planet, and the effect it had on their environment.
- The outer world Is Connected To, And Reflected In, The inner world
- Every single thing, all your possessions, are reflecting an outward image of your inner journey.
- Considering we are energetic beings living in an energetic universe, then we too must have the same reflective rules of nature apply to every area of our life, as there is no separation in energy.
- Nature shows us mirrored relationships in all things; clues left in patterns, in all things, all for the support of our existence and evolution.
- The stillness of water reflects the images that surround its body. Nature has given us clues to her intricate design. 'As within so without,' and we only have to be still in our body (of water) to recognize that the truths of our lives are being reflected to us in our environment.
- Life force—chi—is constantly moving and changing. It circulates throughout all living systems. Coming full circle, it seems to be time for humanity to get back to the teachings of the ancients and celebrate our relationship with Mother Nature—Mother Earth, Gaia, the Creator.
- I have always said that, intuitively—instinctively—we all practice Feng Shui. Somewhere deep in the center of our beingness we are

connected to all that is, ever was, and, will be. The problem is we don't trust it—whatever 'it' is—the feeling or knowing-ness.
- Wind and water (Feng Shui) are essential to all living organisms.
- Success leaves clues and so does Mother Nature.
- When we tune into our 'Heart' and live a consciously aware life in rhythm with our environment, it is possible to live in harmony with the Earth and its inhabitants.

Testimonials

I attended Anita's Feng Shui workshop and found it to be very informative, packed with so much great information that I happily reviewed my notes several times after the class.

At home I immediately started purging, reorganizing, fixing and adding in new elements. I had Anita come over and do a Feng Shui visit to point out what I could change, move, or add to create more energetic flow in my home and yard.

I really liked all of the concepts she put forward. One that really stood out for me was the adjustment of the angle at which one of the chairs in my living room was sitting. We turned it like a quarter of a turn and it completely opened up the room. I have so much more to learn about Feng Shui; however, I love what I have done so far. My home and my spirit have a calm, peaceful feeling. Anita is a great teacher, a great practitioner of the art of Feng Shui, and just a wonderful personality.

…Marnel

We were fascinated by the process of the Feng Shui assessment that Anita conducted.

Her approach and attention to detail was impressive and she was insightful. Anita was very professional, and moreover she was genuinely interested in improving our situation which meant so much to us, and will to anyone else who uses Anita. We have been very pleased and inspired by the results. Anita knows her stuff for sure!

…K&R, Red Deer, AB

Anita is a unique Feng Shui consultant. She is full of compassion and really gets involved following up and checking how things improve. She came to our house and introduced all the tips and options to fix existing issues at a time when our situation was quite difficult and challenging. She is honest and offers very affordable services. She is a true blessing.

…Jihene

I have attended a couple of Anita's Feng Shui Workshops, and hired Anita to do a Feng Shui consultation on my home. Her body of knowledge is vast. In her workshops you will come away with a new understanding of why certain things feel a certain way, and learn excellent tools to get the vibration or energy flowing harmoniously in your home. In a home consultation, her recommendations can instantly change the feel of the house and magnetize positive vibes from everyone who drives by.

As an extension of herself, Anita's new book *The HeART of Feng Shui… Simply Put* is certain to bring you the knowledge to transform the energy in your home and help shift other areas of your life. It's a must read—Anita shares simple techniques that will help you change situations and attract new blessings into your life.

…Carol Uchytil Past Publisher,
Intuitive Artist and Deliberate Creator

After transitioning our son out of his crib he soon began night walking and did not want to sleep in his own bed. We spent over a year of trial and error trying to prevent him from getting up in the night. Anita gave us simple and effective advice that we never found when scouring parent websites and books. The day we made the recommended changes was the first night that he slept peacefully in his room. He continues to do so. Thank you so much!

…Janel. C

FROM A STUDENT OF THE ESSENTIAL FENG SHUI PRACTITIONER TRAINING:

Anita's teaching, mentoring and friendship has changed the direction of my life. I feel in sync. This new journey is exciting and, at times, nerve racking, but knowing Anita's guidance is alongside me is calming and reassuring. My gratitude, for all you've taught and shown me. Thank You.

…Cheryl V.

Funny story how Anita and I met: I decided one of the offerings I wanted to give the world was to help people raise the vibration of their homes. At first this was through organization. It moved to including aromatherapy and color therapy. The more I did, the more modalities appeared on my horizon. When I was talking about this exciting new path, I had a friend tell me that I was describing Feng Shui. But I thought Feng Shui was a fad from the 90's—about fancy furniture placement, so, I went on with my life. Not long after, another friend told me that I should look into Feng Shui. I wondered if the Universe was speaking to me. The following week another friend invited me to a networking luncheon. During the sharing time 'Anita' explained she was a Feng Shui Instructor, and had two courses running. I went home and excitedly told my fiancé. Without hesitation, he told me I had to do this. The course provided eye opening moment after eye opening moment. I finally had an official term for what it was I wanted to be able to offer as a service to the world. Anita has shown to be incredibly knowledgeable and intuitive. She taught with grace and patience and kindness. I absolutely adore her, and will forever be grateful for the experience of learning the beautiful and soulful art of Feng Shui under her guidance. I feel very confident in my abilities having this skill in my tool belt. I know, without a doubt, that the Universe brought Anita and I into each other's experience and I wish her all of the success and abundance that she so deserves.

With gratitude and love
Salina Rose Thien

Resources

www.theheartoffengshuisimplyput.com

www.fengshuisimplyput.com

www.ogcoffeebiz.com

www.vannette.ca

www.mariebeswickarthur.com

Art work by: Cynthia Williams www.raevynberg.weebly.com

www.flfe.net/chi

https://www.womansday.com/health-fitness/nutrition/g2503/foods-that-look-like-body-parts-theyre-good-for/

www.scientificamerican.com

https://careertrend.com/how-to-become-a-numerologist-12525564.html

https://www.monikamuranyi.com/glossary

https://www.menus.kryon.com/

https://learning-center.homesciencetools.com/article/four-elements-science/

https://www.ancient-code.com/earth-grid-ancient-monuments-result-global-consciousness/

https://www.heartmath.org/gci/

https://en.wikipedia.org/wiki/Chinese_numerology#Zero

https://www.yourChineseastrology.com/lucky-number.htm

https://www.numerology.com/numerology-news/Chinese-vs-western-numerology

https://www.wikihow.com/Calculate-Your-Name-Number-in-Numerology

https://www.medicalnewstoday.com/articles/319882.php

https://awakeandempoweredexpo.com/magazine/pineal-gland-seat-soul

https://www.gotquestions.org/Bible-divination.html

http://blog.americanindianadoptees.com/2016/11/gods-plan-mission-schools-his-story.html

https://haradimension.wordpress.com/the-torus-the-zero-point-energy-field-and-the-creation-story/

http://cosmometry.net/the-torus---dynamic-flow-process

https://divination.com/history-of-the-i-ching/

https://quantumgrid.com/

https://www.edgarcayce.org/membership/why-join/

https://www.tokenrock.com/explain-flower-of-life-46.html

https://www.britannica.com/biography/Pythagoras

http://www.thrivemovement.com/the_code_fundamental_pattern

https://www.crystalvaults.com/crystal-encyclopedia/quartz

https://en.wikipedia.org/wiki/The_Secret_Life_of_Plants

https://www.motherearthliving.com/mother-earth-living/the-power-of-plants

https://www.heartmath.org/resources/videos/interconnectivity-tree-research-project/

https://parentingisnteasy.co/messy-home-anxiety/?fbclid=IwAR2sSyqA-K6WjsIrUg4I0tV7d5k3x-CKNmssnW0wBtePemXYhX6J_R3NdFs

https://en.wikipedia.org/wiki/Cultural_depictions_of_turtles

Note: Raymond Holliwell's quote or reference came from the book: *You Were Born Rich*, by Bob Proctor